MORE PRAISE FOR *WOND*

"Sonya Lea tells her extraordin well. She has a rare ability to bring readers to the places where love and sex intermingle, collide, or go their separate ways. *Wondering Who Your Are* is an amazing accomplishment. Every page sparkles with wisdom, candor, insight, and love."

CHRISTOPHER RYAN
author of *Sex at Dawn: How We Mate, Why We Stray, and What it Means for Modern Relationships*

"Sonya Lea's *Wondering Who You Are* is an extraordinary story. A wrenching, deeply honest exploration of love and identity that made me question my ideas about memory, about gender, about marriage and family and faith. About the whole human rigmarole. Her story does what the best stories do: it made me think about life in an entirely new way."

SUZANNE MORRISON
author of *Yoga Bitch: One Woman's Quest to Conquer Skepticism, Cynicism, and Cigarettes on the Path to Enlightenment*

"An incredibly intimate and honest memoir, *Wondering Who You Are* shows more vividly than any work of nonfiction I've read in years the endlessly complex and delicate nature of identity. In particular, the book movingly reveals how mutable all relationships are, how metamorphosis on one side of a partnership necessitates metamorphosis on the other—we are all constantly changing."

PETER MOUNTFORD
author of *The Dismal Science*

"Sonya Lea's closeup, incisive memoir carries the reader breathlessly through her heartache, loss, love, and rediscovery. She delves bravely into the taboos of caretaking and examines the conflicts between love and duty, resistance and submission, distance and desire, as well as the grief inherent in the not-knowing."

NICOLE HARDY
author of *Confessions of a Latter Day Virgin*

"This story is strong and strange and haunting and moving all at once . . . [Sonya Lea] has a voice and tone that are so truthful and authentic."

BRET LOTT
author of *Jewel*, an Oprah's Book Club selection

"An intense and accomplished memoir . . . This sweet, erotic, wrenching story asks quintessential questions about memory, the constructed self, and love—its challenges and deep compensations."

PRISCILLA LONG
author of *The Writer's Portable Mentor: A Guide to Art, Craft, and the Writing Life*

# wondering who you are

# wondering who you are

a memoir by

SONYA LEA



Tin House Books
Portland, Oregon & Brooklyn, New York

Published by Tin House Books, Portland, Oregon and Brooklyn, New York

Distributed by W. W. Norton and Company.

Library of Congress Cataloging-in-Publication Data

Lea, Sonya.
Wondering who you are : a memoir / by Sonya Lea. -- First U.S. edition.
pages cm
Includes bibliographical references and index.
ISBN 978-1-941040-07-2 (alk. paper)
1. Lea, Sonya. 2. Appendix (Anatomy)--Cancer--Patients--Family relationships--United States. 3. Appendix (Anatomy)--Cancer--Patients--United States--Biography. 4. Amnesiacs--United States--Biography. I. Title.
RC280.A66L43 2015
616.99'436--dc23

2015001537



First US edition 2015
Printed in the USA
Interior design by Diane Chonette
www.tinhouse.com

*For our children*

*I'm working on my own life story.*
*I don't mean I'm putting it together; no, I'm taking it apart.*

—MARGARET ATWOOD

## *Author's Note*

To write this book I utilized my journals written in the hospital and the early years of recovery. I also relied upon hospital records, letters to and from friends, family, and colleagues, doctors' and therapists' notes and reports, legal depositions, and, in some cases, interviews with people mentioned in the book. Richard's perspective was created through his own writing on various subjects, as well as interviews on subjects I might not have otherwise known. I have changed the names of many people in the book, but not all of them, and in some cases I modified identifying details so as to preserve anonymity. I omitted some people and events when it had no impact upon the veracity or substance of the story.

# prologue

EIGHT YEARS LATER, in the first hour of July 2, 2011, an immense silvery light comes into our bedroom. My husband sleeps near the door; I'm reluctantly on the left. He needs to be the man; he needs to remember what he has forgotten; he needs me to want him where he is. What he has is a body freshly absent of cancer, an acquired brain injury, a scar down his middle, a gap where the memories of our life used to be, a kind, childlike smile, and a wife who thinks she's a badass. The light saturates the midnight room. A bolt the speed of lightning; a brilliant flash; ordinary blackness. We raise our heads and breathe; there is no thunder.

# part one

# 1
# waking

THE NIGHT BEFORE my husband's cancer surgery, I stay up to watch him sleep. In the featureless hotel room, I think of our first meeting, our college breakup, our marriage, our honeymoon, our reunions, our children's births. We have been married for twenty-three years. I have been a child and a woman with this man. To imagine his death is to imagine the end of myself: I cannot know this loss. Instead, I will us to live with a kind of fierce presence I've never before achieved. I watch. I wait. I witness.

By 5:00 AM, he's signing paperwork and I'm sipping stale coffee in the hospital lobby. Every room has a television. Every television resounds with a cheery morning news show. He's moved to pre-op. He goes in to change into his hospital gown. Soon, a nurse calls my name and hands me a large white plastic bag marked PERSONAL BELONGINGS. The bag is heavy with his size 13 running shoes and tall-legged Levi's jeans and wallet stuffed with discount cards. I don't want to be left holding this dismal bag in the fluorescent waiting room with the televisions blaring Montel Williams and Judge Judy in a bizarre symphony while I clasp the last of his scent.

A few minutes later, I'm called to the curtained space where Richard is being prepared for surgery. His body spills over the sides of the gurney. We've waited forty-six days for this moment, assessing every medical paper, learning all we could from others with the same horrific rare disease.

I think of where Richard might go in the time his body is open to the doctors and nurses doing their work. I hope he'll be in a dream, like the ones he has about running and flying and climbing, and not like the ones I have, which are about the end of the world.

His long, summer-tanned legs stretch from beneath a mint-green gown. A drip is flowing into his arm. He's suddenly scared. I stare straight into his eyes. Steady, smiling, subdued.

"You're going to be okay," I lie.

"You need to say good-bye," says the nurse.

I kiss him like we aren't being watched.

A tear descends across his cheekbone.

I walk back to the surgical waiting room and nod to my sister, who has come to be with us for the first week. Christie is a nurse; she's Grace Kelly on the outside and the warrior Boudica on the inside. You want her on your side in a crisis. We've already talked about this moment. There's nothing left to do but pray and meditate in silence while we wait for the surgery to end some ten hours from now, if everything goes as planned.

The deadly and rare cancer afflicting my husband is pseudomyxoma peritonei (PMP), *pseudo* for the way the mucus that surrounds the organs may resemble a tumor mass. The disease has few signs or symptoms. It develops when a polyp originating in the appendix bursts and spreads mucus-producing tumor cells throughout the abdominal cavity. The cancer can range in malignancy, though every kind of PMP is deadly. Gelatin-like mucin is produced in the abdominal cavity in such large quantities that it squeezes the life out of the vital organs. They call this cancer "jelly-belly." We were not fooled by the cute name. The mucus—gelatinous ascites—that stuck to Richard's insides caused more than a midlife paunch.

PMP is fatal. To watch someone die from this disease is to witness the body starving itself to death. The mucus restricts the intestinal tract, and the tumor absorbs the body's nutrients, then finally results in bowel obstruction and wasting syndrome. This is Richard's second, and potentially more lethal, surgery.

Richard has chosen an experimental and controversial treatment called cytoreduction with hyperthermic intraperitoneal chemotherapy (HIPEC). During this procedure, surgeons will cut his torso from pelvis to xiphoid, take his navel, and possibly resect or remove his bowels, gallbladder, omentum, spleen, peritoneum, and parts of his pancreas, stomach, and liver. After the cancer has been scraped from his innards, the surgeons will pour toxic chemicals heated to 107 degrees into his body cavity. The aim of pouring the hot chemical solution is to kill off any remaining cancer cells, with minimal exposure to the rest of his body. The ten-hour surgery will be followed by five days of additional heated chemotherapy, in which chemicals will be poured into his abdomen to soak the solution through his insides. Survivors call the treatment MOAS, for Mother of All Surgeries. At the time of Richard's operation, there's a five-year survival rate of 53 percent, provided he lives through the surgery. We've read online and in journals that 5 percent of people who opt for this treatment do not survive the procedure.

In the waiting room, there's no space to sit where I'm not assaulted by television noise. I walk into the hall and sit on the floor. Earphones go on my head, and when I press the button on my Walkman, Tibetan monks chant healing tones. I sit like this for hours. The monks' rumbling throat-notes make a fearless zone in my body. Overtone songs compose me; I'm motionless and undisturbed. What returns is the Zen practice that stilled me when I was a young mum and learning to meditate.

I imagine my husband ascending from his body. I imagine him rising from the gurney and floating, high in the sky, toward the mountains, our beloved sawtooth peaks in the Canadian Rockies, which we hiked that August, one month before the surgery. This was a medicine walk, where you go out into the wild holding a question about your life. I want to see Richard as I did that day, in the dark tent the morning we started on our silent walk. He smiled as he tied a purple bandana around his long wavy hair. In that time of preparation, our teenage children, Joshua and Dylan, and I were holding the same question: How do we help him live?

But I can't forget that when we began our vacation in the Canadian Rockies all the national parks were burning: smoke covered Banff, Jasper, Kootenay, Yoho, and Kananaskis. Our campsite reservation had been canceled. On the drive north from our home in Seattle we were diverted twice when fires jumped highways. The air was hot and smelled of soot. We snaked slowly along roads, watching for fleeing deer, elk, sheep. We followed the smoke toward the park or perhaps the smoke led us on. We arrived with our throats sore from breathing ash, our eyes red, and we stood looking over the Bow Valley, the brilliant russet sunset the unlikely gift of the blaze. We unpacked water, sweaters, rain gear, footwear. We pulled out our field guides from the years we had spent living in the Rockies, found the names of old friends: larkspur, glacier lily, red elderberry, prickly rose. And yet, something was going awry. Ranger-planned forest fires had bolted their barriers. We finally found shelter on the Icefields Parkway, in the Mistaya Valley with its protected Waterfowl Lakes, blue spruce, and moose. We placed cash in an envelope, stuffed it in the self-reservation box, and began setting up camp. No incursion of smoke was going to deter me from this quest. That last summer together, I wanted to prepare for this taking apart of my husband's body.

All that time in the forest and still, in the hospital, I don't know how to be without him. I have rarely lived alone. All those days I watched the land burning in the distance and sensed the oncoming danger, my throat tightening, and still I don't know what to do. All those nights spent listening to the silence as the fire lit the sunset, and still I do not really know what I like, who I am. With him alive, I've never risked the discovery.

That afternoon, Christie comes to take me for lunch. In the hallway we meet the CEO of Richard's physical therapy company, an organization he's worked with for twelve years. Richard is one of their best therapists, a managing director who heals patients in his own clinic while supervising twenty other centers. The smooth-suited man has an earpiece attached to his head, a strong handshake, and a confident smile. He tells us he's been at a meeting on the East Coast, and that he wants to be here for Richard when he gets out of surgery. I thank him for the Bible he sent us last week. (When people asked us what they could do to help, we said send us books you've loved so we can read them to each other while he's in recovery. We have a suitcase full. We will not read one book.) When the CEO hears that our budget doesn't include our children traveling to the hospital, he offers to fly them in to see their father. It's the only time I cry all day.

We keep checking in at the nurses' station, but no one knows anything. Finally, a nurse comes to tell us everything is proceeding as it should. My sister tells me to get some rest, and because it's been thirty-two hours since I've slept, I let her walk me to our room in the hotel next door. By the time I lie across the bed, the phone rings and it's the CEO.

"Dr. M is out. I've spoken with him," he says.

We return to the surgical waiting room. The CEO tells me the update the surgeon has given him just minutes earlier: Richard is stable. There are a few more hours to go. I'm so relieved I don't even care that the doctor has broken patient confidentiality. We wait. Christie makes me eat. An exhaustion sets in that even strong coffee can't overcome. I feel as if I'm walking in a dream, as if I'm suspended between Richard's forced sleep and my own state of high alert.

By late afternoon, Dr. M emerges from the operating theater and escorts us to a tiny closet of a meeting room. Christie and I sit on cold folding chairs and listen to a report about the operation. I hand her my red, sequined journal and she bows her head, taking notes. She writes in the language of medicine. My sister-the-nurse knows her sister-the-writer remembers words that appear on paper.

"We had to take his spleen and part of his colon," Dr. M says. "No bag," he adds, after registering my face. "We hope the resection knits itself so we don't have to take more."

"His stomach?" I ask.

"Fine."

His stomach had been surrounded by the mucus deposits, and I worried that Richard would lose one of the greatest sensual pleasures of his life, eating wonderful food.

"We had to take a lot of mucus from the pelvic region," Dr. M says.

Christie looks at my face to make sure I've heard his words, and when I gaze back at her eyes she looks down.

*Pelvic region*, she writes, and then she makes an arrow pointing up. Code. For Hellacancer. Whole colonies of gelatinous ascites, gobs of abdominal mucins. Richard has either the hellacious, rapidly dividing peritoneal mucinous carcinomatosis (PMCA) or the milder form of cancer, disseminated peritoneal adenomucinosis (DPAM)—we won't know until the lab results come back.

While I'm watching the surgeon's eyes, in walks the CEO of Richard's company. I'm shocked, both at the surgeon's statement and at the intrusion of the man from another domain into the private world of medicine.

I can no longer stop anything from happening.

I lean toward the doctor. I hope that my body is blocking the CEO from hearing our words, that the surgeon won't notice I'm staring at the blood on his pants. I will myself to remember the words that are spoken.

"Yes, we knew there might be a lot in that, uh, region," I say to the room.

I want to say, *Fuck you, cancer, for ruining twenty years of rollicking fucking*. I want to call cancer a curse, a rat, a vampire, a fiend, an avalanche. But I don't say anything out loud. I sit there like the nice girl, the good wife, the woman who can cope without decent sex.

"We won't know about functionality for some time," Dr. M says.

I shake his hand. My man is cancer-free. "Thank you, thank you, thank you," I say.

By twilight, an hour after the surgery, I'm holding Richard's hand in the wagon-wheel-shaped ICU. Christie is calling our friends and family from the waiting room down the hall. Only one of us can be in the room at a time. I wish I had my sister near to help interpret what I see.

A round clock on the wall above Richard's feet marks the minutes. He has thirteen tubes in his body. By seven o'clock, he opens his eyes. He locates me. Then he returns to sleep. By 7:20, his blood pressure is unstable, and the nurse hangs a norepinephrine drip to help his blood coagulate. Sixty minutes later, Richard's blood pressure stabilizes. I breathe more easily. This is typical, I think. The body settling after its strenuous ordeal.

The nurses change shifts. The new nurse examines him, and then organizes the multitude of wires that lead from the machines reading his body to the computer box sounding alarms. She focuses on the technology and not on my husband's body, and I keep asking her questions; I want to direct her attention back to him. Minute by minute, I watch as his blood pressure rises and falls. By the time the minute hand has circled the dial, his heart rate has passed 100, 105, 111.

"This isn't what he's like," I say. I mean to tell her that Richard is a fit man; his resting heart rate is 54. Because he hiked and ran and skied and played tennis and basketball, his heart rate has remained in a fit zone for decades. I can't get the words out. "This isn't right," I keep saying.

He moans. His skin is dank, cool. His face is flushed.

By nine o'clock, Richard's blood pressure is fluctuating wildly—systolic in the 80s and diastolic in the 40s. Monitors beep exclamations. The nurse checks the response of his pupils.

"What's happening?" I ask.

"The blood has been ordered, but it's slow to come from the lab," the nurse says.

"He's losing blood?" I ask.

"They won't release the blood. I think they're going on a false reading."

I want to run to get my sister from the waiting room, but I can't risk leaving Richard and not being able to get back into the ICU.

"What's happening?" I ask again.

"I'm giving him more fluid, to stabilize him."

"When was the blood ordered?"

"Hours ago. The hematocrit reading he had right out of surgery was thirty-nine."

I'm confused. "What's hematocrit?"

"That's really good," the nurse says. "Hematocrit is the concentration of red blood cells. It's normally about forty-five percent. Because the reading was in the healthy range, the lab won't release a further transfusion."

"We have to compete for the blood? Where's Dr. M?" I ask.

"He's gone home. Richard is going to be fine. As soon as we stabilize him."

The monitors blare their denial. His heart rate races to 122, the number lit in the acrid color one sees only in technology. The nurse raises the sheets and we both see that the drains coming from his body are filled with blood. There's no way this much blood should be leaving his body. The nurse looks agitated.

"When is the blood going to be here?" I can't tell if I am polite or yelling.

"We had a doctor on staff order the plasma. It's on its way."

Richard's body lurches on the bed. His head moves from side to side. I hold his boxing glove of a hand. His fingers have always been thick, three times the size of mine, yet now his grip is weak, swollen, sweaty. The weight of these hands has offered me such reassurance. I know their density and history. I know how his life shaped these hands.

# 2

# compatriots

"TELL ME EVERYTHING," I said on our first date.

"Sure." He took my hand as we walked past the hockey arena.

"Your hands are huge," I said.

"Once my mother caught me playing with matches, and she punished me by putting my hand in the fire."

"Once I bit my sister, and my father came home from work and took a bite out of me, here," I said, pointing to my right forearm.

Survivors, we were. Compatriots.

We met in 1976, at a high school dance. It was the era of Pierre Trudeau and glam rock and the Sex Pistols. He was the boy from out of town. I was the girl who wanted out. Like young people of every generation, we thought nonconformity and the acquisition of authentic wounds to be essential to our freedom. Our scars were there, waiting inside us, scars of disease and damage, but we didn't yet know how they might undo us.

Richard lived on Blue Mountain, the hill west of Collingwood, Ontario, Canada. His was the place of bohemians, fringe people, adventurers, and artists, the place where I escaped to walk through fields of wild poppies, imagining another, wilder self I might become. I lived in the town nestled in the valley below, next to Georgian Bay, a tiny shipbuilding community full of first-generation immigrants—Scots, Irish, and Italians—a town that would, in our youth, morph into a ski resort for Toronto's privileged class, who could afford a weekend chalet and a ski pass.

I was a month shy of my seventeenth birthday and already bored with everything about that place: its parochial conversations, its hockey culture, its lack of books. My friend Wendy, a blond minx I'd bonded with the day I'd arrived from Kentucky a decade earlier, had made plans to graduate from high school early and leave for the city. I knew that I had to raise funds for university myself because I was determined to make my own way. I wouldn't allow myself to become indebted to my authoritarian father, who had ruled my childhood. I was $5,000 and one year of senior classes from my goal of perfect freedom. I waited tables and babysat children and wrote fantasy lists in my journal, which I hid in the back of my closet, in a cigar box.

1. Find the perfect university.

2. Study literature.

3. Buy a car.

4. Travel.

5. Meet interesting, smart people with whom I can have fascinating conversations.

This was why, when Wendy and I arrived at the high school dance in our frayed bell-bottoms, scuffed Frye boots, and shiny lip gloss, we were dateless. Second-wave feminism had swooped us up, and we had no intention of betraying our dreams. En route to the dance, for about ten blocks down narrow chutes made by sidewalk snowdrifts, we drank bootlegged rum mixed with the Pop Shoppe soda our mothers bought by the caseload. The last dance of the year was to feature a band called Liverpool, who played regurgitated Beatles music that was, we thought, so like the fading hippies: a symbol of lost hope. We smoked a cigarette down the last block, blowing white rings into the icy air, the buzz of the booze warming us. Inside the wide glass doors, I took our ski jackets and stored them in the prefects' room—I'd elected to take on the role of prefect for its obvious benefits of getting away with more while pretending to lead others—while Wen scoped out the scene. In five minutes she swept down the locker-lined hall and took my hand and steered me straight to the folding tables near the front door, where a long line of students waited to pay a few dollars for admission to see the facsimile of the greatest band of all time.

"Don't look. The guy with the curls," Wen said, her back to the line so I could seem like I was glancing without gaping. Wendy was tall, with a mass of blond tresses, not easily unnoticed. I was Skipper to her all-Canadian Barbie: tomboy-skinny with flat brown hair to my waist, bright green eyes, and a shy smile. We'd spent most of our young lives up in trees, and since we'd come down, we really tried to understand what the adult game was about but found ourselves mostly rejecting its conventions. Pippi Longstocking, Anne of Green Gables, Scout—these were our girl models, and we saw no reason to abandon their fortitude just because we were growing breasts and desiring boys. Furthermore, no man really counted unless the best friend approved, but we never withheld affection for rebellion, adventure, and impulse, thus only the truly dangerous ones were ever scuttled. I pretended I wasn't checking out her man.

"He's cute!" I whispered.

"Hell, yes," she said.

Then I saw the guy behind him. Dark hair past his wide shoulders, six feet tall at least, in faded corduroys. He took off his ski toque and ran his hands through his bangs. The girl selling tickets said something to him and he smiled, somehow easy and elegant at the same time, etching dimples into his snow-tanned face.

"That one," I said, as if I were claiming him. And I was.

We staked our positions to observe the boys' movements. They seemed to be best friends who shared jokes, affection, and a sporty style. But who were they, really? Where had they come from? And most important, how were we going to get them to notice us?

A few dances into the night, Wendy was already in the arms of the boy with the curls, and I was dancing at a polite distance with a sweet kid with freckles. I looked over my dance partner's shoulder and saw the boy with the long hair and faded cords watching me. I winked. He threw his head back and laughed. Strong jaw, fast instincts, imperfect teeth. I liked all of him instantly. He had big bones and effortless grace, the kind of ease I longed for. It wasn't love at first sight. I didn't believe in such things. But it was the kind of lust I'd rarely experienced. I didn't want to seduce him so much as I wanted to document his steely muscles, understand why his pelvis balanced like a pivot above long, long legs, and crawl behind his eyes to observe his film of the world.

One song later, Richard and I were dancing to "Penny Lane," communicating in hip thrusts and elbow jerks. Two hours later, in the backseat of a two-door car, we perched on the knees of the boys from out of town while their friends drove us to Wendy's house, where I was staying for the night. I took every opportunity I could to hang out with her permissive family. She lived three houses down from me on Beech Street, in the middle of a residential grid of tree-lined avenues named for trees. This night, our curfew was an hour later than my curfew would be at home, and better yet, I wouldn't be questioned about the car in which I'd been riding with boys.

Richard walked me to the back steps, where we always entered our homes. The back, with its boot trays off the kitchen and its solid stairs that avoided the neighbors' watchfulness.

"Can I call you?" he asked.

I gave him my number, which he memorized upon hearing. "Thanks for the dancing," I said.

His eyes came close to me then, and his arms went around my hips, and I registered their weight. Something in me calmed. His ease transferred. With his thick hands on my back, I felt effortless and free. Exactly the way I wished to be but never could achieve, my mind constantly jockeying my many responsibilities. His lips touched mine, and they were tender, warm, sweet. I hoped he couldn't hear my heart beating through my Wonderbra. His fingers stroked the hair at the nape of my neck. No one had ever touched me there, not even me. The nape had been absent of touch, and he had discovered its need. I enshrined that sensation as if it were an artifact of my aliveness. He turned and walked back to the car full of boys, and I watched his hair, which bounced with his steps.

Richard called me the next night. We began a conversation that would endure for decades.

The following Saturday, he picked me up in his aunt's Volkswagen, and we drove to the local bar, the Arlington Hotel. I posed with a fake ID and got kicked out in a few minutes. Instead of listening to a bar band we walked around on wintry Hurontario Street. I had a chance to study him up close. Broad, athletic, with shoulders like a linebacker's, a shock of black locks, and bright blue eyes, he was well-read and down to earth, a brilliant raconteur.

On that first date, we stood in front of a furniture store and its window display of La-Z-Boys and rocking chairs.

"What kind of home do you want?" I asked.

"One with music," he said. "And you?"

"Children," I said. "Five of them. Really well loved. But not a lot of stuff. Just each other."

We were playing house. We knew that we were young and likely wouldn't last. We wanted to talk in ways we hadn't yet allowed ourselves. We wanted to speak of all of the things we hadn't been able to say to any other. We entered into an unbounded dialogue each night.

"Get off the phone!" my father yelled.

"Okay, I'll call you back," I'd say to Richard, hour after hour. I learned to lift the receiver of the upstairs rotary phone from its cradle and dial slowly, muffling the circular spring with a pillow, and then drag the phone into my room, where I closed the door and whispered, so I wouldn't be heard. In those conversations I learned he was book-smart: intelligence was how he'd distinguished himself when he was moved from school to school, thirteen over the course of his childhood, although he'd skipped the second grade. Loquacious, magnetic, with a quick wit inherited from his Brit mother, Richard was a yes man, one who could get a yes without ever asking a question.

Or this story. He was the son of a single mom, a child of poverty and violence, abandoned by his father, beaten by an uncle and several drunken stepfathers, but somehow he found the mulish will to become the first in his family to be accepted into college, where he planned to go in the fall.

"I've never met anyone with a mind like yours," Richard said. "Can you come out here to my place one day?"

Two weeks later, I told my mother I was running errands and dashed off to his house on the mountain. I drove the Chevy station wagon my mother insisted was "robin's egg blue" but was really an opaque metal beast that rusted orange in the salted snow, its back end scarily skidding over patches of black ice.

Richard lived in a nondescript chalet at the base of the Apple Bowl ski run, close to the lodge at Blue Mountain Resort years before investors scooped up nearby land to build condos, restaurants, gift shops, and amusement rides. His house had burned to the ground the year before; the fire had killed their three dogs and destroyed every object of family life they had. This was why the clothing he wore looked borrowed. He'd been given everything by neighbors, who knew his single mother could scarcely afford to rebuild the house.

Now, at eighteen, he lived alone. His sister stayed with her boyfriend in a nearby town; his brother was on an exchange trip in South Africa; and his mother had left for

Bermuda, a place that seemed to offer her a greater sense of freedom than what she experienced in North America.

Richard met me at the door of his silent, cold house and brought me to the kitchen, where he was eating peanut butter and crackers and drinking milk. Clean dishes were stacked in the drying rack. Dozens of his mother's plants lined the windowsill, most of them still alive. He made me a mug of Earl Grey and we sat on a worn brown couch and held hands and talked. He liked to talk more than anyone I'd known, fanciful discussions that wove from personal lore to politics to philosophy. We kissed a long time, and then he showed me to his bedroom: a twin bed, a poster of Bruce Lee, a polar bear print, a dozen medals and trophies from his high school—including Athlete of the Year—and a stack of textbooks. He was a ski instructor in winter, a tennis instructor in the summer, and a vigorous player of football, basketball, volleyball, badminton, and table tennis, so sweaty gear was de rigueur. He'd cleaned up for me; this would be the last time I saw his bedroom floor free of clothing. On the ground near his bed was a well-worn copy of *The Sensuous Man*. *Here is an expert's guide to becoming the kind of lover that every woman dreams of . . .* the cover said. He was studious, even about sex. I hadn't a clue about my own body, had been waiting for someone lion-hearted enough to unlock its potential. I didn't dream of a lover who would sensually transport me, unless that included a one-way ticket out of town. That year I'd turned sixteen and had intercourse with my dime-bag drug-dealer boyfriend mostly because my girlfriends were having sex, and I wanted to check losing my virginity off my list. Since then, I'd had sex with a guy friend who was decent and funny. But now I wanted an orgasm. I wanted to discover if there was a man who cared about the clitoris. The earnestness of this mountain boy had lots of promise.

My arms went around his waist. When I touched his body, I felt ribs. I was thin because I smoked and was a teenage vegetarian. Richard was thin because he was starving. He deposited his mother's welfare check, paid the mortgage, insurance, and utilities, and whatever was left he used for groceries. Most of the adults in his life knew that he had no car, that he was fatherless, and that his mother had absented herself, and they found ways to provide him with meals several nights a week. Richard learned early to live alone, and with few resources. Like most young men, he was constantly ravenous. He appeared to be surviving by his wits.

"How do you get home?" I asked, as we lay curled in his tiny bed. His school was nearly twenty miles west, in a district that served rural students.

"Hitchhike," he said. "If I want to play sports, I have to. The bus leaves early, and I have to stay late. I've hitchhiked every night for years. How about you? How do you get places?"

"Today, I lied to my mother and took her car. I have a few hours."

His feet hung off the end of the mattress—he'd grown too tall for his childhood bed. He asked if he might explore. Everywhere.

I answered, "Please!" with a look I now imagine—decades later, and through the obfuscation of this particular memory, for who can see oneself?—as entreating. Every gesture he made was gallant. No man I'd met had held me with such devotion. If a woman's first orgasm can be said to mark the loss of her virginity, then that winter afternoon, I gave him mine.

# 3

# leaving

"YOU NEED TO get out of here and get something to eat," the nurse says, as she hovers over the numbers on a massive computer printout.

It's nine thirty on the night of the surgery, and I've been awake nearly two days, since we checked into the hotel the day before Richard's operation.

"I'll go if my sister gets to come in the room in my place," I bargain.

The nurse allows Christie to stay with him. In the waiting room, I scarf down a sub sandwich that Christie bought for me. I'm not hungry, the food is tasteless, but I will myself to eat it so I can be strong for Richard.

By ten o'clock, Christie comes to get me. "It's not good," she says.

A few minutes later, I reenter the ICU room. The nurse has my husband's arms in thick Velcro bands, held against the sides of the bed.

"The restraints are to protect him from himself," the nurse says.

I see Richard thrashing about. I bring my eyes toward his. Though pinned to the bed, he raises his head and looks into my face. His hair is matted and wet. His eyes are terrified. He's fighting to stay alive, and what I see behind the fear is his limitless love. He falls backward. Eyes close. Hands go limp. Consciousness leaves.

Later, I will think of this as the moment that I lost my former husband. Later, I'll say that I saw him leave while he lay in restraints on a hospital bed. I'll tell people that I remember watching him fall away, fall without a navel, umbilicus-less, as if he were falling as the first man, no longer tied to history, his or anyone else's. But right now, there is no story. There is only arguing for his life. I must keep him alive.

"Let me stay!" I plead.

"For a few minutes. And then you have to go. You're not supposed to be in here. Visiting hours ended at nine."

As if that's what I am doing. Visiting. I dig in. I want to make the nurse promise me that he'll be okay if I have to leave. Instead I look at her across Richard's body and place my hand on his belly. I don't know it then, but his abdomen is filling with four liters of blood. One hundred and thirty-six ounces. Seventeen cups. Over three pitchers of blood are pooling inside him.

Christie and I meet in the hall.

"This isn't right," I say.

"They're stabilizing him. You can come back in a few hours," she says. "If we have to break through the doors, we'll do it."

I call a few close friends and ask them to pray. I ask them to call everyone *they* know and ask *them* to pray. It makes me feel like I'm doing something.

Christie and I walk to the hotel. I shower and put on fresh clothing. I lie down on the bed with my sister.

"What are you doing?" she asks.

"I can't waste time getting dressed when they call. I have to be ready to go again."

When I lay my head on the pillow I make a deal with whoever is listening: *I'll sleep for a few hours if you agree to wake me if anything happens to him.*

Ninety minutes later I jerk to a sitting position, as if someone has pulled me by my arms, straight up out of bed. I call the ICU.

"You'd better get over here," the man's voice says. "The doctor is on his way back to operate."

I wake my sister and tell her to meet me there. I fly like in my dreams when my body is light and there are no obstructions.

By midnight, his heart rate has plummeted to 40. An accurate hematocrit reading has been taken to replace the false healthy one they took after surgery. The hematocrit reads twelve. Then, when he's tested again, it reads ten, and then three. I don't need to ask the staff to confirm the danger of the falling number; I watch my husband wrestle for his life.

He is surrounded by doctors. One resuscitates him with a bag valve mask.

"Who are you?" one doctor asks.

"I am his wife," I say.

"You have to wait out there. We're taking him down now."

Christie shows up while I'm standing alone in the hall. My body has begun to chill and my teeth chatter. She places her arms around my shoulders and holds me. When the doors open, we hear the doctors calling orders in the room. We see them moving Richard's lifeless body.

"He's coding," Christie says. I know she means that they're doing the breathing for him now.

I only want his body close to mine.

Three doctors in hospital-blue scrubs and caps start to move the gurney down the long hallway. I follow alongside, holding my husband's leg; there are so many doctors that it is the only place where I can touch his body. When we get to the elevator and the doors open, two doctors move the gurney while the other continues to press air into Richard's lungs. Christie and I stand and watch as he's wheeled into the large elevator. I hold tight to my sister's arm.

"Come if you want," the doctor says.

We follow. Everyone faces Richard. The elevator is quiet. No one speaks. The clock stops, minutes run out, time ends. My heart beats into my ears. The *I-want-I-want-I-want* that runs constantly through my head finally halts. The terror of losing him gives way to another place, a place beyond my fear. I am a lake in winter. I place my cool hands over Richard's heart. The doctors watch me. I lower my head. Their faces turn away: slow, tender, a graceful offering. They proffer a private moment with my husband. The gesture happens in a minute and forever, a gesture so kind that in the years to come, I will turn the moment over and over and over, a holy of holies in my mind.

In the silence, I ask that everything be given to my husband. I will myself to pour into him through my hands while the air is being forced into his throat. His chest raises and lowers. We descend.

# 4

# quilt

WHEN I TURNED seventeen, we were in love. Richard had nine months before he left town to attend McMaster University in Hamilton, Ontario, to study physical education. Until then, we would spend every weekend together. In the winter we went to house parties where I drank too many beers and got dizzy, and he drove me home, then slept on our pullout couch in the den. When the weather turned warmer, we went camping, and skinny-dipped in the icy bay, and walked the Bruce Trail, and lay out under the stars while he named the constellations.

I introduced Richard to my father, who thought he was a misdirected bohemian without a bright future. My mother asked me to tell my new boyfriend to stay out of the refrigerator ("He's eating us out of house and home!"), and so I made Richard meaty sandwiches that he scarfed, unobserved. His thriving was essential to me, instinctual, necessary. I hadn't known love before, but this would become my definition of it: I cared about his well-being as much as I cared about my own.

Our first summer together, my mother found my birth-control pills in my purse, and she confronted me, shocked at my audacity. We were Catholic, and she demanded abstinence (at least of us three daughters; the son, not so much). I had become a disappointment and Richard was the catalyst for my fall. After berating the doctor who had prescribed the medication, my mother asked my father to talk to me.

"You're not aware of the consequences of your choices. You don't know what life has in store for you!" my father said, over a steak dinner out. (We were always treated to the best restaurant meal when we needed a talking-to.)

"No one knows those things, Dad," I said.

"You can't keep chasing after him. When Richard goes away to college, he's going to move on to other relationships." My father sipped his Canadian whiskey on the rocks.

"We're having sex. That's not going to go away. But no man is going to get in the way of my goals," I said, without sarcasm, as I slashed my filet mignon.

My father knew that I was serious about my studies, and for the time being, his fears were quieted. All summer my parents looked the other way, hoping that when Richard and I lived a hundred miles apart, things might settle down. Instead, that September, I told them I'd be visiting my boyfriend at college.

"If you leave to spend the weekend with him, you can't come back to this family," my father said.

"That's your call," I said.

That first weekend visiting Richard in his college apartment he shared with two roommates, I made him lasagna.

He chilled dessert in the freezer while we watched *Star Trek*. I sprawled on a pillow next to him, reading Blake. We smoked hash. Hours later, in a desperate search for satiation, in a tear through his pathetic pantry, in a stoner's quest for munchies, we discovered the forgotten confection. We sat on the linoleum floor and we fed each other ripe strawberries and we licked whipped cream from our fingers.

That Sunday afternoon my father, emitting a stony silence, allowed my return. I visited Richard every month. The distance didn't shake us.

Since I was twelve, I'd kept my three siblings fed many days while my mother slept, her headaches—and the codeine she was prescribed for the pain—removing her from the world. After school, I'd come home and start dinner, usually something easy like a casserole or sloppy joes, while Mother woke from an afternoon nap, folded laundry, and chirped anecdotes at me over the antics of Graham Kerr on *The Galloping Gourmet*. We'd eat dinner at six when my father arrived; then I'd often study at the kitchen table until one or two in the morning.

My mother was not ambitious, stalwart, or confident in raising children. But she was funny and charming. Where she was social, I was studious. This made me outwardly responsible and inwardly rebellious.

In January of 1978, I turned eighteen and graduated from high school six months early. I waitressed at two restaurants, my bank account slowly growing. I felt as free as I'd ever imagined, because I knew I would make it out of the constriction of my family life and because I was so well loved by Richard. Inside my body I could locate a sense of fearlessness and power, an awareness beyond the punishments and rewards of my childhood.

That July, I drove to the poppy fields atop Blue Mountain and lay down in the flowers' garnet shimmer. For a moment, the story of my life did not exist. There was no territory, no past, no mother, no father to possess. I was not relative to anyone. I did not belong nor did I desire belonging. There was only the wind lifting petals. The warbler's call. In the distance, the murmur of a spring. When I was a teenage woman, my body knew what it loved.

After Richard returned from his first year at McMaster, we celebrated the freedom of our summer together through music. We stayed up all night with a hundred thousand fans at Canada Jam to scream along with Kansas and Triumph and one of Richard's childhood favorites, the Commodores. We drove to Toronto to load up on vinyl at Sam the Record Man, to dance to the steel drums at the Caribbean Carnival, to see Fleetwood Mac and Cheap Trick and Rush. We danced at clubs in the city and hotel lounges in town. He knew the words to every album Motown put out and he sang them for me as we wound my used Plymouth Valiant up Blue Mountain's back roads. We had three months until we left for different universities, and we spent much of that time playing, just playing.

Earlier that spring, my father announced he was moving the family back to Kentucky for a job. He needed a challenge, he said, and he thought it would be helpful to return to where we had roots, and family. I'd been accepted to Wilfrid Laurier, which was in Waterloo, two hours by bus from Richard's school, and I told my parents that I would not change my plans. My family and home disappeared, so that autumn, I moved myself into the dorm room a week before school started. It was the first time I'd been alone, without anyone to care for. In my aloneness, I was relieved and confused. That bafflement only made me drink more alcohol, something that went perfectly with freshman year. The daughter of a distiller, I'd become an adept bartender at my father's parties and seen how booze made me braver, less inhibited. Being alone, without anyone to rein me in, only intensified my experimentation.

The weekend after orientation, I took a Greyhound bus to see Richard. He put Todd Rundgren on the turntable and told me that he didn't want to be together anymore. He wanted to date other women. He needed to see what school would be like without a long-distance girlfriend. He didn't want to take the place of my absent family.

I fought against the unknown. I went on a campaign to convince him to see our relationship as necessary for survival, as I did. I visited him the next two weekends. I made a case for giving each other more space. I said that I'd call only once a week. I promised we could take a break, if only he would keep us together. To be without his physical presence seemed unbearable. Finally he told me to stay away, that he couldn't see me.

"Promise me that if you get serious about anyone, you'll call," I said.

"Promise," he replied. "You too."

When I gave him up, I dated a dozen men. I slept around. I met a lovely man who took me on trips and cooked for me and was exactly the opposite of Richard—small, nurturing, quiet—although they had the same name. I dated my psychology professor, who was newly divorced and aching for attention. I didn't have the sense to realize that most of those relationships were clichés. I was sad, and drowning my sadness in beer and speed, a combination that gave me limitless energy and made me feel invulnerable. I lived on Labatt's Blue and a salad a day, and my weight dropped below one hundred pounds, seriously skinny. But I could still go to class in the morning, read Virginia Woolf all afternoon, and, in the evenings, party. Like a patient with walking pneumonia, I looked better than my symptoms suggested. I was heartsick and masquerading as a college feminist, determined to take control over my life but finding only exhaustion.

Five months later, Richard called.

"I miss you," he said.

"I'm seeing someone," I said.

Silence.

"Remember we said we'd be honest?" I said, wanting to put some distance between us now.

"You could have told me!" he yelled.

"I'm telling you now!" I screamed, terrified I'd feel attached to him again. Emotions were so contained, so manageable with the other men. It was easier not to complicate things with love, I thought.

A week later, a letter arrived. Richard was angry with himself for allowing me to go. He hadn't seen any other women. He wanted another chance. When I opened the letter, I was in the cafeteria eating sausages made by the women of the mostly German town, who each day plied us with their wunderbar Oktoberfest menu. I smashed the letter into my plate. Mustard splattered onto his tiny handwriting, his intelligent sentences. When I tossed my meal into the trash, the aproned woman who'd been trying to fatten me up looked concerned.

Still, I relented. Richard and I made plans to see each other before I left to visit my family for spring break. I'd be getting a ride with a whiskey truck driver my father knew, making an eighteen-hour haul from the distillery in Ontario to the bottling house in Kentucky. Richard and I agreed to meet at his home on Blue Mountain. The psychology professor drove me to Richard's house and suggested we make plans to finish reading *Gödel, Escher, Bach* over scotch on the rocks, which he'd been teaching me to drink. I didn't know what the hell I wanted anymore, but I did know that I wasn't enjoying playing roles for the benefit of men, learning to amuse, faking caring. In my first year of college, what was to have been my greatest experience of freedom had turned into the kind of vacancy I saw in my mother's tired face. I was absent. No philosophy could pierce my vacuous melancholy. I could only remember a kind of emptiness that came with loss and disappointment. I said good-bye to the professor in the ski lodge parking lot down the street and walked to the little brown cottage I'd visited so many times.

Richard answered the door and invited me in. His hair was long, past his shoulders, and his biceps bulged from the time he'd obviously put in at the gym. His muscled body handily nullified the memory of the horrible high school mixtape he'd made for me that included both Edgar Winter's "Free Ride" and Marvin Gaye's "Sexual Healing." He sat me on the couch and told his story.

"This breakup was the stupidest idea I ever had. I was afraid of not taking the chance to see other people."

"Did you?" I asked.

"I don't want anyone else."

"You didn't even sleep with the phys ed chicks?"

He smiled at my famous disregard for the monotonously unimaginative female gym rats who were his classmates. "I couldn't even ask anyone on a date," he said.

"What have you been doing?"

"Listening to music."

"Surely someone tried to snog you."

"They delivered muffins to my house."

"I bet they did."

"Can we start again?" he asked.

"I don't know . . ." Suddenly I wanted to run away from everything he represented: intensity, desire, a kind of devotion my recent independence had freed me from.

His hands reached for me. "Sonya, I love you."

We held each other until I could breathe again, and then I pushed him away.

"I need to go," I said.

His head went into my lap, and he sobbed, wracks and gasps that ran through his giant body. My hands unclenched, and I touched his beautiful hair. He raised his eyes and words seemed to unlock from his chest.

"I want to spend the rest of my life with you."

I wasn't sure if he'd made a terrible mistake and said this thing out of a need to keep me close. Was that a suggestion that we marry? Or a desperate attempt to make his pain go away? And how would I, in my aching confusion, know what the difference was, anyway?

"Oh, God," I said. I made a prayer that I might walk away from there, and at the same time, something inside me was watching as I settled into his love. "I'll call you at the end of break," I said. I got out of there, before he could take me to bed.

Two days and seven hundred miles later my father asked me why the hangdog face.

"He proposed."

"Who?" my mother asked from the laundry room.

"The ne'er-do-well," I said.

"What did you tell him?" my father asked.

"I need time to think."

"Well, don't leave him hanging out there."

I surveyed my father for signs of derision but he'd clearly started to like the bohemian mountain boy, at least in his absence. Dad had grown to admire Richard's persistence and his stellar grades. They'd shared conversations about organic chemistry, basketball, and growing up poor. Before we'd broken up, my father had hired Richard to work for him, loaned him his luxe car, and tested him on American history. They were bonded in a way that I couldn't be with my father, for Richard shared none of my bitterness.

The phone rang, and my father answered and talked for a moment before handing it to me.

"Your dad says I can catch a truck and be there by to-morrow," Richard said.

"Don't you have class?" I asked. His spring break had already come and gone. And he'd never skipped a day in his life, a fact I found freakish.

"I want to be with you," he said.

Three years later, we were married at the Toronto Ski Club near his home. Our honeymoon was in a cottage in the Muskokas, loaned to us by a family friend. We took a boat to a remote island, lay naked on the sand, told each other our wildest dreams. Mine: to write, and start a camp where children could live free. His: to live with me forever. And play a little tennis in the summer.

We moved back to Waterloo, where I finished my de-gree in literature and Richard began a graduate degree in exercise physiology.

Five months later, near their home on the mountain, his mother was run over by a drunk driver while help-ing someone on the road. His family came to tell him the news, and because I was unreachable in another city, they waited for me to come home from a journalism conference in a snowstorm. The *Toronto Star* ran a headline on page two about his mother's death: GOOD SAMARITAN DIES, it said. I held the paper folded in my lap in the dim car, unable to read it because of the perilous road conditions. I wouldn't learn of his mother's death until I got to our apartment door.

We grieved. In him, this looked like working long hours at school and sleeping a lot. I worked as the news editor for the university paper and went out drinking at the pubs after press time. Richard and I never argued until after we married, but that first year of marriage was full of conflict. During a weekend retreat called Engaged Encounter, a marriage preparation program courtesy of the Catholic Church, we discovered that we agreed on everything except for how we might raise children (him, laissez-faire; me, with vigor). After his mother's death, he was distant in his sadness, and I didn't know how to help him. And so I stayed out late, partying. My absence drove him further into his private thoughts.

Two weeks after his mother died, I discovered I was pregnant with our first child. I'd skipped a period, and went into the university health clinic to be examined. The test was positive. The doctor looked at my wedding ring and counseled me on all my options.

"You can get substantial grants for married students, if you want to stay in school," she said. "This office has fine prenatal care. But if you need to terminate the pregnancy, I can make some recommendations."

"I'm good," I said, jumping off the table. I wanted to get outside, to someplace I could be alone with this information.

"There are counselors here, any time you want to talk," the doctor said.

"Thanks," I said, grabbing my coat and getting out of there.

Richard and I had made a risky decision. After several years on the pill, we had decided to alter our birth-control method. We'd discussed birth planning with our families, and both our mothers warned us that early marriage wasn't the best timing to make a change. I wasn't sure which night of pleasure had created this embryo. I walked the quad of the university—students rushing to class, young men throwing snowballs—and I pulled my winter coat close in the February chill and shivered past the brick buildings.

We had spent those weeks after his mother died turning to each other in the night, our limbs aching to prove our existence. We were in sex-grief, that complicated twining of longing, acceptance, relief. Richard found solace in lovemaking. One of those nights, we hadn't paid attention to prevention. Now, we were with the sway of a force that could change the direction of our lives. As if that hadn't happened enough lately, I thought. I was worried that I'd fucked things up, a thought I had nearly constantly even when there wasn't a baby involved. My heart beat loud. I made myself breathe in the winter air, cool clean breezes filling my body. Tears froze on my face. If nothing else, I thought, I could make a righteous dinner.

I walked the slush-filled roads to the cheapest market in town and I found the ingredients, confusion winding me up and down the same aisles a dozen times. For two miles, I carried the plastic bags through the darkening city, hoping that I wouldn't run into anyone I knew on the street. I also carried home a card I'd bought for Richard, my music aficionado, a valentine with a picture of a stereo receiver on the front. Inside our apartment, I began to make boeuf bourguignon, a recipe of Julia Child's I'd wanted to try since we married. We didn't have much money for beef; if I made this dish we'd have to eat peanut butter sandwiches for several meals, but suddenly I wanted the elegance that I'd always imagined married life might afford, the kind of grace and calm my own chaotic family never seemed to achieve. The stew simmered. I put the Clash on the turntable, the apocalyptic, angry, post-punk "London Calling," with its warning of the coming ice age, starvation, and war.

The song, inspired by the 1979 meltdown at Three Mile Island, wasn't exactly inspiration for bringing another life to the planet, but it wasn't a thoughtful consideration that I wanted. I danced the kind of dancing one does in the house alone to analog recordings roaring full bore. I screamed. I tossed my hair. I thrust my pelvis and struck a pose. At the end of the album, I stretched out across the floor and put my hands on my belly. I listened. There was nothing in me that could take away this life. I hadn't known I was so resolute, but here was certainty. Whether I could mother well was another question. I'd been mothering my siblings, cooking, and cleaning since I was twelve, but I hadn't had many models for the kind of mother I wished to be. I did have a fierce imagination.

I looked around our two-room apartment. Richard and I shared a mattress, two lamps, cooking supplies, dishes, an old couch, and a kitchen table. We were intelligent and tenacious with a tendency toward adventure. We'd have to give up traveling in the ways we'd imagined when we lay on the beach on our honeymoon. I was twenty-one and he was twenty-three. We'd have loads of time for travel when this kid left home. I laid a blanket and pillows on the living room floor and lit candles everywhere. I wrote inside his valentine's card with the picture of a stereo on the front: "We're not going to be able to afford one of these for a while."

Richard came home from a long day at the research lab. He saw the candles, smelled dinner, and melted into me. We laughed through the meal, making plans for where we'd go on spring break, a road trip to visit friends. After dessert, he opened the card and looked at the sentences, and then at my face.

"Pregnant," I said.

"Do you want to have the baby?" he asked.

"I want to know what you want," I answered.

I nearly always deferred to his greater confidence. He tried to read my desires in my eyes. This was precisely how we were dishonest with each other.

"This would be a change," he said.

We sat in silence. I cleared the dishes. He came to the kitchen, put his arms around me.

"Come back," he said.

We lay across the pillows, and he curled his long body around my back, cupped his hand across my breast.

"I can't tell you whether to have this baby or not, sweetheart. You'd be the one to do the greater share of parenting."

"At least for the first bit," I said.

"But whatever you want, we can figure it out." He kissed my neck, turned my face to his.

"I'm sorry it happened so close to your mum going," I said.

"You'd be a good mother," he said.

"We'd be great parents together," I answered. "We don't have to know right now. Let's see how this feels."

My grandmother Frances sent a quilt she'd stitched for our wedding, and I placed it over our simple mattress. Its ivory butterflies, made from scraps of old clothing, somehow lent ancestral ballast to a time when I walked around in a trance.

A few weeks after that night, Richard's instructors purposefully killed a dog during an experiment in the kinesiology laboratory. He told me how it happened, how the dog's death hurt him, how he knew he could not be responsible for taking the lives of research animals. We sat with our books open at our tiny kitchen table and cried, knowing that we would not ever be the same. He would not finish his final year of graduate school, he would not become a researcher or a teacher, we would return the scholarship money, I would graduate from university four months pregnant—we would not be young and careless again.

That night, we held hands as we lay on the bed in the college apartment, blue moon mottling the wedding quilt, quiet. In the days that followed we'd sometimes wander across to the corner store for potato chips and bread and cans of spaghetti, piling food and books and blue-ruled paper on the bed, surrounding our prone bodies. We didn't know where we would live or how we would support a child. But we did know that we were rootless, and gutsy, and that we didn't need wealth or possessions to be a family. This seemed to us a beginning.

# 5
# cairn

THE LIGHTS ARE off in the vestibule outside surgery where we wait for the doctor to emerge. A janitor sweeps the floor. My sister holds her arms around me as we sit on the chairs outside the door to the operating theater. A hospital employee asks if we need anything.

"Can you get us a blanket?" Christie asks.

But there isn't any blanket that can erase this chill. My teeth chatter so intensely that I lock them to keep from biting my tongue.

All I can think of are the calls I made to my children after they took Richard back to surgery. The buried sorrow in Joshua's throaty question when I'd called him at college, "Is he going to be okay, Mum?"

"He's with the best surgeon in the world, honey," I answered.

The friend I asked to watch over seventeen-year-old Dylan said she would relay the news to our daughter when she woke up, but that "it wasn't the time" to upset her with this information. I sit in the waiting room, knowing that I've made the wrong choice to allow things to be kept from our girl—we don't keep secrets—but I'm unable to do anything now to change it. Our cell phones don't work in the waiting room. The only pay phone is down a long hall. I won't get up and walk those hundred steps to call Dylan; I think that if my body is close to Richard's I can save him. I can't speak of my regret to my sister. She holds me and keeps saying reassuring words: "It's going to be okay, he's strong, they got him back to surgery in time, hang on."

We sit on cold chairs in the cold room next to the room with his cold body. No one comes out. Hours pass. I imagine Richard's body in shock. Ever since I placed my hands on him in the elevator, I've been concentrating on sending him my vitality. If I can force some of my indomitable will into him, then maybe he can endure.

I remember the day we said our new vows in the sunshine, nineteen years married, Mount Rainier shining onto Mystic Lake like a stony buffalo, Richard sitting across an old log in his bandana, leaning in to give me a kiss, me holding the swell of his strong calf. I cannot imagine losing this man. I can't see into a future where he doesn't exist. I imagine whispering into his ear while he lies on the operating table: *Later, I'll tell you the story of today as if I am a cairn and you have forgotten a fork in the trail.* I will him to live, live, live.

Suddenly, I stand up and push Christie's arms aside. I can't keep the news of what's happening from our daughter. I run down the hallway to make the call, and then I hear my sister yell, "Sonya! Come back!"

I pivot on the grey linoleum marked with such serious scuffs. I run back to the waiting room and see Dr. M looking straight at me. His eyes are tired and regretful. "He's recovering. He had four liters of fluid in his abdomen, and copious amounts in his left chest region. This shouldn't have happened. They should have called me right away."

"When can I see him?" I ask. I can't take the doctor's word for it. I want to know that my husband has returned.

An hour later, when I arrive at the ICU to wait for Richard's arrival, there's a man dying across the hall. The family wants to light a candle to honor the man's passing in the way of their religion. They're distressed that the hospital environment will not allow for such a fire. I stand in Richard's empty room and try not to look. Dr. M arrives and says that after a few minutes I have to leave, that the nurses can't do their work if I'm there—it's policy, no discussion. I relent. In a few hours, I'll come back to check Richard's status, see if I can sneak in early, I think.

The steel gurney is rolled in from the narrow hallway. From the doorway of the intensive care unit, I watch three nurses hover over my husband's body, now covered in a thick blanket. Richard won't wake up for hours. I hold his hand, which is huge, hefty, cold. I wonder how we will speak of his near death from the cancer surgery when he awakes, how this story will enter the family lore. My mind searches for something witty I can say to him when his eyes open: *Dramatic enough for ya?* or *Let's try for boring for the next, oh, thirty years*. Instead, I lean over and kiss his eyelids just to feel their tender skin.

The nurses send me away to rest. On the telephone I tell Joshua that his father is going to survive. We cry. Dylan wants to know what happened while she slept. She's shocked by the sudden news; her voice is reflective and sad.

I ask them to be sweet to themselves, tell them that I'll call again after a sleep. We listen to each other breathe. The near loss feels close, like we could disrupt his safety if we say too much.

When I return, Richard is sitting up in the ICU, the tube in his mouth and nose preventing him from speaking. His midnight eyes stare at me blankly.

"Sweetheart," I say, and he cries, silent tears. He's not self-conscious about crying. He'd usually be throwing out medical questions, engaging the nurses, trying to make people laugh at his jokes. Instead, he's all heart. "Why are his hands so swollen?" I ask the nurse.

"Two surgeries. Poor circulation," she answers. "We have a list of things that have to happen to get him released from the ICU and onto the hospital's digestive cancers ward."

"So he can start chemo," I say.

"He's already completed the first step. He's sitting up and interacting with us. Then, when we know his lungs are safe, the breathing tube can be removed. The NG or feeding tube remains until he can safely digest food."

I lift the blanket and count the tubes running from his chest, abdomen, nose, arms, penis: thirteen. I'm not as shocked by his body's appearance as I am by the childlike way he watches me. His eyes are wide, unblinking, soft. Everything about him—his muscles, his manner, his rhythm—has softened.

The nurse gives Richard a piece of paper and a Sharpie. He writes the same questions over and over, in black marker on a white page: *Who is here? Who has been here? Who is coming?*

He will write these questions again and again for days, and I will answer them again and again: "My sister is with us. Your boss was here. My father is coming."

Within a day, the breathing tube is removed, and he leaves the ICU. He looks like he's improving. His eyes track me in the room. His cheeks are pink. But when he can speak, there are more questions: *What happened before now? Where do I work? Where are the children? When am I going home? Where is home?*

"He doesn't know who he is," I tell the nurses.

"It's just the morphine," the nurses say.

In three days he's moved to a private room. Across from his bed is a counter with a steel sink and a fluorescent light. Near the window is a bathroom with an industrial toilet that has a chain and lever, and a loud flush. Bottles marked URINE and containers marked WARNING: CHEMO sit on the floor. There is a small shower with cracked tiles and an emergency cord. I sleep on a rollaway bed tucked under the window ledge. The view from the window is of a gravel roof. One foot away, close enough so I can reach out and find his skin, Richard sleeps on a high bed surrounded by monitors that beep alarms and pump breaths. At night, when the room is dark and the equipment casts its unnatural light, I lie on the cold sheets and watch the helicopters arrive each hour like steely birds, their blades piercing the sky. The helicopters bring trauma patients. This first night, they bring a boy whose legs are severed. I hear the stories when I sit in the cafeteria and I eat the food that tastes like it's never been alive. I push myself away from the table and walk to the tiny wood-paneled chapel where there is no talk, only weeping and prayer.

Before we came to the hospital, we left our home on Tiger Mountain near Seattle, a place with ravens and owls and peaceful winged ones, but that was before we said good-bye to our friends, before we placed our worldly goods in storage, before we flew across the country to meet a surgeon who, it had been said, could save my husband's life. His body has been saved, though I no longer know if the husband I married is located inside that body.

When Dr. M comes to examine Richard, there's fluid on his lungs. Until he's stable, the five-day protocol of heated chemotherapy cannot begin. The protocol also cannot begin too late in the week, or he's at risk of organ failure. If the chemotherapy isn't possible, they can't kill the microscopic cancer cells, and the disease returns.

"What happens if we don't get the full five days?" I ask, but I already know the answer. We have to wait for the pathology results.

PMP happens to one in a million; fewer than one thousand cases are diagnosed annually in the United States. The dominant prognostic factor for survival is the pathology—is this a low-grade cancer, or the more malignant high-grade tumor that's likely to respond as poorly to treatment as colorectal cancer? Complete surgical removal of PMP is extremely hard to accomplish, and the best chance for survival lies in early detection, choosing a PMP specialist for a surgeon, and completing HIPEC, the heated chemotherapy. Residual disease is common, and treatment involves more surgery to a body already wounded. Outcomes aren't pretty for very many; I know the disease recurs in nearly three-quarters of the survivors. Still, for those with a complete cytoreduction and chemo, there is a slender chance of never requiring treatment again.

Richard is moved to the floor we will live on for weeks, for those with digestive cancers, gastrointestinal malignancies. We live now in a place that serves disease. The halls form a square, with wings for patients with stomach cancer, appendix cancer, colorectal cancer, and cancers of the abdomen and pelvis. The bulletin board outside his room looks as if a primary school teacher designed it: in bold letters are GASTRIC CANCER, PERITONEAL CARCINOMATOSIS, HEPATOBILIARY OR LIVER CANCER, PANCREATIC CANCER, PERITONEAL MESOTHELIOMA, and ABDOMINOPELVIC SARCOMA, as well as my husband's disease: PSEUDOMYXOMA PERITONEI, the cancer that once grew like inflamed jam through his abdomen.

We lie in the room where the monitors beep and the equipment casts its cyaneous glow. When Richard is resting, I think of our former, cancerless life: the house in the woods, the liberal-minded city, the artistic friends, my career in marketing for museums, a good income I gave up to pursue writing and teaching. I think of the generations of family violence that we left to become the kind of couple we'd always wanted to be: kind, adventuresome, passionate. I think of our children, thriving teenagers who sometimes enjoy our company, who have said they find our family "amazing."

I don't feel very amazing at the cancer hospital. I resent cancer for its intrusion into our lives. I thought myself in my prime, midforties powerful, and my husband a handsome, magnetic leader devoted to our family. Instead, here in the hospital, there is death everywhere. Instead, there is no past, even one into which we might be borne back ceaselessly. Instead, we are lost.

While I'm trying to sort out why Richard appears so confused, his lungs continue to fill with fluid. The tumor removed from his diaphragm has caused flooding in his pleural cavity (the space between the lungs and the thoracic cage). During the surgery, Dr. M placed tubes as a preventive measure to drain any fluid that collected after the operation. They aren't draining fast enough. Dr. M shows me how to clear clotted blood from Richard's chest tubes, and I carefully watch for black globules inside the plastic tubing that falls from the holes in his mid-right and mid-left ribs to the linoleum floor. I learn to press my fingers against the hard plastic to draw the knotty clots toward the bulbs that hold them like thrombus petals. Once I would have been disgusted by such a task, but now I consider myself essential, beyond taking offense. Richard's body requires my care. I'm not just his advocate. It's a relief that the doctors and nurses have included me in their work.

On the second day after we arrive in his private room, his heart appears to be weak and compromised. There's a window of a few days to get Richard healthy enough to begin the chemo. Every day when I call the children, I sound encouraging, but I'm scared that their father will fall again, that the bare consciousness he reveals will slide toward blackness, toward death.

Every night Richard falls asleep asking, "What is happening?" The helicopter blades *slice-slice-slice*. The compression machines on his legs *pft-pft-pft*. I stare into the sky wishing that I knew what to do.

On the third day on the hospital ward I lean over, find his dark-blue eyes, make them fix upon my mostly steady gaze. "Richard," I say, "the doctor is coming soon and we're going to get you ready to talk to him, okay?"

And he closes his eyes and nods, not able to speak much for the tube that is running into his nose and down the back of his throat, not able to take in a deep breath for the liquid that is filling his lungs.

The nurse changes one of the bags that drips constantly, and I look at her with hope for reassurance. As if she is reading my thoughts, she says, "It may take a while to get his strength back after a surgery like this. But he'll be up and walking the halls in a few days, won't you?"

And then Richard grunts, lifts his eyebrow, using the least energy, never arguing with them, never wanting to make it more difficult for anyone who is watching over him.

The daily round is staffed with residents, specialists, and researchers, a dozen white coats grouped against pale walls, the floors edged with lint. I tell the medical team that my husband cannot remember his life.

"Let's start the chemotherapy and see if his cognition returns," Dr. M says.

Before she leaves for home, Christie and I pull Dr. M aside. "What about the blood loss during surgery?" we ask.

"The internal bleeding he suffered could have caused an anoxic incident," the surgeon says.

It's the first time I've heard this term. "Anoxic?" I ask.

"Lack of oxygen to the brain," my sister whispers.

"We want to get as many days of chemo as we can."

"We're doing five days of chemo, right?" I ask.

"The chemo can't happen too far out, so with the complications he's experiencing, we're likely to get four. We have to make sure that his lungs are more clear," says Dr. M.

I understand that we're on to the next thing, that saving his life is more important than figuring out the mystery of his mind. But I can't believe that this man is the husband I kissed good-bye a few days ago, when he left for surgery.

This husband is now a shell. He has gone to surgery one person and come back another. I don't have any way to tell someone that I have lost him. I know Richard no longer remembers where he lives, or the life we share with our children, or the work he does. I know he has fifty stitches running from his heart to his pelvis, where they have opened him up, taken out his organs, unraveled his bowels, and scraped the cancer that clung to his entrails. I know he has thirteen tubes running from his body, each of which puts something into him or takes something out. I know we have twenty-four hours to clear the fluid from his lungs and ensure his heart is durable enough so we can teem his gut with chemo emptied into his belly where it will scorch his organs, killing every last cancer cell. I know this will be painful, and he will have to endure 345,600 seconds of this pain before it will be over. I know when his eyes rest upon me they are calm, but when they look about the room they are wild, as if he can't quite sort out how this happened to him.

I walk the halls of the cancer hospital and I observe men sitting up in bed reading the *Wall Street Journal*, coordinating their calendars with their spouses and colleagues, laughing with their children when they come to visit, remembering what they just did five minutes ago, for God's sake. Compared to them, Richard is living in the fog of a distant land, an underworld that he can't even report from, since he has little language. I gaze at the white paper on which he wrote notes in the ICU, and I see the same question over and over in a slanted, strange scrawl: *Who is here?*

I have the same question for my husband.

# 6
# scout

BY THE TIME our son Joshua had his first birthday, we were doing everything we could to become a steadfast, reliable family. None of it worked.

Richard had taken a job as a pharmaceutical sales rep, traveling through Ontario, though he was able to return home most evenings. We lived in a worn-down bungalow north of Toronto, in an Italian Canadian community where little English was spoken.

"Hey darlin', let's take him to the pub," Richard said on nights when the baby wouldn't sleep. He wrapped Joshua in blankets and we walked down to the neighborhood tavern, where the kid usually settled to loud rock music.

"He calms with the bass," Richard said, "just like when you were pregnant."

We had roommates to help pay the rent, and we threw parties so we wouldn't lose connection with our college friends, but we were struggling to take care of our son. Joshua cried for hours every evening, and I met Richard at the door many times already dressed in my coat, ready to leave the house.

"Rough day?" Richard would ask as he stashed his briefcase, loosened his tie, and took the baby in one arm like he was cradling a football. "Come on, little man. Let's give your old mum a break."

Those nights, I read at the library, took ballet classes, walked around the block. An hour of being childless soothed me enough so that I could continue feeding the baby through the night, every two hours. Those first months, I would learn our child was sensitive and active, a combination that would challenge us, since we had few parenting skills to cope with our stress. Richard met whatever his little boy gave. He churned the kid's legs, sang him James Taylor songs, tucked him in a sling for walks in the snow.

"I've never seen a kid like this," my mother would say when my parents came to stay, so Richard and I could have some time alone.

"He's going to be a tennis player!" Richard would tell her, as if that were clear from our firstborn's early crawling. And when Joshua walked at ten months, heaving himself up onto his feet by clinging to shelves and turning the dials on the stereo receiver, my mother said, "How are you doing this?"

I knew she meant allowing him to try things she would have forbidden. "I can't keep saying 'no' to him," I said. "I've got to find some 'yes' or else we'll crush him."

But I also knew that I had to find a way to give myself that kind of freedom.

One day that spring, after returning home from a stroll with Joshua in the used pram our home nurse helped me find, I saw a postcard from Wendy in the mail. A photograph of panoramic mountains near Banff in the Canadian Rockies, the place where my friend had traveled for a summer job, then ended up staying. I stared at the image for a long time. Turquoise Moraine Lake and the Valley of the Ten Peaks: images we'd grown up seeing on the twenty-dollar bill. Banff was located in Canada's largest national park, one hundred miles west of Calgary. With 2,500 square miles of mountains, ice fields, glaciers, rivers, waterfalls, canyons, caves, forests, and those famed turquoise lakes, and surrounded by the national parks of Yoho, Jasper, Kootenay, and a network of provincial forests in Alberta and British Columbia, it was a vast ecological sanctuary. People could live there. People with families.

Changes in location always made me feel more alive. Richard longed to settle down, to make the stable home he never had. I wanted to wander, to cast off ideas people had for me, test my mettle. Being raised in Canadian culture had given me an outsider's sensibility, and I was never nostalgic for a restrictive suburban America. My childhood move north brought me everything—nature, fine storytelling, my man. Now I wanted to see if the archetypal Canadian experience of survival, unlike the American frontier story of conquest, could play out in my choices. Mountains allured. Wilderness beckoned. But could we survive their harsh conditions?

That evening after dinner I showed Richard the postcard and told him that I wanted to leave the city. He pumped Joshua's little legs, flew his scrawny body toward the ceiling, tossed him a foam ball—our nightly ritual to exhaust our child's nearly ceaseless energy.

"How are we going to live?" he asked.

"I'll work. You can stay at home."

His eyes flashed possibilities like fireworks across his angular face.

"What about the money to move?"

"Let's sell some of our stuff. We'll reduce our expenses. We can do this."

"I want to stay for the Serious Moonlight tour," Richard said. David Bowie would be in Toronto on Labor Day weekend.

"Let's stay until Joshua's first birthday."

We would not arrive in that land of glaciated limestone and shale until the New Year, after I had secured work as the editor of a local magazine and Richard was ensconced in daddydom. He was thrilled to walk all over town, his boy on his shoulders, comfortable in the winter clime among skiers, mountaineers, adventurers. Richard shared that alpine wanderlust; he knew what to wear; he was a robust furnace of pink-cheeked happiness.

To me, the Canadian Rockies were a romance and a devastation. The postcard image hadn't translated the sensation of forty below, and eight months of snow, and the isolation of living encircled by ten-thousand-foot rocks, the weather arriving only overhead, the distant horizon always obscured. I hadn't counted on the hard work necessary to acquire the skills to endure. I hadn't realized boots would be required for warmth and stability, not fashion; that, many months, skin froze with exposure of under a minute; that the beauty of the vast mountain temples would slay my composure. We arrived in that town with no car, our only entertainment the turntable and hundreds of albums we'd carted across the frozen plains. We left behind rugs and the washer and my wedding dress to bring musical memories encased in protective sleeves of white frost, like snow.

In Banff, we carried groceries home in our backpacks and skated on the Bow River. We walked quiet trails where bull elk shed velvet and cow elk mewed to their copper calves. We stared at glaciers. We soaked in the hot springs. We went to Pop's Bakery, ate buttery cookies, and made snow angels. When Joshua turned two, we enrolled him in a day care whose leaders taught us how to parent, their encouragement a balm to our shame-filled childhoods.

Richard took work as a tour bus driver, and he tried out his new knowledge on me everywhere we went: names of mountains and mountain ranges and mountain passes, geological history, indigenous tribes, early alpinists, early settlers, railroad stories, river systems, wind patterns, waterfall depths, animal tracks, habitats, forests, tundra, even how to back a bus full of scared foreigners up a steep switchback. He picked up Joshua many afternoons in the massive motor coach, the children pressed to the window of the day care in awe of the kid who got to ride home in the fifty-seater.

Each night, when we returned home to our apartment at Squirrel Corners, we put an album on the turntable, grimacing every time the rumble of the nearby Canadian Pacific Railway crossing caused the needle to skip a line or two of a song. I'd hear the train whistle in the distance and imagine the worn echo resounding from the faraway sandstone hoodoos and the Kicking Horse River, through spiral tunnels, over the Continental Divide, past ice-capped Castle Mountain, and then straight to the Banff station, a block from our home. Then I'd wait for that train's arrival, all of its romance and earnestness and archetypal longing splintered into discordant notes and my husband shouting

"Noooooo!" and the baby laughing to see his father's large body lunge toward the stereo. I should have been the happiest woman. But something skipped clashingly inside me too.

I left my writing work to take a money job entertaining media for a grand hotel, and started spending many evenings drinking with journalists on the company's expense account. I escorted fashion photographers and people from film companies and ski magazines around Banff by day, and drank expensive wine while telling amusing stories to Japanese, German, British, Aussie, and American media by night. I liked not feeling like somebody's wife, not identifying as somebody's parent, and I found reasons to extend the work into all-night parties.

Alcohol emboldened me. In its grip, I could loosen whatever strictures a dogmatic Catholic upbringing imposed on my young mind. It never occurred to me that I might avoid the substance and simply change my thinking. Who would I be if I didn't belong to someone? Who would I be if I didn't have a drinking problem? Who would I be if I didn't need something to set me right? I didn't wonder about these questions, except alone, in the disgrace of some drunken binge.

Sometimes I went out with girlfriends to bars and walked home after midnight on snowy streets. "I don't know," I'd shout over my shoulder when Richard wanted to know what time I'd be back, even though I knew that his worry would keep him from sleeping.

Once, Richard got tired of my irresponsibility, walked into a party, threw me over his shoulder, and carried me home. My friends laughed at my stubbornness. When we arrived back at our house, I slammed the door.

"You can't leave me with the kid when I have to go to work in the morning," he yelled.

"I just wanted to be myself without people to take care of for a while," I yelled back.

He threw the push-dial landline phone across the room. I jumped out of its path. The phone smashed against the wall, the long beige cord a snake across my feet.

We stood toe to toe, yelling things we knew would hurt the other: all of the you-always, you-never, I-give-up stories we believed about ourselves.

Later that afternoon, I called to apologize. He came home and we had makeup sex and resolved to start anew. This pattern kept me from realizing what I wanted: to be a good mother in an unconventional marriage. Living under the shadow of someone so magnetic kept me hidden. Richard tried so hard to be the best at everything, and I grew bored with his one-man show.

Richard began working at Sunshine Village Ski Resort, marketing to skiers, managing media, carving turns like a he-man in his svelte ski attire. He taught hotel guests and townspeople to play tennis in the summer. In between, he did nifty gigs like a modeling stint for GWG, Canada's leading jeans brand, in which he was paid to take a trip and stand on a mountain ledge while a helicopter camera captured his ridiculously fine ass. I was envious of his ease, and tired of standing in his light—the same light that drew me to him when I fell in love with his intelligence and wit—and the only way I could get out was to become the wild girl.

Eighteen months after we arrived in the mountains, we bought a house, and I found myself pregnant again. The pregnancy was unplanned, but I was joyfully expectant. This was my chance to change. During the pregnancy, I (mostly) quit smoking and drinking, and took long walks alongside the river. That spring, as I looked out high hospital windows onto resplendent Mount Rundle, our daughter Dylan was born. Our girl was tiny and big-eyed and solemn, and I felt like a part of myself could calm now that she had arrived.

Through the day care I'd met a group of parents who were artists, and we took our children to karate lessons with a man we called Sifu, a Zen master and recent immigrant from Korea, who spoke in poetic sentences and told stories that had mysteries at their center. That summer, the short, pot-bellied man with a beard like Confucius and a booming, theatrical demeanor took me into his office and made me tea. He swirled the leaves in the cup, then poured the whole thing out onto my saucer.

"You do not take who you are into practice," he said, making a *ckee* sound in his nose and pointing at the tea debris. "See what happen?" he asked, staring at my overflowing saucer as if I had forced him to spill the leaves. "No Zen without first empty cup!"

"Believe me, I get it," I said. I'd spent most of my twenties trying to conform to some version of myself that I thought others wanted. I was willing to dump any of my habits, functions, history, if it meant that I'd get a chance at reinvention.

"You come here tomorrow night," he commanded, and I did, sitting for an hour that first evening with three women friends and several climbers who had their own reasons for stilling their minds. I sat two nights a week, evenings filled with silence and laughter and koans that I thought Sifu must have designed to split our brains.

"You have your own treasure house. Why do you search outside?" Sifu asked. "Always 'where is my treasure house?' *Ckee.*" And he laughed, big-bellied chuckles, while we sat, our spines tall, our faces serious, as we tried to crack his code.

"I don't see why you have to be out all night at meditation now," Richard said, angry that something else was taking me away.

"Sifu invited you," I said.

Richard tried to cross those long legs on the cruel basement floor, but his sharp mind wouldn't be blunted by a boot-camp method. When Sifu helped me quit smoking through his crazy wisdom blend of acupuncture and mental toughness, Richard decided to support my practice. He was relieved that I wasn't partying at clubs and pubs and coming home tipsy, but he still wished I was happy doing all of the things that satisfied him: watching television, playing sports, staying home.

"You can go to those full-moon all-night things, but I can't have the kids three nights a week by myself," he said.

"That sounds fair to me," I answered.

Then Sifu, up to his own shenanigans, insisted that I bring the children to practice. Joshua jumped on the bed in the spare room like it was a trampoline. Dylan crawled on my lap, inserting her fingers into my nose.

"Great strength!" the Zen sadist said.

Sifu introduced our family to his own teacher, whom we called the Wolfmaster, a lean calligrapher from Japan who climbed mountains like a goat. We hiked in the backcountry with our strange troupe, and threw parties where we painted and danced. We enacted something called "stupid practice," time on a stage acting silly, so we could relax our too-solid egos. I returned home feeling I was shaking loose much of my old, insecure self. I could do something difficult, persist in a discipline my capable husband had given up on.

"There's my spiritual scout," Richard said, proud of my effort.

He was grateful that I hadn't killed myself in one of my alcoholic blackouts, that I'd found some peace with a group of people who were weird but obviously not going anywhere dangerous. And Richard was correct: I had become his scout. In these early years of our married life, I discovered that my job was to locate my truth. Not his.

One day, with the toddlers tucked into day care, I climbed from Lake O'Hara to its ledges at eight thousand feet with Wolfmaster and Sifu, the spring-slanted sun buttering snow patches and early poppies at the edges of an icy stream, and my feet a shocking blue cast after I thrust my bare toes into the glacial melt. The Wolfmaster wore a straw hat and walked on the rocks across the river, calling my spirit name, Sunyata—Sanskrit for "emptiness." I squinted into the light, watching starbursts erupt from alpine snow.

"If you like snow, don't be afraid to freeze to death!" he said, and I smiled, scared to ask what he meant. "Someday you will know this meaning," he said. "You will not forget."

I swear it happened just like that.

# 7

# serum

WHEN RICHARD WAKES up four days out of the surgery, his lungs have stopped filling with fluid. He had one round of chemotherapy in surgery, and now the ongoing treatment begins. One nurse supports his body while another changes the sheets under him. They roll him from side to side while he grimaces in silence. I'm scared one of the tubes coming from his body is going to be jerked out of him, that blood or urine or morphine is going to be unleashed on the room, though the clean, spare gestures of the nurses make their maneuvers look like Tai Chi. I unstrap the pressure wrap machine that forces a band of oxygen around his legs to prevent blood clots from forming. The hair on his legs is wet with sweat, and I lay my cool hands on them, wanting to offer some relief.

The nurses ask me to bring them clean cloths and spotless sheets and unmarked soap, and I'm thankful to be useful. They speak in measurements of what is being eliminated, and I write their words in a little notebook: *10 cc. urine*; *12 right chest tube*; *13 left chest tube*. Nurse Jen leans in with a wide shoulder and lifts Richard's upper body to bring him into a sitting position. This is their goal for the day—to get his legs over the edge of the bed, to help his body strengthen by allowing it to sit for a few minutes. They strip the gown from his seventy-six-inch frame and hand the clothing to me. I look down at the patches of dried blood over its even stripes. Near the door is a large bin where the soiled linens go, and I walk the gown there, placing it with the sheets that are still warm from his body. I can hear the shouts of the shift change on the other side of the door, and I peer through to the light, watch the interns laughing, listen to people talk about the weekend. My hand is on the door and there is part of me that wants to walk out and get a hotel room, order a pizza, and sit in front of the television watching movies—to pretend that none of this has happened.

I want to be a woman whose main problems are getting the kids through college, finding meaningful work, dropping the extra fifteen pounds. I want to stop asking the doctors why there's something missing. I want to make things easier for the nurses, to ask the doctors the right questions, to be loving and kind and gentle with my beloved. I want to pretend I don't know what I know: the man I have known for decades has gone somewhere else. Instead, I walk to the supply closet for new gowns, a comb, baby powder. When I walk back to the room, his naked back is to me, and I am dumbfounded by his frailty.

His shoulders hang low and his back is bowed. He is forty pounds lighter than he was a few days ago. His is a body without strength, without vigor, without lust, without intention, without memories. A body taken apart and reassembled, a body that has not settled into the space of gravity, a body that knows nothing about its own scars, crevices, grumbles.

"Would you like to bathe your husband in private?" Nurse Jen asks, and I walk across the hard linoleum. I come to his side and say, "Yes." She brings me a pink bowl filled with warm water and in it soaks a bar of soap. She lays out towels and a washcloth. She walks across the room, pulls the curtain, and exits, closing the door fully behind her, not leaving it a few inches ajar as it has been before this moment.

My husband closes his eyes, and I take his hand in mine. The light of the new is in his thick fingers and large square palms. I squeeze the water from the cloth and rub it across the soap, beginning to make swirls in his palm, pressing into the flesh of the life line, stroking through each of his fingers. I lay the dry towel across his knees and place his hand to rest there while I glide the cloth up his arm, softly caressing against the grain of his wispy black hair, smoothing over his wide shoulder. I lift the arm onto my shoulder and rub under it, silky soap making a trail into the pit, its dark curls slick with lather. Once I could lick there, swirling his hair in my tongue, breathing in his scent as if to memorize its salty musk. Now there is no odor, except of chemotherapy, the smell of ice on steel. It is the fragrance of his first treatment, a burning liquid they poured inside him while his organs lay on the table near his open body. I imagine the synthetic medicine binding to his cells, the sick cells dying, the dead cells pouring out of him, onto my cloth.

I soak the cloth in water again and rinse him in its warmth. Droplets slide down his forearms, where I want them to wake something that wants to live, where I want them to rouse some fire under the pallor. I dry the length of his arm, almost as big as half of me and so weak it flops to his side without support. I rub down his broad back, pat his left arm and hand, touch the skin tenderly. I walk around the pole that holds his IV lines, avoiding the tape and tubes near his wrist. I wash the dried blood near his chest tubes, keeping the water away from the tape down his middle, a wide bandage over two feet long where his skin is quietly restitching itself. My hand travels down to clean his penis, and I gently swab around the catheter, my hand finding his testicles, holding their weight in the way I would if I wanted to make love. I wipe him with sweet strokes; I look up to his face. He opens his eyes. Tender, surrendered eyes. Tears fall down my chin at the dignity in his submission.

I wrap him in his clean gown and lean him back into a fresh pillow, strapping on the leg bands that will pulse his blood through the day and night, making the sound of wind as it is carried, a measured music in our unsteady life.

Later that afternoon, the nurse fills Richard's peritoneal cavity with a chemotherapy called 5FU, or fluorouracil, a toxic agent that acts to interrupt an enzyme required for DNA replication, killing cancer cells permanently. Once his belly is full, he moves from lying on his right side to his left side every thirty minutes, for a total of six hours. This is so the chemo can reach all of his organs. It is incredibly hard work for him, as hard as any workout he has ever done, and once he moves onto one side, we prop him up with pillows and foam pads so he can stay fixed in one place. After the moving is complete, the fluid stays in him until it's drained out eighteen hours later. Then he is refilled, and the moving begins again. The fluid presses against his ribs and wounds, and the intense pressure is the source of his pain. During the time the chemo fluid enters him I sing a song, no words, just sounds. The melody seems to calm Richard.

I take off my amber beads and press them to his back for their coolness, and because I imagine that the gems he's seen me wear might be comforting on his skin. I run a damp cloth over his forehead, and his languorous eyes open. He is an inchoate being, newly drawn but fully aware.

I don't speak much because I know he's trying to stay alive. I understand that he craves the quiet. He isn't worried about who he used to be. That desire for a solid identity is mine.

The man who survived on smarts, charm, and looks has vanished. Who he was, isn't.

I hold his face in my hands, his black whiskers under my palms, my fingers pressed to his temples. I hear: *Everything that you take to be your story is gone. All that there is: touching, telling, making things. If no thoughts arise, there's no experience of anything.*

"Quiet, right baby? No thoughts. No thing. Nothing," I think I whisper. But then I wonder if I'm speaking, or if my mind is transmitting those thoughts to his mind.

His eyes close. He nods.

Dad comes to stay for five days. He sleeps at a hotel near the hospital each evening, while I'm in Richard's room. When my father comes back in the morning, he gives me his key and urges me to leave and get some rest.

"We have to keep the room calm for him, Dad," I say. I show my father how to assist Richard as he turns his long, reclining body from right to left so the scalding solution travels through his innards. I show my father how to refill the aromatherapy diffuser I have placed on the counter, so the fragrance of rose attar and rosemary fills the room. I ask him to speak softly, so Richard can get some sleep. My father comes to Richard's side and punches him three times in the shoulder.

"He's going to be fine!" he says.

"Dad."

My father, who is always reliable in a crisis, who is generous with all his resources, who, during my childhood, hit first and talked later, repeats his gesture of love, the one he learned from a family whose way of expressing affection was roughhousing: he punches Richard on the shoulder.

"If you do that again, I'm going to have to ask you to leave," I say over my husband's body, staring my father down so he knows I'm serious.

When I return to the room an hour later, NASCAR blasts from the television and my father claps his hands loud enough to shake the nurses from their perch. I fume.

Richard opens his eyes and looks up at me and whispers, "It's okay."

Four days later, in a letter to friends, written from the hospital, I say:

> Today is Richard's last day of chemo. The doctors have opted for four rather than five days. His second day was excruciating, but they changed his pain medication yesterday and he was able to rest rather than fight his way through it. . . . He is almost always watching from far away. The medical term for this is lack of lucidity, but it sometimes seems by his language and questions that he is seeing in two worlds now, the one in ordinary life and the one heading toward death.

At eight in the evening, Richard receives the final round of chemotherapy. It's been a week since the surgery, and Richard has had nothing more than ice cubes to taste. My father sends me to the cafeteria. The food is terrible; even the salad is a sodden, brown mess. I walk past the greasy sandwiches, the fried foods, the hot table where entrées sit in soupy goop. I eye a Krispy Kreme doughnut. Looks like dinner. I eat it in three bites. I am proud to be able to live on even this ridiculous repast. I am alive. And strong. I think I can will Richard's body and my own into continued existence.

When my father leaves and Richard is sleeping, I walk the halls. I'm alone now with my thoughts. I cannot sleep when he is resting in the day, and I cannot sleep at night when he is restless. I want to take my shoes off and run in the grass. Since the night of the emergency surgery, I have not left—and I will not leave—the hospital, not even for a walk outside. I take to the halls, listen to screams of pain, and I cry. One of the nurses insists on taking me for a drive. I'm agitated as she steers through roads lined with gritty tenement buildings. I ask her why she is doing this. She says she thinks I could use a break.

I walk the stairs six times a day for exercise. I cry a lot. I decide the staff will have to get used to the woman who cries as she moves through the building. I peer into the rooms with the doors left open. A wife grabs my arm to ask if my husband is here for PMP too. Her burly, brusque police officer of a man is in constant agony.

"Has anyone told you how long the chemo pain lasts?" she asks.

"I don't know," I tell her.

"He won't let me go out of the room! I told him to stop crying and keep focused on what he needs to do to fight the cancer!" she says.

I nod my head. My husband is angelic, sweet. I do not tell her that he didn't used to be so peaceful. I do not say there is no one here anymore to fight. I do not tell her that Richard's memories are not returning, even in our second week after the surgery.

I slide into bed after checking Richard's urine output, making sure he's warm and dry, since he tends to sweat through his sheets. Soon after I settle in, he bolts upright straight out of sleep and says: "*Sera-sanguineous*. I like that word. It reminds me of the grassy steppes of the African plains." He will barely speak for another month, but there he is, uttering complex metaphors. He's never been to Africa, though I recall the steppes were the habitat of the mammoth and the first humans, about ten thousand generations ago. My husband hasn't uttered either *sera* or *sanguineous* in the twenty-five years I've known him. I have no idea what he's talking about. When we return home, I go running for the dictionary. The phrase means "the serum involving bloodshed."

Truth is also sera-sanguineous. Truth is the serum involving bloodshed. Truth can save us, I think.

When we read it in the preparatory notes, we knew it was going to happen. Still, it's a shock to see it, or rather not to see it: the belly button, the navel, disappeared. The eighth day after surgery, Richard's left lung having finally been drained of its excess fluid, the left chest tube is removed. (The right tube will be removed days later when its draining is complete.) Dr. M peels back the dressing running from just under Richard's xiphoid bone on his chest to the top of his pelvis. Lying there, like a snake, a pouched pink zipper, are fifty stitches, scarred skin with no sign of ever having been connected to an umbilical cord.

I try to hide my shock, cover my tracks, imitate the face of calm in the way that partners do: we communicate without ever opening our mouths. I'm quiet until the doctor leaves.

"Maybe you can get a tattoo on the scar," I joke.

His empty body frightens me. I wonder if he can read me, if he remembers what I used to be like, if he knows if I am fearful or brave.

"Does it hurt?" I ask.

Richard moves his hands down the sides of his abdomen and lifts his head to look, as if the navel might have fallen, slipped to the side while he was sleeping.

We cry for the missing navel, this remnant of having been nourished by his mother. I wonder where they sent his spleen, the big bucket of cancerous mucin, the foot and a half of his lower colon—all likely sent packing to the incinerator, along with the other outworn organs. I imagine us walking through the halls, searching for Richard's navel among the bins of the surgical unit, a dimple of an "innie" lying among abandoned parts.

The surgeon comes by for rounds every morning. Our hours are ordered by the schedule of the doctors. Every morning I ask Dr. M about Richard's absence of memory, and after ten days, the doctor offers to provide a consult with neurology.

The neurologist saunters into the room, blocks me with his back, and leans into Richard on the bed: "Is this your concern or your wife's?" Richard raises his shoulders, lifts his palms, a favorite gesture since his time in the ICU, the *comme ci, comme ça* of opinion giving, the big Whatever sign, showing his postsurgical lack of defensiveness.

"I am just living through this," Richard answers.

The bow-tied neurologist answers, “Hmnn. Now count backward by sevens, starting at one hundred.”

When the neurologist quizzes him, Richard remembers the president, the year, and my name. He tells the neurologist that he does not remember how he got here, what his life was like in the months leading up to the surgery, or much of his past.

“He’s already ahead of ninety-five percent of the population!” the neurologist declares after twelve motor skills tests in five minutes, as if that ought to satisfy our cravings to have Richard remember his life, then and now.

Perhaps he’ll remember his life if his family comes for a visit, I reason. Two weeks into our time at the hospital, Dylan arrives for the weekend. She’s harried trying to find her way into the hospital. I go down the stairs to bring her to the room, to ease her transition to the strange and unsettling cancer floor. She comes up the elevator. We miss each other. She arrives in the room to see her father naked. She’s not scared by his nudity; she’s unsettled by his lack of modesty. He’s a youngster in a man’s body, uninhibited, unaware, an innocent. She has come face-to-face with a man who is no longer her father. She has no way to speak about the sudden change. She massages her father’s Flintstone feet and takes me to get food. In a few months she will write her college-entry essay and hand it to me to read. That’s when I will realize what happened for her on that day.

Joshua doesn’t come to the hospital.

Days, I’m completely focused on getting Richard well. He’s working like a bear that’s come out of the springtime cave, lumbering toward survival. But at night, when he’s sleeping for a few hours between tests, I run the events over and over in my mind. Everything that didn’t happen that day of his surgery angers me—not protecting our privacy, the incorrect blood tests, the lab refusing to release blood, the staff not calling our surgeon, that I didn't argue more loudly on Richard's behalf. Being confined makes me irritated. I'm cross about the terrible food, the unclean room, the lack of information from the doctors, my inability to resolve the mystery of Richard's missing memories. To cope with my anger, I write lists in my journal. I came to the hospital hoping to record our dreams, conversations, and healing journey. But I find myself writing lists.

THINGS THE NURSES AND DOCTORS TELL ME THAT I BOTH APPRECIATE AND RESENT:

1. Get some sleep.

2. This is within the range of normal.

3. You're not used to seeing him this vulnerable.

4. You really ought to get more sleep.

5. How much sleep have you had?

6. His short-term memory loss is normal.

7. It's not useful to remind him of his memory loss by saying, "Do you remember . . . ?"

8. Why don't you take a nap?

9. How is he today?

10. How is he this morning? This evening?

11. It's lucky your sister is here to help you understand the doctors.

12. You have enough time for a rest.

13. How many times have you walked today?

14. Your husband is so peaceful. The engineers, they're the worst. They want everything fixed right away.

15. Well, of course he's confused! Is your husband on narcotics at home?

16. He needs to get out of here without any further complications.

17. Memory lapses can be caused by thyroid problems and vitamin B deficiencies and narcotic drugs. And oh yeah, syphilis. Says the attending physician.

18. The trauma of the second surgery and the loss of blood and the potential decreased blood flow to the brain could have contributed to brain changes. Says the surgeon.

19. It's good it's nothing serious, then?

20. Patience.

There's not a lot of patience in me. It's forced on me, by the rules. Richard cannot eat or drink anything until his belly begins to make grumble sounds. His digestion must mobilize (he has to pass gas) before he can ingest. The only way to make this happen is to walk. He walks the hallways leaning on the pole holding his IV, the blue cords draped over the frame. We run into other recovering patients making this same circumambulation. When we meet people in the hallways, Richard cannot speak. He nods his head, a few words at a time. It's like he's a newborn—gentle demeanor, wide-eyed gaze, stunned silence. When other patients stop to tell us their stories of being out on the golf course a couple of months after their previous surgeries, or of returning to work robust and renewed, I can no longer imagine such a fate for my husband. I don't know how he will return. I only know I can help him start to eat again.

Every time a new person comes in the room, he pleads for food. My sister Shelley sends me a basket of fruit, and I hide it behind the curtains so he cannot see the tempting contours.

"Juice," he says, like a broken record.

After Dylan leaves to go back to high school, Richard's body gets stronger—he can walk once an hour—but his digestion remains as silent as his speech. We spend most of the days ambling along the hallways. He's unspeaking. I talk to nurses, doctors, other caregivers. I keep up a near constant chirp of encouragement for Richard. It's as if he's slowly waking up from a dream, and he isn't sure what's real.

On the seventeenth day, he farts and we rejoice. I take pictures of him famished for his first meal of weak broth. He eats everything that's brought to him, including foods he detested before the surgery. He smiles wide, like a child content with his nursery meal.

Around the time we went to live in the cancer hospital we purchased a digital camera, our family's first. Following the HIPEC surgery, I begin taking pictures of my husband, so I can document his state, so I can make sense of what is happening. I shoot him frail, in his first shower after he can stand again. There are close-ups of stitches and sunken eyes, long shots of being weighed and walking with IV lines, and pictures of him with Nurse Tim. My husband can't remember the day before today, sometimes even the moment before this one, and I want these images to help him find his way back to his memories, if he chooses. I am still his scout, searching for some way to be of use.

But the faith I came into the hospital with is eroding. I know that I should be thankful that my husband is alive, and that dozens of people prayed for him during his ordeal—and I am grateful for the support. My time in the cancer center among the screams of pain, and the surgeons who, for all their earnestness, cannot control deadly cancer, has diminished my God. Maybe my God was the childlike belief that nothing terrible would happen to us if we did everything right. Maybe my God was the love I'd found again after years of avoiding our problems. Maybe my God will be revealed in the body of the man whom, I am starting to see, I do not know.

When he begins to eat, Richard improves rapidly. In three weeks, he's ready to be discharged. Dr. M checks off a list of requirements. I read the discharge sheet: Keep contact with your hometown doctor. Send a Christmas card to your surgeon to tell him your cancer status. Do a CT scan of your chest, abdomen, and pelvis every six months. Complete recommended treatments. Stay strong, just in case you need surgery again. Do not drive for eight weeks. Do not lift more than fifteen pounds. Eat a nutritious diet. Keep your insurance statements. On our form, the surgeon has written NO in block letters beside the recommendation to watch the tumor markers. Another NO next to the requirement to exercise to get ready for the next surgery. There won't be another surgery, in this doctor's opinion. And then the number: 85%.

"What's that mean?" I ask.

"Richard's probability of living ten years is eighty-five percent," Dr. M says.

"What about after ten years?" I ask.

"There are no statistics for that," he answers.

And when I look perplexed the doctor repeats: "We don't have statistics of people living after ten years. This is a new treatment."

I had forgotten that we are the first generation of PMP cancer survivors enduring the Mother of All Surgeries.

Just as Richard has been a model student, a model employee, a model athlete, he now is a model patient. We have done everything asked of us. So why isn't he back to his former self? It's the question that no one has the answer to. I'm determined to understand what has happened to my husband, and to see if I can return him to the man he used to be.

# undoing

WE WERE SETTLING into our family life. And then we found ourselves unhappy with what we'd settled for.

Richard kept taking promotions, jobs with greater responsibility and longer hours—he wanted to prove himself. He came home tired, his temper sharp with our kindergarten-aged son. I'd taken a terrific job working for the Whyte Museum of the Canadian Rockies and was scrambling to transform their marketing program. For two years we both worked too much and were unable to support each other emotionally. The more he confined me with his expectations, the more I wanted to rebel. He wanted a woman who would come watch his tennis tournament. I wanted to play games at a pub. He wanted me to take care of all matters related to the children's education. I wanted to take weekends away. I drank, he yelled. I was living in one of the wildest places on earth, yet completely unable to access my own wildness. When I looked around me, I saw athleticism, countless people who excelled at sports I'd never had the resources to learn. In my mind, Richard kept me from becoming who I really wanted to be. I couldn't yet look at him and see myself reflected there. So I punished my body with alcohol.

Every month or so, I'd stay out dancing at the luxury hotel's club, sipping wine and sweating it out under the lights. But the booze-fueled exercise wasn't enough to compensate in a body just over a hundred pounds, and I got drunk fast, somehow never realizing my altered state. After last call one night, I drove a few blocks toward the tidy houses on Sulphur Mountain, where we lived. The road was icy. I veered into a snowbank.

"Fuck!" I screamed, as the car's front bumper slid into solid ice.

I spun the wheels, but the car only dug in deeper. I wouldn't leave the car and walk home because I couldn't face this scene in the morning, under the town's gaze. In those early hours, I called Richard to rescue me. Still believing that I needed to be rescued by someone else. Scorching shame seared through my body. Richard arrived with a shovel, silent in his fury. I watched him dig out the car. He poured sand under the wheels and expertly maneuvered the vehicle out of the tall bank of frozen snow. I bit the inside of my mouth. There was no way I could promise him I wouldn't act like a maniac again. I seemed to be incapable of reining in the self that refused to obey rules. We went to sleep pretending we were going to be okay.

"I can't do this anymore," he said one night not long afterward, as we cleaned up after dinner.

I'd never heard him surrender.

He sat down at the table, his hands against the sides of his head, his eyes closed. I leaned over to kiss his black, cowlicked crown.

"You need to quit that job," I said, expert at deflecting and denying what was really at stake.

"And do what?" he asked with a kind of desperate curiosity. It was in his voice; he wanted me to name something that might return us to our former magic.

"Tell me what you've always wanted to do," I said. Richard had been trying to take care of the family for so long that he'd forgotten he could choose to work at something that he loved.

"It's impossible," he said.

"Try me."

"I think I'd like to be a physiotherapist." He looked shocked to hear himself say the words. "But I can't. That's four years of school. How would we take care of the kids?"

But we flourished when we were in motion. In a few weeks, we discovered a two-year physical therapy program at a university in Louisville, Kentucky, where my family lived. My father offered us a house he owned to live in until Richard graduated and found a job. Immigration for my Canadian-born husband and children went smoothly. Richard called the college placement office every week to see if he'd been accepted. He was given the good news that spring, and the following summer he started back to school. Our children were four and eight. We packed up our few things and headed south.

After we settled into our new home, we rolled the first garbage bin to the curb, our son following behind. Joshua looked at the easily sideswiped container and frowned in deep thought.

"Daddy, what about the bears?" Joshua asked.

Until that question, I didn't realize how fully we had altered our children's experience. And changed our own frames of reference. America ran on a bootstrap ethos that was difficult to describe, especially to Americans, who didn't realize the country to the north was governed substantially differently. Richard and I had grown up in *la mosaïque culturelle*, and now we'd been tossed into the melting pot, assimilating as fast as our thirtysomething minds would allow. I took a job writing press releases for a public relations company. We had our first encounter with the terrible problem of gun violence when a rageful man brandished a gun at our daughter's preschool. Our children played games that didn't involve snow. On one of his internships, Richard went to live with Mimoo, my maternal grandmother, in western Kentucky. He did four rotations to physical therapy venues: a hospital rehabilitation, a neurological rehabilitation, a hospital burn unit, and an orthopedic outpatient clinic. He charmed my grandmother, charmed his patients, charmed his teachers, charmed his colleagues. He was passionate about his work and thrived when learning anything. In the summer months, he took a job at the distillery my father managed, charring barrels in warehouses where the temperature reached over one hundred degrees. Richard came home covered in soot, with burns on his arms. We took the kids swimming on hot summer afternoons and wondered at how fast a life could change.

Richard graduated second in his class and was honored with an award for professionalism. My family blew horns and whistles in the audience. He took a job to learn about treating spine injuries from one of his mentors. My husband had found his calling. Every day he leapt out of bed, helped get the kids ready for school, and marveled at how he was able to get patients moving again. He was excited to help people, and he was great at it.

I was happy for Richard, but disconnected from myself. I'd taken a job to help transform a sleepy history museum into a technologically adept science center. This was the kind of work I excelled at. To much of my world, I was a wonderful professional, a good mother, a loving wife. But my close friends and family knew that when liquor entered my body, I became another person. I blacked out when drinking now. Sometimes I blacked out for a few minutes, other times most of a night would go by and I wouldn't know what had happened. I didn't know who had shown up, said things, and when I woke the next day, I'd wait for details of my history to arrive from my friends and family. Richard was embarrassed by my behavior. He played sports to cope with his anger, but sometimes it spilled over in insults spit through gritted teeth, in sadness that kept him alone in a dark room, waiting for me.

I was often tired and needy. One morning, I pulled at his coat, asking him not to leave the house we shared with law students, who lived upstairs.

"I have to get to work," he said.

"Please. Just call in sick," I begged. We were whisper-yelling at each other, to avoid scaring the children, who were getting ready for school.

"I can't do that," he said, ever the responsible one.

My arms went out to him, to hold him back.

"Let go!"

I blocked the door of our bedroom.

He turned and pressed me up against the wall.

"Sonya! I can't do everything you want!"

I slid down the wall, crumpling into my fears: that I was losing my mind, that I couldn't really be known by the man I loved.

Living so close to my family of origin was thorny. My parents had divorced, and I was out of touch with my mother. She had left for California to start a new life, and had never been good about wanting contact with other people. I would sometimes call her, to let her know how her grandchildren were doing. But after a while, I grew tired of the responsibility and stopped reaching out. My father was impatient with my boisterous, freethinking son, and dad had a clear preference for ambition, in himself and others. We were reliant on my father's assistance for two years, something I'd never been willing to take for myself but was willing to accept for the sake of my husband. I secretly wanted to be a writer, but couldn't give myself permission to do anything other than the big career. I resisted my father's influence, yet longed for the patriarch's approval. Barely thirty years old, I didn't realize that I'd be saner if I lived by my own choices. Contradictory impulses—to belong and to rebel—ran my thinking. While I drank Canadian Mist whiskey, the very brew that had once brought my family to Canada, my mind reasoned that I couldn't be an alcoholic because my father was a distiller. Insane logic, and a trap.

Two years after graduation, Richard moved farther south, and the kids and I drove down to look for a home a couple of months later. He'd been offered a promotion—director of a clinic in Memphis—and I urged him to take the job. Our worn Corsica pulled up in front of Richard's downtown apartment, and behind us came B. B. King's luxury tour bus, with its stately hum, its burgundy shine, its side panel painted with the iconic Lucille, the name of King's famous Gibson guitar. We thought this was a sign of our good fortune.

In the city of the blues, I drank. I tried to stop drinking. Then I drank again. Big blackouts of drinking. The kind where you forget what you did after the first sip. Our children were in the third and sixth grades. We struggled to understand the city's history of racial division, its citizens' apathy, and its socioeconomic disparity, which was so severe that the majority of public school students were eligible for the subsidized food program. I took a demanding job for the city, which was planning to rebuild and rebrand several major historic attractions. In a few years, our son was experimenting with drugs, our daughter was singing her heart out in a girls' chorus, Richard was managing several clinics, and I was pouring whiskey into a coffee thermos and sipping it between costume changes at the child beauty pageants where Dylan's troupe of tiny troubadours entertained.

Even the friends I made were—like me—distraught, forlorn, sinking. My friend Jo, whom I'd met at yoga class, became suicidal and threw herself in front of a truck, an event that ended not in death but in brain injury. I stayed around long enough to ensure she made it home to her children after she was released from the hospital, but I couldn't stand the cheery milquetoast she became in place of the transgressive sprite I had adored.

"He got the wife he always wanted," I said to Richard, after running into her and her husband at a Thai restaurant, my sadness showing in my pathetic cruelty.

I dragged myself out of bed hung over most mornings, Richard already at work, the children having made their own lunches. Sometimes I'd drive them to school, come home, and sleep another hour. Or I'd go into team meetings at work smelling like alcohol, trying to mask the scent with mints. Unable to quell the alcoholic onslaught, Richard reverted to the domination that had been effective with his four alcoholic stepfathers. He screamed. He bargained. He used his physical power to control.

One day, when we were leaving to go out for dinner, I was in the bedroom getting ready when I heard Joshua mouth off to his father, some mumbled complaint, and then a loud scream, "No!"

Before I could walk around the corner, Richard had thrown the twelve-year-old down to the ground and was holding his arm to the child's neck. Dylan screamed in the corner. I ran into the den and pushed Richard away from his son.

"Get out. Now," I said to my husband.

"Mum, make him stop," Joshua said through his tears. I patted my son's chest over his heart, convinced that I could change our family's behavior.

I knew I had to quit drinking, and for four years I had tried to quit, but I couldn't figure out how to do it. I'd start by running and lifting weights, by dieting. I went to couples' therapy, telling Richard he could talk about everything except for my drinking. Then one day a year after the violence with his father, Joshua's high school principal called me at dinnertime.

"Ma'am, you'd better get ahold of your child quick, because he's in trouble," the principal said.

"What do you mean?" I asked.

"What do I mean? You must know that his grades are sliding! Are you and the father still together?"

"Yes!" I said, wanting to defend my family.

"I'm telling you right now, the kids he's hanging out with are dangerous. You'd better get on it."

All I could hear was my father's authoritarian voice, telling me that I'd screwed up. I drove to the gym and worked out for hours. When I returned, I locked myself in the office and called a colleague, a lovely, calm woman who I knew dealt with an alcoholic in her life.

"I don't know what to do. I've tried everything," I whispered over the phone.

"Well, you've come to the right person. I'm what you call a double winner," Carrie said.

"What's that?"

"I'm an alcoholic in recovery married to an alcoholic. Stay where you are. I'm coming to get you."

She took me to a church basement with a long table lined with candles. Twelve women sat around it, all ready to tell me their stories of how they'd found themselves right where I was. I cried through every one.

At the first twelve-step meeting I went to on my own, I stood at the door in a long coat, with a hat hiding my eyes. A man came to stand beside me. When I finally had the courage to look up, one of my bosses, a museum trustee, looked into my eyes.

"Glad you made it," he said, nonchalantly.

After I'd been going to meetings for a week, I knew that I was ready to tell Richard that I was quitting drinking. I dropped the kids off at a church-supervised skating program and sat on the floor in the den of our suburban ranch colonial, waiting for him. We'd purchased the home from a decorator and everything about it was prettier than I wanted: heavy floral drapes, blue-painted barn-board walls, curlicue fixtures, custom wood blinds that had to be dusted. The place felt too much for me. I craved something spare and clean, my old Zen practice room, an outdoor waterfall, a mountain cabin.

"Sit beside me," I said when he walked in, seeing me serious, my hands fluttering like I wanted a cigarette.

"Where are the kids?" Richard asked.

"Freedom Friday," I said, referring to the church program that would feed our kids dinner and let them roller-skate in the gym, hyped up on Big Red and Swedish Fish. I watched him look down beside my lap and see no tumbler, or even a tea mug disguising its contents.

"Let me get through this. No interrupting. Okay?" I said.

He nodded. Looked at my face. Something clearing there, something returning. He watched my eyes. I was sure that he hadn't seen them unclouded for a long time.

"I know I've tried before and I haven't been successful but I'm doing something different. I don't expect you to trust me. I know I have a lot to make up for. But you need to know. I'm an alcoholic. I have to go to a meeting every day. I want to live."

His throat caught. He man-sobbed, that full-out cry before it's reined back in, the surprise swallowed.

"What do you need?" he asked.

"I can't touch the booze. Can you dump it?"

I walked him from room to room, all of my hiding places, pointing at the whiskey bottles in drawers, on shelves, inside boots. I went outside while he dumped them down the sink and put them in a bag. I heard the clank of the bottles in the recycling bin.

We went out to eat burritos, and I told him I was resigning my job, that I couldn't do it and save my ass at the same time. I looked up at the big and tender man who had been with me since I was a girl. Despite the alcoholism in Richard's family, or perhaps because of it, he had somehow stayed married to me when I was a ruin of blackouts and bruises.

"I so wanted love that I drank to avoid being myself," I said.

"I know, sweetheart," he said.

Two weeks later I told him I was going to take the kids someplace healthier. A place that didn't have constant reminders of times I'd been drunk. A place where Joshua could get a fresh start too. A place with pristine wilderness, progressive schools, and well-funded libraries.

"We're not going to make it if we stay here."

I'd said the same thing in my afternoon meeting, to Joy, a woman with an upswept hairdo, hot-pink nails, and what seemed to be a form of dwarfism, and she'd met me in the parking lot later.

"Sweetie," she said, "I had an old robe I used to drink in. I burned that damn thing up when I got sober. You just go ahead and listen to yourself. Don't worry about those sayings about not changing anything the first year." She pointed to my heart, raising her plump arm nearly straight up. "You trust yourself," she said.

That night, after we returned home and finished dinner, Richard held me for a long time. "Where are we going to go?" he asked.

I got out my high school atlas. Opened it to the North America page.

"I want to stay with my company and keep my salary, so it has to be the States," he said.

"What's the closest place to Canada you're willing to live?"

# 9

# shattered

WHEN YOU SAY you'll take him "in sickness and in health," you don't think you'll be cleaning up vomit in the airport. Even if you think cancer, you certainly don't think he'll forget the day you married and the day you buried his mother and the days you had children. But you're not thinking about any of this when the skycap wheels him from the limo to the airplane that will take you across the country to your new home in California—the one you barely had a chance to move into before the surgery—where your girl is finishing school. You're thinking how great it is to be doing something normal, out of the wretched cancer hospital, on your way to eating real food again, when you look down and see that his eyes are as wild as a frightened puppy's.

You say, "What's wrong?" and he can't tell you, he has no words, and so you stop the wheelchair and come around the front. "You need to rest?" You're asking like he's a child, and you suddenly see, he is. His head turns from side to side, and you know that he can't stand being among people again. You move him behind a partition, and you put three chairs together to make a bench, and you turn him toward the wall, and you cover him with a jacket, and you tell him he doesn't have to get on the plane until the end, after the people have all gone. Still, you don't know how you're going to get him on this plane without him feeling bombarded. The first soldiers have started coming back from the Iraq War and you watch them in their camouflage gear, and you wonder if they are on their way home.

Your husband falls asleep, and after a while you wake him and you take him by the elbow and you raise him to a sitting position. He looks up. You see that the crowd milling at the gate terrifies him. You ask if he wants to go to the bathroom and there is no answer.

You say, "You can't move yet?" and he nods his head, agreeing with you.

Boarding announcements continue. You wait until most passengers are on the plane and you wheel him toward the toilets. He tries to stand and he wavers and you yell, "I'm coming in!" in case there are men at the urinals, and when you go in, you see a man looking at you strangely, then pityingly. Your husband stands to urinate and you turn your back and wait at the door. You listen for him to finish and then you place him back in the wheelchair. When you leave the bathroom, you strain to move him across the carpet toward the gate. All the passengers' eyes turn toward you, and then they turn away, fast.

"No!" he says.

You turn the chair away from the gate and toward the quiet corner. You kneel in front of him. He retches.

You say, "Do you think you can get on the plane?" and he raises his shoulders and there are tears in his eyes. You say, "It's okay, we can catch another one," and you touch his face. You say, "We didn't know it was going to be like this, honey." You like to speak with assurance when things no longer seem rational.

While your husband waits, you stride to the gate and you describe your plight to the flight attendants, but you don't tell them he is a baby suddenly. You say "chemo" and "nausea" and "just have to make it home" and they tell you they will come and get you after the people board, and before the plane takes off.

When you make it back to your husband his face is pale. He says, "I am going to throw up."

You wheel him back to the bathroom. He raises up, vomits. You run paper towels under the cold water, wipe his face, clean the sink.

You help him into the chair and you say, "One more try."

When you enter the corridor it is empty.

The agent says, "We're holding the door for you."

The flight attendants are wheeling him onto the plane then, and you discover that passengers inside have shifted so you can sit up front together. You hold on to your husband's arms and you say, "Look down," so he can walk to the seat. People bring you water and pillows and a blanket. After you buckle your husband in the window seat, you look at his face where the terror still swarms. You take the ends of the blanket and you make a cave for him. You hold it so he cannot see other people and soon he falls asleep. You touch his forehead and you ask what it is like to defy death. He tells you from his dreams, which you can suddenly hear.

He says he isn't afraid of having no story. He will learn whatever past will be necessary to stay here in this place.

He says death was like any other moment. He slipped away, and then he was present. There were no white lights, there were no ancestors or gurus to meet him, there was no pain. He doesn't know if pain exists. He says he likes having a body. A body reminds him that he is fresh here. For example, when he is thirsty, he must drink. He opens his eyes. You hand him the water.

It will go on like this for a long time.

We arrive home to a three-room apartment in Laguna Canyon, a tidy, transient building with an outdoor pool and a party room that always seems to be full of off-duty strippers. Palms and pepper trees surround the sunny property. Our rooms are on the edge of the sandy hills of the Laguna Coast Wilderness Park, where there are rattlesnakes, rabbits, red-tailed hawks, and coyotes that yelp in the distance. When we first arrive from the hospital, our teenage daughter has cleaned the house and arranged flowers and stocked the pantry with nourishing foods. We're happy for the simple things. We put away our clothing. I talk to Dylan about the homecoming dance. We go for walks in the morning fog.

Every day I expect to wake up and discover that the morphine has worn off, as the nurses promised, and that Richard is back to the man he was before the surgery. Instead, quiet. A stare. A step or two. A question repeated. I make him breakfast and I bring it to our bed. I get our daughter off to high school, clean the house, make doctors' appointments, wrestle with insurance, write thank-you cards, open bank accounts, order film from the MRI laboratory, email other PMP caregivers we met at the hospital, take the car into the dealer, take the car for a smog check, attend Dylan's voice recitals, organize her college audition tour, consult with friends about alternative healers, fill out college financial aid applications, apply for Social Security disability, manage our finances, talk to Richard's employers, send letters to family and friends to update them, work with people in recovery for addiction, meet with Dylan's teachers and vocal coaches, hunt down research on the brain, organize visits from friends and family, write stories, send my work to magazines and editors and agents, plan Thanksgiving with my son and father, plan Christmas vacation with our families, take Richard to a doctor visit every week, and talk to friends and family about our new state of affairs. My calendar looks like the work of a madwoman who cannot endure a moment of silent repose.

He sleeps. He sits and falls asleep. He reads and falls asleep. Each morning, I cajole him to get out of the bedroom, to go for a walk around the parking lot, to take a dip in the pool. He does not want to leave his bed. I promise him he can come back to the apartment if he's uncomfortable. We walk a few feet in the sunlight. I hold his arm, place my hand on the middle of his back so he can sense his own body. He tucks his head, unable to take in the bustle of daily life, the noise, the movement, the aromas, the intentness of everyone around him. Every day I push him to go farther. My voice is gentle, and inside, I'm terrified. What if he doesn't come out of this infant state? How will we live then?

After we return from the hospital, we start to sort out what happened in there. The cancer center had its own laws and dogmas and edicts. Being home at least allows us to live by our desires. There is good, organic, beautifully cooked food. There are walks in nature. We have our daughter getting ready for college. We are in contact with our son, who is attending to his college education back in

Seattle. A couple of hours up the Pacific Coast Highway, I have writer friends I can talk with every week.

I wake up at six most mornings so I can make Dylan's lunch and get to a twelve-step meeting by seven. Richard is awake by the time I return, and I'll make him breakfast, coax him to step outside for a few moments, and take him to his doctors' appointments. He'll sleep much of the day, his body recovering from the two surgeries, chemotherapy, and forty pounds of weight loss. He's a rail, with huge sunken eyes. I had planned to learn more about screenwriting during this time, make some contacts. Instead I'm researching online, interviewing medical professionals, and talking with friends, trying to understand what happened to his memory.

When the brain loses oxygen, it's said to have experienced an anoxic insult: not an insult in the sense of a demeaning or offensive remark, but rather a trauma, from *insilire*, "to leap upon one." What leapt upon him, what leapt upon us who knew him, was the disintegration of his personality: the loss of traits, gestures, and expressions that burnish the behavioral patina one has grown to know. Following his anoxic insult, when people ask how I feel, I answer, "Uncomfortable." It's an itch under the skin, an unease that keeps me feeling uprooted, a desire to find the correct answer when there isn't one.

The lost part of him that our family most misses is his enthusiastic desire to communicate. Without the craving to converse, there's little self-reference, self-regard. No need to impress anyone. He has no wish to have his self reflected back in word or deed. The charm he lived by and wooed by is erased. Now that we are in this transition house, I have no idea if he will be able to work again. I know that it's too soon to tell, and I also know that something has seriously changed in him.

The first Monday, two days after we arrive home, Richard is examined by his new general practitioner, Dr. V, who will become our advocate for all his future care. She sets up a baseline MRI the next day, and answers my questions about the memory loss. We learn about the stagnant anoxia that results when internal conditions block oxygen-rich blood from reaching the brain. Brain injury specialists say that the death of brain cells results in the interruption of electrochemical impulses and in interference with the performance of neurotransmitters—the chemical messengers that transmit messages within the brain. The neurotransmitters regulate body functions and influence behavior. We need to get someone to clarify if he has had an anoxic insult, Dr. V advises, and to what extent he has been debilitated, and what his prognosis might be.

That autumn day we leave Dr. V's office with a referral for a neurologist and a speech therapist. Tracking down the cause of Richard's mental condition feels useful. People have been remarkably uninhibited about confirming what scientific information is available, and quick to admit the limitations of their knowledge. I'm thankful that the operating surgeon, Dr. M, had the integrity to share his opinion about the anoxic insult Richard might have experienced. In having this lead, I'm able to argue for my husband's case, and to make quick decisions to spend our savings on getting him the best care we can while we wait for the insurance approvals to arrive.

Before we left the hospital, Dr. M handed me suture scissors. He demonstrated on Richard's chest-tube stitches how I might remove the fifty knots that climb from my husband's pubis to his xiphoid. In the past month, I've already massaged blood clots that lurked in transparent plastic tubes, threatening to ascend to his lungs and choke him. I've cleaned up urine that overflowed buckets when night nurses failed in their duty. I've used tiny scissors to cut his long hair when it became greasy and matted from weeks when he wasn't able to shower. A few dozen stitches do not scare me.

A week after we arrive home, the fated day arrives. I tease each stitch from the skin with tweezers. The tip of the suture scissor slides under each knot and clips it. Richard watches for a few moments and then closes his eyes. He sleeps. The sun from the desert hills slides across my back. I hear my breath, panting, and his, slow and steady. I think of the two-foot-long seam splitting, his insides coming apart, red, red blood seeping over the white blanket on our bed. My hands shake. Now that I am without the hospital professionals, I imagine the disaster that I could cause through my mistakes. I track backward through time, sourcing this sense of responsibility. I cannot find a time when I *didn't* think *I can fuck this up*.

Richard opens his eyes. Since the surgery, they bulge wide, a stare without a blink. My fear of making mistakes turns into resentment that seeps toward him. Viscous, silent seeping.

"Eyes," I say. This is our new code word to let him know that his flat affect, the fixed stare of the brain-injured, is becoming uncomfortable for others. He blinks. I tug at a stitch and watch him wince. Tears come to both of us. Catholic-girl guilt. Guilt that my mother suffered from some unnamed malaise I couldn't fix. Guilt from my decade of binge-drinking and blackouts that I'd halted just in time for Richard to find his cancer. Not yet, but soon I will discover that cancer has changed the game on my anger. When there's no one to volley anger back, cementing marital guilt in its pathetic, pitiful story, that's the end of that sorry party.

When we are finished I take the stitches outside and I bury them in the earth, along with a toy soldier I find on the patio. I kick the dust with my toes. In the distance, coyotes scream.

Being without identity is a terrifying thing. Or so it seems to me, watching Richard in those first months. He's cut off from his memories, cut off from his preferences, cut off from his beliefs. I'm not sure if he'll regain any desire at all. He's lost not only his own sense of self but the one we share, our marriage history, our familial ties, our community connection, our political and social selves. Day to day, he can't remember what makes me "me," what makes us "us." And that doesn't stop him from wanting our pleasure and ease.

In our marriage, he was my wild man, my field guide. I want a rich and complex intimacy again. Instead there is innocence and spaciousness. Sweet as he is, we seem shattered.

Two weeks after we return home, we visit a new neurologist, a woman this time. She shows us an MRI of his brain.

"No definite acute intracranial abnormality. No evidence of lesions or infarctions or hemorrhage." The only indication: "An increased signal in the posterior limbs of the internal capsules bilaterally, slightly greater on the left . . . suggesting chronic ischemic change."

Brain research in the twenty-first century provides more clues than ever about the way our minds function, behave, relate, relay, imagine, interpret, explore, examine, detect, and understand. Severe brain injuries—ones that manifest in comas, with no voluntary activities, no cognitive response—are easily detectable, both physically and in the person's behavior. Mild to moderate brain injuries are often not physically detected, though they can create the kinds of deficits that seriously affect the person's life, work, and relationships. It's difficult to find "hard" proof of tissue damage or chemical malfunctioning in subtle brain injuries because brains are the most variable of all of the human organs. We don't know what a normal mind looks like. (This is not a metaphor, or a joke.)

We have obtained enough confirmation from medical professionals to know that Richard is likely suffering from the effects of a hypoxic anoxic insult. This is the kind of brain injury that occurs when blood flow is interrupted, starving the brain. From Dr. M, his surgeon, to the neurologist, to the general practitioner, there's a consensus that a loss of oxygen to the brain during internal bleeding, even if it was small, likely caused the injury. I wonder if the hospital's delay in noticing and responding to the internal bleeding was a significant contributor. Brain cells begin to die after just four minutes without oxygen. Perhaps Richard's brain injury was a side effect of the three pitchers of blood that pooled in his abdomen while he was in the ICU. But none of our effort will go to assigning responsibility for the cause. Right now, all we want is for him to regain his capabilities.

An injured brain is not less smart than it was before. Richard processes information more slowly, giving the impression of a diminished intellect. But that brilliant mind of his is still vital, wise, dazzling. I believe that his intelligence is simply locked inside. In my view, my husband does not have access to the *use* of his brilliance.

"He can't speak; he was altered during surgery," I say to the neurologist. "We need to find out what's happening with his speech."

The neurologist confirms the need for a speech therapist. Ten days later, after we get approval from our insurance company, he has his first appointment. For two months, I will drive him there three times each week.

"Name animals that start with *c*," she says.

Richard looks up at me with big eyes.

"Eyes," I say, reminding him to soften his gaze.

His eyes fill with tears. He can't find one example.

I want to say, "Camel! Cat! Caterpillar! Cougar! Canary!" Instead I place my hand on his shoulder. I look at the therapist.

"Now what?" I say.

By the end of the first month at home, Richard gets dizzy when he stands up. One afternoon Dylan and I return from the grocery to find that he has passed out on the floor and pulled a twenty-pound sculpture of a mother and child onto himself as he reached out to break his fall.

I call Dr. V, who asks us to bring him in right away. Dr. V sends a note to the neurologist noting "short-term memory loss and difficulty with directions and spatial orientation." We take Richard off salt, check his iron. Perhaps, we think, this is a low blood pressure issue. In six months we will learn that balance issues are common in brain injury, and that 65 percent of people with a brain injury suffer from dizziness and disequilibrium at some point in their recovery. At this time, we know only that we cannot leave Richard alone. If I have to go to a school event for Dylan, we bring someone in to stay with him. Richard resists, but he keeps getting dizzy, and he learns that he needs to have someone present until his body stabilizes. My husband is like a child—sweet, tender, toddling, and terrified to leave the house, mostly spending each day napping.

I watch Richard's wide eyes as he tries to understand the world around him. On our daily walks, he stumbles because of weakness in his entire right side. Although the neurologist can't confirm the location of the injury, I remain convinced it's in his left temporal lobe because his right side is hunched like the maimed wing of a bird.

As I observe him, I wonder if he's managed to reach one of those states that people meditate for years to achieve. He's injured and he's also somewhere else. From my perspective, it appears as if his former self has died, and he awoke in a new life. To me, he's another man. But Richard didn't awaken like those people who have spontaneous spiritual events. He isn't the Buddha, or Byron Katie, or Jill Bolte Taylor. Yet he isn't unlike them either. Richard has no context for creating meaning. He can't recall what happened to him yesterday or a year ago. He can't explain recent events to anyone, not even to himself. His only motivation is love. As far as I can tell.

"Why did you come back to this body?" I finally ask him weeks after the surgery, after he's gained ten pounds, after he's stopped fainting, after he can walk more than a few steps, after he can form sentences.

"I wanted to be with you. It didn't feel like I was finished," he says.

# 10
# sobering

DECIDING WHERE TO live so my recovery from addiction could be supported took us five minutes. Richard's company had clinics in Seattle. The city was beautiful and progressive. There might not be so much God talk at meetings. I just needed to find a way to make the move happen. Within a month, I had an interview for a museum job. I moved across the country when I was ninety days sober, and stayed alone for four months, the first time I had ever lived by myself.

In the first week, I found a twelve-step group where kind women told me their stories, took me for brunch and walks and what seemed like buckets of espresso. Dylan left sixth grade at spring break and came to stay in my little apartment on Lake Washington. She listened at the edges of meetings in church basements, and we went for drives around neighborhoods and visited schools. Six months later, Richard and Joshua drove across the country, and we began our new life in the foothills of the Cascade Mountains, nearly an hour from the city.

I hoped something rural would save us. That tall trees and waterfall-filled pools and spring frogs would make us anew. Instead, now that Richard was safe, his anger seemed to spout like molten rock. I was no longer the one who fueled all of his resentment. One weekend, Joshua wouldn't comply with being grounded. He grabbed his pack and left the house. Richard followed him onto the porch and pushed him back inside. Joshua hit his father, and then Richard was on top of him, holding him down, the same way I'd seen him behave with his son years before. I pulled Richard away from our child, but he refused to walk away. I dialed the police. Richard stepped back, shaking with fury. Joshua kicked over the barbecue and fled, walking up the long graveled hill that led out of the forest where our home was tucked, a woodland cottage that seemed idyllic only in my imagination. In the weeks that followed, the two of them battled in sarcasm, curse words, criticism, shouting, and shoves.

Nearly eighteen months sober, I offered my husband a way out of his pain, though we both knew it was an ultimatum.

"Therapy or you move out," I said.

"There's nothing wrong with me," he insisted.

That spring, we separated. He moved into a colleague's cabin in the middle of a floodplain in Kent. The Green River rose. Water drenched everything. We began therapy.

"You haven't been married to your wife for eighteen years," I remember our therapist saying in our first session together. "This is a new marriage."

We'd been sitting far apart on the couch when we heard these words, and I stole a sideways glance at his beautiful profile, the ruddy cheeks, strong nose, solid brow. Was he excited about the possibility that we could leave behind the old relationship, stop holding grudges against each other for our habitual reactions, forgive what we had done? Could we do the earnest work of letting go of our ideas of who we *were* in our story of each other? Richard turned toward me and registered my fear in the way I bit the left side of my mouth. Our marriage had shown us that we were willing to have our hearts broken, but by the time he moved out, we seemed to prefer constant disappointment. Now, here was another possibility: a new marriage. Something of that notion felt brave and worthy and possible.

"You mean her recovery," Richard said. "Because she's changed so much, since she stopped drinking."

The therapist watched us contemplate a reset on our relationship.

"You're saying we'd have to stop relating to our history," Richard said.

"I'll teach you new skills. You'll practice them at home. But Richard, this isn't just about her changes. This is about the identity changes in your relationship. I want to show you how to turn toward each other."

We had to unlearn everything. Through weekly meetings with our therapist and homework assignments over the course of a year, we learned how to listen, how to fight well, how to bond in the aftermath of a "regrettable incident." We began to share our fondness for each other, to say the kinds of things we'd said in the beginning: *Baby, the way you never miss a day of work is highly impressive.* I told him how I adored his grace and charisma, his observant mind, his principled and empathetic heart. We learned to share our dreams for our life again. And what we spoke was risky, powerful, uncomfortable. Now I had to look beyond our tumultuous past and see who this man had become. He had to give up the rebellious, timid girl who fought against the harsh strictures of a demanding father and a stringent upbringing. We had to learn how to communicate to each other beyond reactive stances like stonewalling and defensiveness.

We luxuriated in our newness. After years of arguing, we began to work together, to envision the marriage we wanted. One Saturday, we sat on our bed with the windows open, listening to the frogs croak in the pond in our front yard, while we tried to share how we felt about money. Coming out of poverty, he was a lifelong saver, with a strong desire to minimize risk. Having had children so early, I had a craving for adventure, and would rather throw vacation expenses on a credit card and pay them off through the year. That afternoon, while the frogs rasped throaty interludes, I heard the story of his childhood in a way that I never before could.

"We sometimes didn't have heat, so we'd sleep in our clothing. I scrounged for coins on the street to play pinball. There was such chaos, thirteen schools, crazy parties, that I couldn't ever count on things being stable. I want to give you what you want, honey, but I also have this number in mind that I'd like to be in our savings account," he said.

I listened to his dreams for paying for the kids' college and retiring debt, then I told him the list of all the countries I wanted to visit. How I wanted to become a decent mountaineer. That quitting alcohol had made me realize how much I wanted to live, but not a safe life: something wild, daring. Then we hiked to the top of the driveway, which backed onto Tiger Mountain. The gravel road met the state forest. We followed along the fire road where truckloads of paragliders climbed to a lofty jump above the city of Issaquah, on the hills they called the Alps. Instead of slogging upward, we wound our way into the forest and its secret springs. We rolled up our cuffs and plunged into transparent pools. He put his hands along my hips, and I felt the safety that didn't come from his body alone, but from mine also, and from who we were together. We walked back to the house, made a fire in the little pellet stove, and ordered pizza. We stripped our wet clothing and put on pajamas and made a plan. I would support his savings dream by staying out of debt; he would ensure we visited one place on my bucket list every year.

He gave up his sarcasm and righteousness; I surrendered defensiveness for curiosity. We were passionate, supportive, and clear about our vision for our life together. Weekends, after we'd dropped our teenagers at the movies, we shopped for groceries at Costco and then sat by Issaquah Creek, licking soft-serve ice-cream cones and finding ways to ask questions we'd never, in all of our nearly two decades of marriage, thought to ask: *Would you live your life differently if no one knew you? Do you wish for a break from the way we've always done things? What would you do if you had a year to live?*

While we were rebuilding our marriage, Joshua changed his life, finding the tools he needed to live without harmful substances. At sixteen, he was too angry to be with us, so he left to live with a friend's family. We helped him pay for his expenses while he stayed in the basement apartment and then, months later, he moved home again. We were not flawless, and we weren't trying to be. We were trying to avoid living by habit and inattentiveness.

On our nineteenth anniversary, at the suggestion of our therapist, we made new marriage vows. We'd made the first vows in our twenties in a Catholic church, because that was what my family wanted. Now we were adults, in our forties. We wanted to do it our own way. We climbed a trail at Mount Rainier, just the two of us, on a weekend in July. We had no campsite reservations because we forgot to plan the trip. We piled sleeping bags, a large camp stove, and a too-large family tent on our backs just in case there was a camping spot at Mystic Lake. Five hours in, past the Carbon River entrance, up five miles, over a suspension bridge, parallel to a glacier, through zigzagging forest paths, across the Wonderland Trail, above the tree line, into a subalpine meadow, past marmots and pikas, through Indian paintbrush, alpine aster, and pink mountain heather, over two small ridges, down a descent, around the lake, we realized there was no room at the campsite.

We walked to the sunny side of the lake and we each said vows written for the occasion. The mosquitoes were there to witness the ceremony. There was no cake. I broke off a triangle of a Toblerone bar and Richard scarfed it down. After ten minutes he said, "We have to go. It's another five hours back." I was sad about leaving. We were both exhausted from the climb to the lake. The elevation was as intense on the way back as it had been on the way there. We were hiking a long trail with a 3,900-foot gain, but neither of us mentioned this. When we watched a lithe young man practically levitate up the trail, my new husband said, "Skip along, little man," and I laughed. Oh, how he liked to make me laugh.

"Under that joke, is there anger?" I said, because we'd become honest like that, asking dangerous questions.

He delivered the truth: "It's the way I get certain things done."

"Like marriage?"

He gave me the look like: *I'm not wandering into that territory.*

Instead, he asked: "What did you think marriage was going to be?"

I told him: "When I was a girl, I thought marriage would be dressing up in ball gowns and going to fancy dances. When I was a teenager, after the sixties, I read *The Harrad Experiment* and I thought I wouldn't have a conventional marriage, but instead a feminist one, though I still wasn't sure what that meant."

I told my husband: "There have been plenty of men I've wanted to fuck, but I haven't ever wanted to live with anyone besides you."

"I didn't know what I was doing when I married you at twenty-one," I said, stretched out over a bridge, trying to relax under the weight of the twenty-pound pack on my back, "but that's okay because who the hell does know about something they've never tried?"

"Maybe this hike has turned out just like the marriage," he said.

"How's that?"

"We set our sights too high and we carry more than we need. There hasn't been any rest along the way and somehow we keep going."

When he told me this, I cried. He reached in his pocket and handed me his bandana. He didn't ask any more questions. There were miles ahead, and if we stopped to talk we would not make it back to the car. Later, he bought us ice-cream cones, and we licked each other's flavors, and kissed with our sweat-salty lips. We drove home in the twilight talking about the honeymoons we would take, if we could get away.

Nine months later, in June of 2000, while undergoing a yearly examination for physical therapists, Richard scored a false positive in a tuberculosis test, and a subsequent scan of his lungs showed a strange substance around his stomach. He stood in the kitchen buttering a piece of bread when he told me this, like it was no big deal.

"What are you going to do?" I asked.

"Some doctor thinks I have to get on medication," he said, shrugging, opening a beer.

"You're going to keep asking questions though, right?"

Over the next three months, some doctors said the substance was nothing. They told Richard he ought to wait it out. But his colleague Sigrid, who was a doctor near Richard's practice, who saw him every day, who wasn't satisfied with our watchful waiting strategy, kept pestering him to find a diagnosis for the mysterious matter growing inside him. That August, after an x-ray and a CT scan, he had an answer: a slow-growing tumorous mass had descended through his abdomen and pelvis. Inside, he was growing a shadow of himself.

When I looked at my husband, it was unfathomable that there was a cancer taking over his entire torso. And so when cancer first appeared, we spoke of it as if it were a stranger who'd invaded our home late one night and gobbled the last of the Thanksgiving pie. We spoke of cancer in whispers and questions and disparaging asides:

*She's got a nerve, messing us up like this.*

*You're the one who asked her in.*

*Me? I don't think so!*

*Well, let's get her out of here, then, before she makes a real disaster.*

I was in the room when a doctor tried to take a biopsy of the cancer. The needle slid into Richard's skin and aspirated nothing. We watched the confusion on the doctor's face. They sent us home to wait.

That September, in the surgeon's office, we heard the name of the disease for the first time: pseudomyxoma peritonei, a rare cancer of the appendix. Without surgery, Richard had perhaps a few years to live.

The surgery, scheduled for October 2000, was supposed to end the cancer. Called a debulking, the procedure would remove the tumor and as much of the mucus as possible, without infringing on the organs. It would be performed near our home in Seattle.

The day of the procedure, the surgeon, Dr. T, emerged from the operating theater after many hours, his scrubs splattered with blood, and thrust his palms wide apart. He told me how much of the cancer had been taken from Richard's belly: "Three family-size fried chicken buckets!"

A few days later, we left the hospital. We continued to raise our teenage children. We hiked the mountains of the Pacific Northwest and Canada. We attended to our demanding careers. We had romantic dates. We took family vacations. In the brilliant concord of mutual denial, Richard and I quickly forgot. We thought this had been the first and final surgery. We thought we'd lost the cancer and returned to our beautiful life.

Three years after the first surgery, the cancer returned. We asked questions. We got down to business. We took on this rare cancer like we were managing a rare economic downturn. Soon, Richard was bringing home pages of research about a surgeon across the country, a doctor who was doing an experimental treatment called cytoreduction with hyperthermic intraperitoneal chemotherapy (HIPEC).

I read the blogs from survivors and others online. "They call it MOAS, for Mother of All Surgeries."

"Sounds like a slash-and-burn," my husband said, trying for a joke to make me relax.

"You really want to do this?" I was shocked by the torturous treatment.

"This is my best chance to survive."

Our Seattle surgeon, Dr. T, didn't think so.

"I think it's a death sentence," he said to us when we went by for a consultation the following week. "Look, you're being used as a guinea pig for this guy's research project. The morbidity rate is seventy percent. The survival rate at ten years is thirty-five percent, and we're not even sure if these are accurate reports."

I'd never heard the term *morbidity*. Dr. T saw my eyebrows raise and my hand touch Richard's arm.

"Morbidity is the number of people potentially disabled by the surgery," the doctor said, answering my silent question. "HIPEC is a treatment with a high morbidity. This doctor cherry-picks optimal patients to reduce toxicity and complications. But the complications—they're still happening. Very high risk of death."

"What if I have a chance to be cancer-free?" my husband asked.

"Richard, you're fit, and you're otherwise healthy. We can control this disease with a much less radical surgery. Every few years, that's what the commitment is."

We left the doctor's office even more confused about a course of treatment. The doctor arranged for us to meet with an oncologist, who sat us down in a steel-blue room and blurted out, "HIPEC is torture. This surgeon you're considering—his protocol results cannot be reproduced. The cancer is cellular. We have to fight it aggressively."

"With what?" we asked.

"Thalidomide."

"The birth defect drug? Jesus. For how long?"

"A year. At first."

"And then?"

"We would give his body a rest."

"And then?"

"He would be on chemo the rest of his life."

"I want to be healthy again," Richard said.

"I know you do," I responded, "but I'm terrified I'm going to lose you in what sounds like an extreme treatment."

On a scorching August weekend, five months after the CT scan confirmed Richard's cancer had returned, we flew out to meet the experimental surgeon, Dr. M, and when we arrived at the hospital we witnessed a depleted young man being carried across the parking lot by his mother and grandmother. We were at the threshold of killer cancer.

Dr. M had wise eyes and a no-nonsense disposition. He reviewed Richard's CT scans, conducted a physical exam, and gave us details of the surgery and expected recovery. When we expressed surprise at the months-long wait time for the surgery, he reminded us that PMP was a slow-growing cancer and told Richard he'd need that time to get strong for the treatment. Dr. M suggested that when we come for the surgery, we live at the hospital for three to six weeks; instead of arranging for a hotel, he advised, I should sleep in Richard's room to help oversee his care. Dr. M answered all of our questions and informed us that the operation would likely take all day and into the evening.

"I have an Asian woman patient who is half his size," the surgeon said. "This big guy is going to take some time."

I scrawled the surgeon's words on a legal pad that Richard and I had written our notes on during the flight. We knew the recovery was going to be strenuous, and this doctor certainly didn't minimize anything. We toured the hospital, got on the waiting list, and flew home for Sunday dinner with the kids. We hadn't told anyone that we were not sure as to the right course of action.

When I did mention to a friend that we didn't know what treatment to follow, she offered Richard her cabin on nearby Vashon Island, so he might spend the weekend in contemplation of his choice. I spent the weekend alone too, to face my fears. In three days, Richard arrived home with a bouquet of roses. He handed the blood-colored flowers to me in the driveway.

"Thank you for letting me go," he said, and I knew he meant toward the cancer treatment and his own healing, wherever that might take him. Even as he stood there, I could tell by the somber bow of his body that he would choose the most arduous route. He'd already moved into a grave gaze, a disconnected stance, a serious lexicon, one that I, who had never had cancer, did not know. He was preparing himself for a taking apart, a transfiguration. In that moment, I thought that I'd lost him to something bigger than us.

Aboriginal shamans enact death and resurrection with ritual symbolic removal or rearrangement of body parts, including symbolic disembowelment, and journeys into strange realms. The "chosen one" is ritually killed, set loose on a wondrous journey with the sky gods, and then returned to life as the tribal shaman, with the otherworldly awareness intact. Richard would enact the modern-day version: an extreme cancer surgery and chemotherapy ritual that would scrape his organs and ignite any remaining cancer with a fiery poison. To live through it, he would need to give everything he had. At the time he made this choice, we did not know what this meant.

Richard was placed on the hospital's schedule earlier than expected. In six weeks, surgery. We steeled ourselves to the task ahead. Preparing for this moment made us work as fast and efficiently as we ever had. Everything was about the details, the getting ready. Making things more challenging was the fact that we weren't simply going to travel to a cancer hospital and then back to our stable lives. We had decided to uproot. Again.

Three weeks before the surgery, just before Labor Day, I moved with our daughter to a tiny apartment in Laguna Beach, California. Dylan wanted to train at a performing arts high school. She has a beautiful voice, and wanted to study opera. We were willing to change our lives so we could help her do this; it was a decision we'd made two months before Richard's cancer returned. Joshua was already enrolled in college studying media and communications technology, happily living on his own.

After Richard's diagnosis, he and I decided that I would still stay with Dylan in Orange County for her senior year, and that Richard would recuperate there for a few months before returning to his job in Seattle. He knew that the cancer recovery was going to take a great deal of energy, and he had resigned from his position as the group director of twenty-one physical therapy clinics; he didn't feel he could maintain his career in good conscience while trying to heal. In the twelve years he had been a manager and director, he had never taken a sick day. Some people would think they were owed a few. Not Richard. As soon as he learned the extent of the treatment, he began to work with his bosses to make a graceful exit. They told him they would hold his position open for him, whenever he wished to return.

Before we left Seattle, we walked our favorite neighborhoods—Capitol Hill, Wallingford, Belltown, Phinney Ridge—and imagined returning as empty nesters. We toured flats near our favorite vintage theaters and sat in cafés, imagining what life might be like with our youngest off to college, our son happily attending college nearby, and our parenting having shifted to another phase.

In the weeks before the surgery, we concentrated on packing our home, putting our house up for sale, resigning Richard's job, saying good-bye to all our friends and family, moving to a new apartment, finding a new twelve-step group, enrolling Dylan in school, buying a car for her to drive, making sure we had care for her while we lived in the cancer hospital, coordinating visits with family, managing the medical insurance approvals, and budgeting for months of recuperation. In addition, we entirely changed our diet. Richard underwent a rigorous fitness regimen to prepare himself for this extensive treatment. As a physical therapist, he was already active. He had been lifting more weight, doing daily cardio routines, and now we were eating lean food, mostly following an ayurvedic diet. He was muscled, vital, and strong. By the end of forty-six days, we'd checked everything off our lists. The children were safe and protected. The only thing left was to drop the plan and see what happened.

Richard had gone through his checklists with me. I knew where the wills were located, when to call the family, how to expedite the power of attorney, what I was to do if he couldn't have sex again (find a lover and not let him know unless he asked). We had spoken of everything. The only thing to do was to wait.

In the weeks to come, I would hear the doctor's prophetic voice. Turned out, Dr. T was right. There was morbidity and there was mortality—the man we knew as Richard died to us. And with his former self, any notion of an "us." I hadn't yet experienced my own collapse of identity, which came in the wake of Richard's shift out of a personality-driven self. I had yet to realize that the purpose of his body was only ever to be. There would be a hundred thousand *why*s before my existential mind rested in this easy wisdom.

# part two

# 11

# servant

MEMORY IS A servant, faithful not only to the believed past but also to the imagined future. This is what I think when I hear how people want Richard to be some version of the man they remember. It's important for visitors to say something positive when they arrive. *He looks good*, friends and family say, when they come to town. They look up at Richard's tall, manly frame, and though his shoulder hunches toward his ear in postsurgical postural disregard, guarding his maimed side, they picture him as strong, reliable, mindful, competent. The shell is the thing important to preserve: *behold, after our likeness he shall be created*.

I thought I knew what made Richard my lover, his children's father, his family's brother. When I look in his eyes, permanently wide with that stare, I witness the absence of forethought. Experience is writ upon his face the very second of its apprehension, as if he's a newborn, as if some Demiurge has just fashioned him from clay.

We learn the nature of forgetting. We begin to notice what has already been forgotten by him—forgetfulness streams into yesterday and today, shadows tomorrow as a flooded Lethe. Gone are even the most mundane things, the things we take for granted: how to form sentences, make a call, go places, get angry, use a computer, remember ideas and names and people and his children's lives and his work and his family and the muscles in his anatomy textbooks. My former husband, I am starting to see, is no longer present.

I want to learn about the workings of his brain, and the parts of his mind and memory that may not ever return. But right now we are stalled, waiting to see if speech therapy changes anything.

In the meantime, some friends think it's a good idea for us to have a meditator around, to create an environment of peace. People make calls. We learn about a group of Tibetan Buddhist monks who have come to a community center near Dylan's school. They are spending a week meticulously nudging grains of sand into a mandala they will then sweep to nothingness. I drive Richard to see them. We take a tiny bag of sand from the beaches of Bermuda, a gift his mother left behind before she died. We hold it out to them.

"We have special sand for this purpose," the monk says, rejecting our coarse grains.

We tell our story to the monk in charge.

"Can you send the lama to come see my husband?" I ask. I already know by the look on his face that a home visit is impossible. But the next day we get a call from the monk I spoke to, telling us the lama's assistant will be coordinating their trip to our apartment. I'm asked to make special food and home preparations.

"He's never done this before," the monk says.

"What's that?" I ask, confused.

"Come to the home of a family."

On the day of the visit we have prepared a meal these Tibetans will eat—vegetarian—and we've cleaned the house, and dressed in clean clothes. We sit in our tiny apartment, barely big enough to hold the three of us. The lama and the American translator arrive. We're introduced. He is Lama Lharampa Geshe Ngawang Lungtok of the Gaden Lhopa Khangtsen of the Monastic University in Karnataka, India, home to six thousand monks, and also a place where the Dalai Lama teaches. The translator tells us that the lama will transform himself into the body of Vajravidaran, a Buddha of radiant light and healing. Dylan and I smile at each other across the living room. We can't wait to see what that looks like.

The translator takes clay from a plastic bag and makes bowls that he tells us will hold our "poison"—all of the negative words, acts, and deeds we have ever done. He gives us herbal water that we swish in our mouths and then spit into this dough effigy. He asks us to give up all of the unkindnesses that have ever been done to us. The lama chants around Richard's body. The translator tells us he's transforming all Richard's negative energy into pure, radiant bliss. There hasn't been anything other than wonder in that man's mind for a month, I want to say, but I don't say a word because the ritual is nonstop spitting and swishing. Then the lama makes the magic signs on Dylan and me, and when I start to giggle, we try not to look at each other. Herbed water is poured over our heads. The translator tells us the lama is blessing us. Next, the lama takes a peacock feather and swishes it around our bodies. The translator says he is making a protective sphere. The lama ties a red thread necklace around Richard's neck and asks him not to take it off. The translator hands us three packets of red-brown pellets.

"What are these?" I ask.

"The crushed remains of the lamas for generations and the prayers of ten thousand lamas including the Dalai Lama," the translator says. (Or this is what I hear. Years later, Dylan will tell me that she thought he said the *tears* of ten thousand lamas. Whereupon I think, wow, that would be some medicine.)

"Would you like to have anything else blessed?" he asks.

"Like what?"

"Medicine, lotions, water."

I go running for my flower essence cream, bowls of water, Richard's vitamins.

"When these are used, now each being will be transformed by this same radiant light."

"What about his memory loss?" I ask.

The translator and the lama exchange words. They look at Richard, then toward me.

"From the Tibetan perspective, the memory loss is not such a bad thing," the translator says.

We all laugh. I think he is kidding. We sit down at our tiny table in the kitchen nook, and the Tibetan eats nothing.

"They don't eat salad," the translator says, "only hot things."

"I can make him a sandwich," I say, but they shake their heads. It's time for them to go.

After the Tibetans leave, I'm not sure why we invited them. My faith that any ritual, remedy, or medicine can change things is already unraveling. I really want to believe in something, anything, that will bring Richard healing, which we define as a return to his former self. I'm not yet willing to see that coming to peace with reality may be an easier path. We take the lama pellets, and we drink the water, and we use the blessed cream on his scars. I will not stop imagining there is a cure for silence and forgetting.

We try everything to help him remember. We repeat things. We tell stories. We show him photographs. Dylan continues the practice of taking pictures. She discovers the camera lens can swing 360 degrees, and she becomes enthralled with capturing herself. Arm extended, she snaps images of herself in wigs, togas, tights; dressed as a man; coifed for prom; putting on expressions from dainty to disgusting. She posts some of them online. She says she's tracking who she is in these given moments and she wants to know how she's perceived, she wants to know how people respond to the snapshots she's posted for public view.

I think these kinds of self-portraits come from the same place as Frida Kahlo's painted images of herself; they're for emotional catharsis, to track the self in its ongoing mission to hide and to reveal. Dylan doesn't want to lose the father she's known, the capable, clear, commanding one. Our daughter cries, always away from her father, usually about his uncomprehending eyes, his distant expression, his empty persona: "Mama, why is he so much like a child?"

When people from his past hear Richard has lost his memory of his former life, they send photographs from his boyhood: inevitably, pictures of the theatrical, gregarious person he used to be, portraits of him mugging, striking a pose, evoking guarded macho-shadow in his gaze. Our daughter places these old images in the album next to the photo of our family taken after we came home from the hospital. In it, her father is lean, calm; his eyes are gaping, exposed. When you look closely, though, you can see the part never lost is his urge to love.

A shaman of Nimiipuu (Nez Perce) and Celtic lineage comes, along with a writing mentor, to do a shamanic journey on Richard's behalf. I met them at a writers' retreat years ago. They were each called to healing after being afflicted by their own "sacred illnesses." They offer this traditional indigenous ceremony as a gift to us. We're not afraid to consider whatever might be most healing: Western medicine, Eastern medicine, ancient forms. Not only do we have a history of being spiritually curious, we have nothing to lose.

In the time we've been married, though we are not churchgoers, we have experimented with a variety of spiritual traditions. Sifu, the Zen master, taught me discipline and acceptance of life's conditions. We attended a Sufi Movement camp high in the Canadian Rockies. We tried a communal council and healing ritual called a Daré, from an African tradition. I explored nature-based faiths, our Celtic ancestors. I researched the scientific basis for prayer and meditation. So while the specific spiritual practices of various traditions came and went, our sense of ourselves as spiritual people living with the conditions of the everyday did not change. Among our lasting practices was saying grace at supper; our meditations came in daily activities—cooking, sex, walks in nature. We stayed quiet a little bit every day. We learned how to be kind to one another. We practiced speaking the truth, as we knew it to be. We tried not to fake life, but to be really ourselves.

When Richard first became ill with cancer, he was comfortable in the role of healer; he was not at all proficient in accepting help. He identified as adept, accomplished, athletic, and sometimes smartass. He was not dependent on others and he had made a habit of requiring almost nothing from anyone he knew. When we were healthy, before the cancer arrived, we held a healing ceremony in our home once each month, where anyone could come and be heard. Eventually, after the diagnosis, Richard allowed himself to be drawn to the center of the circle, to accept support from others, to tell of his fear of loss.

In my shock and grief, I want to do anything I can to recover my former husband. When people ask us if they can do a ritual on our behalf, we receive it. So the healer and mentor bring in their drums and spiritual artifacts. As part of the ritual, the women ask Richard to make an offering.

"What is an offering?" he says.

I go to the room where they're preparing and ask the shaman women to clarify. I walk back to where Richard is lying on the ground, a patchwork quilt over his body. I lean into his face and whisper.

"It's something of yourself that you can offer up to the spirits on behalf of this ceremony," I tell him.

"I offer my life in service to healing others," Richard says.

The rest of the ceremony is beautiful, but it doesn't impact me as much as those words. I already see that my husband knows something I do not know. Something about resilience and generosity and love. A door opens.

The anxiety that kept him isolated in his bedroom lessens. Two months after our return home, he can walk into a dark movie theater in the middle of the day as long as the film is kind.

During the early stages of his recovery, when we can't find anyone to confirm the brain injury, I'm swimming in the desire to believe and belong. I talk with mentors, healers, and friends in recovery, hoping that someone has the magic that will shift our situation.

"Richard stays in bed for days on end," I whisper into the phone. "He can't talk to anyone about what's going on inside him. He can't do many of the things that he used to do."

When I stop feeling sorry for my situation, I write in my journal, in our newfound silence:

THINGS THAT HAVE CHANGED (IN RICHARD)
AFTER THE BRAIN INJURY:

1. He rarely speaks.

2. His eyes are watchful.

3. He calls me "sweetness."

4. He can't remember five minutes ago.

5. Instead of sleeping on his back, legs splayed on the bed, arms behind his head, he sleeps on his side, legs and arms tucked close to his body, taking up the smallest space possible. He sleeps like this a lot.

6. He can't go out where there are people.

7. All of his appetites return, and are more pronounced.

8. He cries. Every day. He doesn't laugh; he smiles.

9. He rarely looks to others for validation.

10. He doesn't complain.

11. When asked what he wants, he asks what you want.

12. He has no agenda. He does what I want. He does what anyone asks of him.

13. His body thrums at a beat-beat-beat instead of a rat-a-tat-tat-tat. (I met another man with a TBI who said his wife divorced him because she couldn't stand to lie next to his altered energy at night.)

14. Hours, days, without words.

15. He wants to know who I am, even if he won't remember it.

16. His reaction time is slower.

17. He's afraid to enter the world and yet he has a deep longing to help others.

18. He does one thing at a time. He isn't thinking about other things while he does this.

19. He likes foods he used to hate.

20. He forgets the distant past. He sometimes forgets the recent past. There is no pattern or logic to what is forgotten.

This will take us years to know.

# 12

# waiting

WHILE WE WAIT for medical confirmation of his brain injury, we go on easy walks in the Laguna Hills, after which Richard takes long naps. Every day he reads his anatomy and physiology texts, hoping to hold some of the information from the day before. Dylan comes home from school and sings to him. Joshua calls and tells him stories about his DJ gigs, or what he's studying in college. Richard listens, says a word or two. *What's going on in your life?* I write on a pad we keep bedside, and I hold it up. My husband recites the words back to his child. He can't remember what people care about, why they open their mouths to speak. Unless he does. He can't remember having been with us, or having heard what we said. Unless he happens to. But he does know how to sleep. Two naps a day and one twelve-hour stretch each night.

While he's sleeping, I read the surgical files. Perhaps there's something I missed, some clue as to why he can't remember his life. We've been focused on the cancer, for essential reasons: the probability of his survival without the removal of the cancer was zero percent. Cytoreduction surgery is experimental. Few surgeons perform peritonectomy procedures. The heated chemotherapy protocol is not FDA-approved. Could these procedures be causing brain function problems? If so, then perhaps the medical research might provide a clue.

Richard's former crisp, block-like handwriting stares back from our personal files. (His handwriting is now slanted and shaky, as if he must start over after every gesture.) There are notes from presurgical interviews he did with several surgeons and their business managers, survival statistics, tumor-marker data, lists of postoperative effects. As a well-respected physical therapist, he had access to a number of doctors for advice and support, as well as a complete understanding of how to do medical research. His training in kinesiology, physiology, and anatomy gave him a language that placed him as a colleague to the doctors and their staff. Richard's extraordinary intellect gave him the confidence of a doctor, and he projected that to everyone he met, but especially to the medical community with whom he worked every day. I finally read the abstracts he placed in the file prior to our visit to the cancer hospital: "Factors Predicting Survival after Intraperitoneal Hyperthermic Chemotherapy with Mitomycin C after Cytoreductive Surgery for Patients with Peritoneal Carcinomatosis," and "Quality of Life after Intraperitoneal Hyperthermic Chemotherapy (IPHC) for Peritoneal Carcinomatosis."

Before the surgery, I was removed from the medical analysis, wanting to focus instead on supporting him emotionally, offering nutritional support and suggestions of ways to prepare for surgery. He allowed me to shift our diet, to organize the family support, to have prayers said by people all over the world. But I didn't have access to two critical areas: extensive research on the hospital, the surgeon, and their practices; and what he'd negotiated with his employer about his time in recuperation. Now, Richard has no recall of any of that information. I kept myself at a distance from the research, a denial I now see as a kind of rebellion against making cancer my friend. The papers he placed in these files, and my own meetings with his doctors, are my only clues. While Richard sleeps, I sleuth.

I sit on our purple couch, in our tiny apartment in Laguna Beach, and I read the report from the hospital, the description of the procedure, and my notes in my journals. Midline abdominal incision including the entire xiphoid bone. Excision of tumor from the abdominal wall. Large volume of tumor beneath the right and left diaphragm. Pelvis with moderate tumor but larger amount of mucus ascites (those deadly culprits). The entire left quadrant, including the omentum and the area surrounding the spleen, covered by tumor. Lesser tumor growths in the bowel. Tricky bowel loops adhered to his former surgical incision. The surgeons stripped away the mucus tumor between the liver and the diaphragm. Then the gallbladder, like the spleen before it, was removed. The surgeon writes: *Now painstakingly we skeletonized the distal 50% of the pancreas.* Even though I don't even know what this statement means, it makes me want to drink a large whiskey, straight up.

The tumor was removed from the liver, the pelvis, the colon. Ten inches of the pelvic colon were "sacrificed," with hopes that the remaining colon would eventually bond and keep Richard from having to wear a colostomy pouch. Biopsies. Sutures. Bleeding points. Delicate avoidance of the vas deferens and testicular arteries (for which we will be ever grateful some months hence).

All the cancer that the eye could see was scraped, stripped, peeled, removed, ligated, incised, burned, electro-evaporated. The first surgical data shows no report of the bleeding that was quietly happening near his stomach; that comes in the second surgical analysis. There is no medical data here that supports a theory of "chemo brain," since the protocol for Richard's treatment was not systemic chemotherapy but a localized chemotherapy delivered into the abdominal cavity in surgery and a five-day postsurgical wash. These chemicals didn't appear to permeate the brain. Still, there are other common reasons for memory loss after these surgeries: post-op malnutrition, stress, sleep deprivation, narcotics, and the effects of anesthesia. Being put under two times in one twelve-hour period took a toll on Richard's body, but weeks later, any remaining mental confusion should have cleared. He's eating and sleeping well, and he's off all drugs. The only stress he seems to be experiencing is that of not knowing what happened to him.

We've done everything we know to help his body begin to restore itself. Richard threw away the hospital-prescribed Percocet, and instead, we take him for cranial-sacral work and acupuncture. He's on a diet of organic foods, garlic capsules, chlorophyll drinks, detox teas, unsweetened juices, and healing broths. No drugs except a few ibuprofen for muscle aches. He remains like a baby, seemingly requiring nothing but nourishment, rest, and sunshine.

There isn't anything to do but proceed with treatment and see what information can be found by the specialists. After a couple of sessions with the speech therapist, I ask for her evaluation.

"Cognitive communication disorder," the therapist says. "The kind of deficit that is both expressive and receptive."

"What's that?"

"He can't find the words to express himself, and he can't sort through what is being communicated," she says. "We haven't had a chance to make a full evaluation. And we can't do that right now. Because we haven't received approval from his insurance company."

"The company he worked for is changing providers. Can we start right away anyway?"

"You don't want to take on these costs yourselves," she answers. "It's thousands of dollars."

"How long do you plan to give him therapy?" I ask.

"Eight weeks. Then we have to switch gears and help him find coping strategies for working with his disorder."

Waiting is nonsense, I think. I hire a practitioner who specializes in Brain Gym, a movement-based program to enhance memory, concentration, and physical coordination, and a method that we've used with positive results for our son's challenges in school. We go for a few sessions, until we know enough to practice on our own. Richard stands in the pleasant suburban office touching his left palm to his right knee, then his right palm to his left knee, a movement he finds challenging.

"These activate the brain's ability to retrieve information across both sides of the brain," the therapist says. She has Richard draw figure eights in the air, and teaches him to breathe differently.

"I don't like it," he says when we get into the car. He sits on the passenger side because his reactions are too poor to drive.

"It's just a different kind of learning," I say.

Richard shrugs his bony shoulders.

I remind him to do the exercises several times a day. He complies. Nothing changes. Brain Gym is to his brain injury as a flyswatter is to an elephant.

For Thanksgiving that November, Joshua comes to see his father for the first time since the surgery. My father decides to join us. Everyone is quiet. The children need more time alone with their father, and my dad's presence keeps us on edge, like we can't really say what needs to be said. We walk the beach. We talk about school and avoid talking about our fears for our family's future. There's a strange sensation of being suspended. Our politeness is uncomfortable, as if we've lost access to the honesty that kept us vital. Through the visit, we swim and walk and make meals in our tiny kitchen. (Richard cringes at the thought of going to a restaurant.) When everyone leaves, I keep trying to find purposeful activity, because action makes me think that I've recovered from what I witnessed in the ICU. When Richard and Dylan sleep, I write, sometimes in my journal, sometimes letters. I send a note to a few friends:

> I am not in fear of anything that is happening to us, or might happen, but I am intensely lonely. The transition from being with a loved one who was so talkative and energetic, and from days filled with conversations, ideas, and dreams, to days of mostly silence is difficult. I am conscious of not asking more of Richard than he can do now . . . I am so very grateful for the love and support you have shown us while collectively we have been focused on Richard's healing. I trust the Great Spirit enough to know that this small "disorder" is not all that is present at this moment, and that Richard has gifts that are emerging that are healing for him and will be so for others too. I trust

> that all of what we are encountering is healing us, in ways we can't even know yet.

This is such a farce. I don't know anything about what's happening for my husband, or our relationship. In this moment, I'm determined to reshape him into the man that he was before, so he might serve our needs.

My new friends from my twelve-step group come to sit with Richard while I take our daughter to school activities or go get supplies. I'm grateful that though I've lived here less than two months, these people want to help.

"Have you got food? A place to live?" Rebecca grabs me the first time she sees me sobbing in the meeting room, mistaking my meltdown for that of someone who might be homeless. She ushers me out for long walks on the beach and slips me a lawyer's card; she listens to everything I have to say when I'm nervous about sharing my terrible fear of loss with my daughter. Even though Rebecca's going through a tumultuous divorce and raising two children, she's thoughtful and calm and reassuring.

One Saturday, she takes me to brunch. There are tables full of others we know from the meetings, but we sit on our own, on the sunlit Laguna patio. We order eggs Benedict and sip strong coffee.

"What does he forget?" she asks, not realizing he is constantly in the act of forgetting. Both his working memory and his long-term memory are faulty. The RAM and the hard disc are shot.

I look at Rebecca's long black hair, her elegant carriage, sensitive eyes. She's the kind of woman I'd want to be friends with, even if I weren't throwing myself at her mercy.

"My husband as I recognize him is gone," I say.

"That man died to you," she says.

I push the food around on my plate. I don't tell her what I'm thinking: *Sometimes death looks like bodies decomposing. Sometimes it's the death of a memory or history or identity, a consciousness that slips away, a ship listing past the curve of the horizon.*

My recovery friends offer their kindness. They make sure we're invited to social events. They don't let me get too far away. This despite the group having been recently manipulated by a woman feigning a cancer diagnosis. One day after a meeting, Grace, newly sober and grieving the loss of her mother, pulls me aside and tells me of the group's encounter with a woman with Munchausen syndrome, of the lie calculated to collect sympathy and thousands of dollars for "alternative treatments" that were actually vacation trips to Europe.

"Jesus H. After that, how can you be so generous with me?"

"You can't let that stuff ruin you, honey," she says.

Generosity isn't the first thing on the mind of the American health-care system. Richard is covered by COBRA, an extension of health-care benefits for eighteen months after his last day of work. When his company's health insurance changes, no more therapy can be approved. We wait. Two months pass.

Richard's health-care providers tell us they will not pay for his brain-injury treatment because they can't confirm that he's actually had a brain injury. They tell us that if the hospital had given us a diagnosis of an anoxic insult, then we wouldn't have to endure this scrutiny. Now it's up to us to prove the degree of his injury. Proof that we must secure by enlisting specialists. Specialists whom we can't enlist because we have no insurance approval. It's the catch-22 nearly every American without health insurance in this era knows intimately.

Because we grew up in Canada, Richard as a Canadian citizen and myself as a landed immigrant, we didn't have to rely on the American health-care system. Even though we've lived in the United States for over ten years, we were always healthy, rarely requiring coverage except for annual checkups. Richard's company, a national physical therapy corporation, does everything it can to help. But it can't make the new health-care provider decide to cover us. Despite the stories told about the Canadian health-care system, that there are delays for treatment in socialized medicine, we never had to wait to be seen by a doctor or hospital in our lives, we never had to have treatment approved in advance of our care, and we never had to struggle to pay a bill. Even when we were a poor married couple with no car and two toddlers, we seldom paid more than eighty dollars a month for our entire family's medical care. We grew up with the notion of a social safety net, used when necessary. With the clock ticking on a possible brain injury, and early treatment being imperative, we're losing valuable time.

The insurance coordinator for the speech and hearing center writes, *Without a written "predetermination of medical necessity," payment will not be determined until the claim forms are received. By the time we bill and they [the insurance company] respond, the charges could be substantial.* The treatment specialist describes how critical it is to begin work on Richard's aphasia, the neurological damage to the portions of the brain responsible for language.

Weeks pass. When there hasn't been insurance approval for the rehab program the speech therapist recommended, we decide to pay out-of-pocket to continue with Richard's therapy. We hope that the insurance company will cover the invoices we'll submit after he has a diagnosis. As the first few therapy sessions have shown us, he'll have to learn the same things hundreds of times before his memory will start to absorb the new information. We ask the speech and language specialists for a plan, and we begin his sessions and homework assignments. My goal is for Richard to improve so dramatically in the first weeks that he will not require intensive therapy or long-term disability. This is a complete misunderstanding of our situation. It's the kind of delusional optimism that will get me through the first years of our new life.

We wrestle with several insurance administrators to get approval for his care. I put Richard on hold for one while I'm talking with another. We juggle our days trying to get the information that will unlock the care that we've already paid for in our monthly fees. I refuse to believe that he will not reach his former capacity. I still can't accept that he might not make it back.

Since the time in the cancer hospital, I've been sorting the family finances. We're luckier than most people who have a serious illness. After paying our portion of the hospital bill, we have $10,000 in savings that we can use to get his treatment started. We tell the children that they will have to get through college with scholarships and loans, that we can't afford more than a few thousand dollars a year for their education. Our home near Seattle has been for sale for months. The week Richard nearly died, a lowball offer had come in from a prospective buyer, and I'd called my friend-the-therapist for reassurance that I could turn the offer down. Since that offer, nothing. Richard's paychecks ended while we lived in the cancer center. For twelve years, Richard paid into his short-term disability program, and now it's the best resource we could possibly have. He has ninety days of nearly full-time salary, essential since I can't work outside of the home while he requires this much care. We live frugally. We have no debt. We wait at the whims of the system.

When we receive medical bills from the hospital totaling over $90,000 for our preapproved surgery, I panic. We call the surgeon's office, hoping this is a terrible mistake. In 2003, there's not enough clinical data to support the use of the HIPEC treatment for Richard's rare cancer. Only about a dozen hospitals in America and Europe offer the treatment. HIPEC will eventually become a standard of care for PMP: over 150 treatment centers will provide the surgery and chemotherapy. Still, many insurance companies will refuse to cover the procedure. This denial of treatment resources, combined with the lack of availability, means the costs for surgery and chemotherapy will remain highly variable. According to a 2011 article in the *New York Times*, price tags range from $2,000 to $345,000, depending on the surgeon, the hospital, the complications, and the length of hospital stay.

We call Dr. M and tell him about the ongoing need for care, how we aren't sure if Richard has a permanent brain injury, but that we're determined to do everything we can to treat him.

"We'll take care of the hospital invoice," Dr. M's business manager says.

"Thank you," Richard says and hangs up the phone, stunned.

"Ninety thousand dollars? Is that possible?" I say. Richard shrugs his shoulders.

We never receive another bill from the hospital.

Three months later, he's approved for treatment. Providence Speech and Hearing Center sends us a report that's so comprehensive in listing Richard's deficits that I fall into silence. I stuff the report in the medical file to save him from depression. And Richard forgets there's been a report minutes after being told of it.

SPEECH AND LANGUAGE EVALUATION

DIAGNOSIS:
Appendiceal mucinous carcinoma with pseudomyxoma peritonei syndrome
Anoxic insult
Cognitive communication deficit

INTERVENTION:
Richard has had no speech therapy since an evaluation at Newport Language and Speech Centers 11/25/03 due to a change of insurance. In November 2003 he was diagnosed with a cognitive communication deficit as a result of anoxic insult. Weakness was noticed in expressive language, auditory comprehension in noise, reading comprehension, basic math skills, executive functioning and high-level reasoning.

PLOF [PRIOR LEVEL OF FUNCTION]:
Practiced as a physical therapist
Immediate family consists of wife and daughter
Patient reports his wife is his primary emotional support

EVALUATION AND TEST RESULTS:

**Speech skills**
Weaknesses in speech production noted in patient's

monotone speech and decreased facial expression during conversational speech.

**Oral motor skills**

Oral motor strength and range of motion was found to be within normal limits.

**Expressive language skills**

Decreased conversational initiation
Use of monotone during speech production
Accurate use of higher-level syntax and grammar
Decreased skills in random enumeration
Hesitations during speech
No paraphasias noted
No circumlocutions noted

**Receptive language skills**

Decreased auditory comprehension of reading materials with background noise present
Decreased comprehension of higher-level reading materials
Difficulty planning and executing a multi-step plan
Decrease in comprehension of word problems
Decrease in recall of words over time

**Pragmatic skills**

Decreased use of eye contact; patient had increased length of eye gaze with decrease in number of blinks and gaze shifting
Decreased use of facial expression throughout conversation
Decrease in topic initiation and maintenance
Decrease in vocal variation

SUMMARY:

Patient continues to demonstrate a cognitive

> communication deficit, which is characterized by decreased abilities in executive functioning, short-term memory, pragmatics and expressive and receptive language. It is strongly recommended that he receive speech and language therapy once a week for twelve weeks and be referred for in-depth testing by a neuropsychologist.

Neither of us is working at any real-world job, yet it feels like we are working harder than ever. Richard's body is slowly gaining weight and strength. I've been avoiding researching online, but now that we have reliable medical information, I find a list of common effects of brain injury: poor balance, slack muscle tone, unself-conscious posture, dysphasia or difficulty expressing one's thoughts in words. Richard has them all.

I make a list of treatments suggested by brain injury survivors, ones that we can pay for with our savings: Chinese medicine, Tai Chi, massage, hyperbaric oxygen therapy, acupuncture, flower essences, physiatry (to plan his rehabilitation), speech therapy, and psychological counseling. He refuses all but the speech therapist and Brain Gym. I know that he trusts me implicitly and will do whatever I ask. But I feel there's some sense that he'll know what's right for his body. I don't press him to do more.

But the speech therapist says their treatment isn't enough. To get a sense of Richard's brain's functioning, we need to find a good neuropsychologist who will test him to determine changes in information processing. Executive functioning, memory problems, emotional changes, attention deficits—all can be assessed. We ask friends to help us find a neuropsychologist who can take Richard through testing, training, and getting him the support he requires to get back to work. We wait another two months for the insurance company to approve the neuropsychological testing, and another month to get an appointment to see the doctor.

While we wait, my identity peels like old wallpaper from a neglected home. At first, I think I'm reinventing myself with the move. This is what my gypsy self does, I reason. But soon, I begin to see that I'm being altered in subtle and profound ways. I make a list.

THINGS THAT HAVE CHANGED (IN SONYA)
AFTER THE BRAIN INJURY:

1. She is five foot four inches, and she forgets that she is not tall.

2. She wears vintage slip dresses in ecru and burgundy because they are a nostalgic reminder of a time that she never had, never will.

3. More than ever, she isn't ready to look her age. She dyes her mostly grey hair black.

4. She thinks she might like a tattoo but she can't choose a design for the same reason she has no fine china: she can't settle on something she'd have to be with the rest of her life. This despite the fact that she's been with the same man for decades.

5. She speaks in a soft voice, speaks with and without looking people in the eye, speaks as if she knows what she is talking about, speaks on matters ranging from marriage to motherhood to money, but while she is speaking, she knows she doesn't know anything.

6. What others want for her is different from what she wants for herself. She's known this before. She just hasn't come out of hiding about it.

7. She takes control. Well, more than ever. She tells Richard that he doesn't need the cookies as she gives them to the guest. She organizes the calendar. She acts like she owns the place. (And she does. She's been running this home since his first cancer diagnosis, and it will be years before she realizes that the family manager is an outworn identity.)

8. She doesn't have any trouble fighting the hospital management, the insurance company, the medical establishment, the Social Security administrators, the disability providers, or the ones who get in the way of Richard's healing.

9. In the house's new silence, she becomes quiet.

10. She goes more and more into the wilderness.

11. As he cries often, she cries less. Except for at twelve-step meetings, where she cries every time she speaks. Truth is, now that life is full of real problems there's less desire to create any drama.

12. She cringes when her husband calls her by the new name "sweetness," completely unable to find the sweet within herself.

13. She fills her calendar with seven, eight, nine very important appointments and to-do items each day to avoid thinking about their situation.

14. She doesn't always realize she is living with immense grief.

15. Grief looks like being unable to read for the first time since words denoted sounds.

16. Grief looks like smiling when she doesn't want to.

17. Grief looks like helping her mother, her grandmother, her daughter, her sisters, the landlady, and quite a few drunks, so she doesn't have to be inside her own life.

18. In the midst of her grief, she really would like to find a new way to hurt her body, but she has closed all those doors.

19. This is why, when her new friends come to her door and propose a dip in the water or a walk on the beach or a funny movie or a meeting, she takes their hands and she follows. This is why, when her writer friends offer to read her pages, she says yes. A friend says, "The witness wants to be witnessed," but she can't tell. She's just living it.

# 13

# virgin

IN THE TIME leading up to his surgery, we calculated our risks, we decided what would happen if we couldn't have sex again. If we couldn't use makeup sex to resolve disputes, well, we'd have to communicate more; if he was impotent, I would take up running; if the erotic wasn't alive, I'd help him locate the sensual; if he couldn't take me to bed, he wanted me to take a lover; if he was partly disabled, we'd find other ways for sex to happen; if he couldn't feel anything, he would derive more pleasure from my pleasure; if we couldn't find ourselves through fucking, we would learn other strategies to connect; if the wild man disappeared with his sexuality, we'd live in the mountains again, restore wildness through empty trails and cloudless skies. But in all of our best or worst-case scenarios we never could have prepared ourselves for what eventually happens.

In those weeks after we return home, I wait. I wait because he has lost the memory of our life and this feels fragile. I wait because I don't know what he's thinking, because he can't speak, because he doesn't know who he is, because he has become an innocent, because the nights in the mountain desert are slow, because I am not sure what his body can do, because I don't know if he's going to want me again. I stare at the ceiling, waiting, pretending to read. He sleeps, on and off, day and night, a quiet trance of breath and perspiration.

As I wait, I am rewriting the narrative. He is not a child. He is silent, dark, and handsome. If I think of him in this way, perhaps his muscles, manliness, and might will return.

He sleeps, naked. His hands are by his side, his body flat over a comforter embroidered with flowers. His purple scar is a brilliant vine up his middle, its skin tender and new. An open textbook lies on his belly. You take the book and place it on the side table, and you dry your wet hair with a towel, watching him breathe. You stare at his legs. His legs are an epic, a beatbox, bel canto, a tango, a fresco, a gastronome. Neoclassical. They are a balm to you; even though his masculine assertion has vanished, his legs are evidence of the athlete and lover he was. In the silence you hear his organs rumble with the soft food and vitamins and medicinal teas that you have plied him with, to help him gain weight. The hair they shaved from his pelvis is starting to grow back. You think about running your palms over it, but you're frightened you will hurt him. You stand beside the bed, and you watch his sliced belly rise and fall.

The November wind moves across the chaparral and sagebrush and goldenrod of the San Joaquin Hills and down to Laguna Canyon, where it winds through the screen window carrying sand and the sense of erosion. The wind lifts tufts of your husband's hair where it is greying: across his chest, the sideburns of his side-parted, freshly washed mane. His eyes open. They are indigo, wide and unblinking. His eyes disguise no thought; they are alight as if to legitimize your belief in innocence.

You lean over to kiss him. Rise up. Smile. When he looks down at his body, you follow his eyes. You see the flesh-familiar shape. You smile, catholic and evil, giggly and silly. No doctor knew if his sexual functioning would return. It's been two months since the surgery, and you weren't sure if you'd ever be with him as a lover again. Your hands go to your satin slip, and you feel your thighs under your palms. You raise the hem of your slip. You don't even think, you just act, the hours and days and months of quiet having made you more instinctual. He watches as you climb on top of him.

He is silent. He is not without words, you think. You imagine words locked inside, where they are waiting to be discovered. And you will. You will search for your relationship's former identity, your marriage's fixed history, your lover's unaltered state. Because you haven't surrendered yet. You still think you want to find your way back to who the two of you were before. You touch his skin. The only thing unchanged is the way he feels upon your skin. You've got to have some reassurance that the "we" that you knew was not altered, crushed, ruined, deformed; is not derelict or dead. His body can give that to you. You remember. You're willing to use his body to take your safety, security, stability, if you have to.

You remember his body, his luscious body, his erotic body, his carnal body, his animal body, the body he has shared with you for longer than he has been alone. You want to remember how his body feels inside. Everything in you wants the memory—your muscles, your skin, your sight, your pulse, your heat, your heart, your breath, your everything.

Everything slows. You lower yourself. You watch his already enormous eyes enlarge, rapt, his posture slouch in easy receptivity, the last surreptitious instinct having been drained from him in surgery: he is defenseless. You think this is strange, this is beautiful, this is precious. You know you've never been here before, and you don't know why you know this.

His eyes are never for a second removed from your eyes. He doesn't turn away from your face and so you do not turn away from him. You do not close your eyes. You watch and watch and watch. Which means you must really see him. You see a face completely unaware of its expression of pleasure, the simple stare of a man who senses all and relates to nothing. You lean back, balancing your body on his legs, keep your hands away from his scar, suddenly frightened that your rambunctiousness might tear him apart. By the time you adjust yourself a few seconds later, he comes to orgasm, and it surprises you both—the fast, sharp impulse, the release that he doesn't seem to recognize.

You watch him closely then, both of you silent, his face remarkably unlike the man you have known, guardedness replaced with the purity of an open gaze. You move off him and lean against the pillow, watching his expression. Across his face, none of his former gestures. He hadn't known what you were going to do, what your touch was going to be like. That orgasm came as directly and forcefully as a teenage boy's.

"Honey," you say, "I have to ask you. Whatever your answer is, it's okay."

He nods, eyes sleepy, still taking in every inflection of your demeanor.

"Do you remember sex?" you ask, your voice a whisper.

"I don't think so," he says, and then he watches your eyes for reaction. He says this without shame, without guilt, without remembering. You look at his face for a few moments, and then you look away, toward the crimson-painted wall where there is a dark column of ants weaving in an unbroken line toward the ceiling. With your finger you smash the ants. The ants reform the line as if you were never there, destroying their lives.

His hand reaches out, enfolds your hip. It is the first time he has moved toward you since the surgery. You do not cry, though you wish you could. In your mind, you add sex to the list of things forgotten. You think about the ways you have made yourself a "we"—who we are, what we like and what we don't like, what we do and what we will never do—and you watch those things vanish too. After a while, you watch him sleep. The man who taught you to explore has become a virgin.

# 14

# mysterium

BY MID-DECEMBER, JUST a few months after the brain injury, we're packing to travel to Atlanta to be with our families for the holidays. There's a new baby, Richard's brother's first child, who will be a welcome distraction. Even though Richard's short-term disability is running out and we haven't won approval for long-term disability, our home in Seattle has sold. We're excited to have some cash that can sustain us during his recovery.

The week we leave Laguna Beach, Dylan puts on "The Christmas Song" and Richard joins in on the chorus. The first notes sung since the surgery. It's a shock to hear the low rumble of his beautiful voice. Richard walks toward his daughter, both of them singing with Nat King Cole, and they hold each other, singing and laughing. After hearing him speak just a few sentences, we're amazed to listen to effortless expression.

This is the first time most of our family has seen us since his surgery. We stay in Richard's brother's large family home on a hill overlooking a golf course. My husband backs himself against the bar in the living room as everyone walks in, sixteen of them, the sisters and the "outlaws," as we call our partners, their children, my long-divorced parents, our children, Richard's brother and wife and baby, and Mimoo—my grandmother—who bonded with Richard long ago over the early loss of their mothers. They grab him by the shoulders and hug him, and after greeting everyone, Richard stands straight, staring, the bewildered face of overwhelm. Mimoo finds a place near Richard, where she can hold his huge hand in her frail one, and she looks away, shaking her head in disbelief, tucking her lower lip to stop herself from crying.

Everyone is thrilled to see him alive and unsure about how to relate to him. In the past, Richard has been the vocal one, rallying people for games and adventure, keeping a steady beat of music going, singing and dancing along. This Christmas, he stays quiet, reading and resting. He tries going out to a hockey game and a movie theater, to see how he will do. He sleeps long hours after each of the outings. Our extended family makes delicious meals, and we talk with the children about their lives.

A week later, when we return to our apartment, Richard will leave only for therapy and the walk I insist he take each morning. But something unusual is beginning to happen on our strolls along the sand. Just as he has begun to sing, now full memorizations spring from his mouth. First up: the entire soliloquy from *Hamlet,* otherwise known as the "What a Piece of Work Is a Man" monologue.

Then, on the drive home from one of Dylan's vocal performances, out pops the announcer from the *Adventures of Superman* television series: "Faster than a speeding bullet! More powerful than a locomotive! Able to leap tall buildings at a single bound! Look up in the sky! It's a bird! It's a plane! It's Superman! Yes, it's Superman, strange visitor from another planet who came to Earth with powers and abilities far beyond those of mortal men. Superman, who can change the course of mighty rivers, bend steel in his bare hands; and who, disguised as Clark Kent, mild-mannered reporter for a great metropolitan newspaper, fights a never-ending battle for truth, justice, and the American way!"

"Where did that come from?" Dylan asks.

"Some memory he had since he was a child. You used to do it for the kids," I say to him. "Remember?"

"No," he says.

And, inside me, the crush of arbitrary forgetting. Life is available only in the present moment, say the gurus. But they remember what happened yesterday.

The "you" in Richard has disappeared, and in its wake a mind appears in random flashes of gestures, words, expressions. There's so much silence that being with him is like being with the spaces between things, between words, between sounds. I'm unmoored by his apparent nothingness. He's a living embrace of impermanence, in dude form. But I don't want this bodyspace called husband, absent of ideas and longings and history. I want him to be as he was. I want to have what was once mine, even though I know he really didn't belong to me. But this man does not stay. He goes and goes and goes. Whatever has done this to us cares nothing for what I want.

In January his company calls to see if he'd like to attend a yearly conference, the same conference where Richard has received outstanding performance awards in previous years. It's all the way across the country, in Washington, DC. I'm not sure how to describe what he might find when he sees his colleagues again. Should I tell my husband that his co-workers might be appalled by what they see in his lost-boy expression? Should I make Richard aware that he risks frightening his colleagues with his childlike behavior?

"You're too fragile," I argue. We walk up the hill behind our apartment. He opens the chain-link gate that leads onto the Laguna Hills path. I watch his body move awkwardly, his shorts belted so they won't fall down. He's still thirty pounds below his presurgery weight.

Richard's mouth moves into a straight line. He's determined to reconnect with the fulfilling career that makes him feel capable.

"I want to go alone," he says.

"Without anyone?" I kick the dry dirt with my feet. The cars drive alongside the old creek bed below, an empty gorge once full of river life. So many cars that roads are being widened. In this canyon, rock ledges and concrete culverts have been constructed, coastal sagebrush planted, to veer flash floods to the ocean. The Tongva tribe used to fish for abalone in these creeks. Now the land is managed wilderness. I'm caught between two internal forces—one that wants to keep him safe from those who can injure him with a frozen image of decline, and one that wants him to reconcile with the truth of his predicament.

"I can travel alone," he says.

"You've only been inside a grocery store by yourself," I say. He has no clue about the support that holds his life together. Richard has no formed sense of himself, or of his relationship with the corporate culture he once found so amenable to his skills.

"I have to go," he says. He is squinting into the ever-present California sun when he says this, and his face looks like a little boy's: innocent, resolute.

I realize that I can't really tell Richard what others might think because I can't actually know their minds. At the same time that I want to control his story, I also want to stop defining who he can be.

"I'll need to coach you on how to do everything—take the flight, take the train, introduce yourself, remember manners. Okay?" I say.

"Yes," he says, and he turns around and walks the trails without caring that there might be rattlesnakes upon the rocks.

Later that afternoon I call the woman who has been his business manager and confidante, and ask her to watch over him. "He doesn't know people anymore," I tell her, and she reassures me that his former colleagues will re-introduce themselves. I place a label with my contact information in every coat and jacket. I drill him on various "what-if" scenarios: what if he gets lost, what if he gets sick, what if he decides to come home early. While he's preparing to go, he continues to read his textbooks and sleep a lot.

He leaves three weeks later. He makes it to the hotel.

"How was the flight?" I ask him later that night, when we check in.

"I can't remember," he says.

"The train? Did that go okay?"

Silence.

"Are you raising your shoulders? Because I can't hear you," I say.

"Everyone says I look great," he says.

"How are you feeling?" I ask.

"Tired," he says.

Three days later, when Richard returns, he sleeps, hard.

"Well, *that* happened," I say, when I take him his morning juice.

"I slept through most of the three days," he says.

"Meetings are boring," I say.

"I went to the Holocaust Museum," he says.

"Really? How was that?" I ask, trying not to choke on my coffee at the thought of choosing so intense an experience straight out of cancer surgery.

"I saw my friend Damien."

"Who used to work for you in Memphis? How is he?"

"Good. He was kind to me," Richard says.

"Then what?"

"I went back to the room and slept until I got on the plane."

"Oh," I say, like it's no big deal. But he's crying already. I lean in and kiss the gentle man on his wide forehead. Something about his incorruptibility is instructing me. He's precious in his purity. It's been a long time since I've seen my surroundings without complication.

Though I spent fifteen years in management for museums and science centers, I left that work to consult and write part-time. Before Richard's brain injury, I thought that the move to California would allow me time to write every day, creative work that I wanted to do from the time I was a girl, work that I never allowed myself in my effort to be responsible. I haven't always been forthcoming about my own dreams. I was afraid to declare them, afraid I would fail, afraid I would give up.

While in California, I work with my writing mentor, who lets me into her retreats for free in exchange for preparing the meals. I'm grateful for this community, and I'm willing to do whatever it takes to continue writing when Richard cannot work. It feels like a compulsion, less a choice than a survival skill. I reason that if we live simply on Richard's disability, then I can help Richard with his recovery, and write a novel and some screenplays. I also do a few consulting gigs to pay for Dylan's college auditions and for travel to see Joshua.

Dylan's vocal studies at the Orange County School of the Arts have kept her engaged throughout her senior year, but in the time I've had to focus on Richard's recovery, our daughter has become more independent and resilient. By the New Year, I'm planning a five-city audition tour for Dylan, who wants to find the best university to study vocal music, and locating companions who will stay home with Richard while we travel. Our plan calls for her to visit two schools on her own, and for me to join her for the more demanding auditions. In February, Dylan flies to Cincinnati, and I join her a week later in Rochester, Philadelphia, and Bloomington, Indiana.

On the East Coast, the clouds open and pour forth snowflakes. Dylan's throat closes. We find a café, and I ask for ginger tea. We take off our mittens and hold hands while we watch the barista grate thin slices of fresh gingerroot, place them in a gauze pouch. I try not to talk about her upcoming performance, since it makes her nervous. Instead, we talk about our impressions of each campus so far, and the student guides, and what it might be like to settle in this geography. After the tour and a successful audition, we find our hotel and go out for burgers and tell jokes. For the first time in months, she has the full attention of her mum, and we play like when she was a little girl, staying up late telling each other silly stories, and joking about family memories, and making fun of the kinds of structures and judgment that stifle personal creativity. We say what frightens us—that Richard will remain emotionally as a child, that we won't be able to reach him, that we will grow angry or, worse, bored with him. We talk about how we will stay connected, even when we don't know what remains of our family.

Upon returning, we're able to know in the lift of an eyebrow what's required of the other. She lost some of her carefree youth through her father's cancer, but having to study and practice in the middle of this upheaval made her self-reliant. She knows that she'll soon be leaving this chaos and entering her own life. I want this for her, and I'm fearful of the silence on the other side of her departure.

The groceries in the trunk melt in the scorching midday as I drive across the parking lot near our apartment. It's late March, and the afternoon air stifles inside the metal car, quite unlike the subdued, dreary Northwest we left behind. When my phone rings, I see an area code matching Richard's company. I'm driving too fast because Richard is worried every time I leave the house. I pick up the call anyway. The CEO says my name. He's on speakerphone with the head of human resources. After the small talk, they ask the question, the one I've been dreading, just as I hit a speed bump. I pull over and take a deep breath. I imagine there's a room full of people listening for the answer, so I'm trying not to sound like an asshole.

"I don't know when he'll be back to work," I say.

They prod. "Three months? Six months?"

"I don't know."

"What do you think it's going to take to get him back to work?" they ask.

It's as if they're speaking in code, some code I haven't ever bothered to learn. I pull at the sundress sticking to my legs and think of the way people expect rational responses to an event so mysterious it hasn't yet found a name. I want Richard's company not to lose hope in him, but I don't even know what has happened to his mind. *He can't remember his past. He passes out when he tries to stand. He's read the same book every day for the last four months.* I don't say what I'd like to because I'm afraid the company will think he's too far gone to ever work for them again. The possibility would crush Richard's motivation; he's getting out of bed because he needs to return to his job.

"Going to take a lot of hard work!" I say, trying for cheery.

They're not impressed. They want to know what our plans are.

"Honestly, I don't know whether he's coming back," I finally say, as I break out in a sweat. This is the most truth I've told all year.

"What is it going to take to know?" they ask.

I'm on a roll now. Might as well give it to them.

"Could be a few months of therapy, could be a sabbatical to the Himalayas in Tibet. I have no idea what we'll do next."

Silence. The kind of silence like that time I stood up in the restaurant after too much to drink and fell face first on the floor.

I cannot find the words. Just like my husband.

Richard has already resigned his position. There isn't anything we can do to make life easier for the corporation. I'm thankful for their support, for the way they flew our child out to see her father, for their help in preapproving and financing the surgery. I've said all of these things. Now, I want them to sit in the discomfort I feel every day.

If only the doctor had told us the hospital caused the brain injury, if only the medical insurance hadn't delayed us in getting the diagnosis, if only I'd screamed louder when the blood wasn't available. You can kill yourself on the poisonous "if-onlys." But there isn't some magic time machine that will transport me to the past to change the outcome. Life now seems to eradicate the past. Richard and I are corpus, bound by scars of the dermis, scars below the surface too. I've loved him and I've hated him, and I'm no longer sure if any of it was because of who he really is.

Still, the persona loves the narrative of change. This is the story I want to give to the corporation—*he woke up and he's getting better!*—but that story is already unraveling. I want to say, *We're eating and sleeping and walking. What more do you want?*

Instead I say, "I'm sorry. I'm sorry. I'm sorry."

By April, seven months after the brain injury, when we finally have approval from the insurance company, we make an appointment to see a neuropsychologist. We wait another month to get in to see Dr. L, who meets with us in his modest Lake Forest office, on a spring day that's California ever-bright. Certified in psychology and clinical neuropsychology, Dr. L specializes in rehab medicine and leads international symposiums on brain injury. With polite charm, kind eyes, and the mild-mannered repose that comes from his black belt in karate, Dr. L instantly makes us feel like we're not insane. It's as if we have been spit out of the rapids of the cancer hospital and the sporadic aftercare and into a gentle river.

His waiting room is filled with vivid watercolors.

"Dreamy paintings," I say.

"Former patients. Most with brain injuries," he says.

"Really?"

"Lots of people with TBI have latent artistic abilities," he says, like it's no big deal.

His bookshelves are lined with clinical works and those by popular writers: Antonio Damasio and Eric Kandel and Michael Gazzaniga and Daniel Schacter. Names I will grow to trust as I learn about the enshrined experiences of memory. Tucked on a top shelf is Dr. L's frame drum, just like the ones Richard and I made to celebrate our twentieth wedding anniversary. Dr. L speaks matter-of-factly and reassuringly about the process Richard will undergo so he can be evaluated: three days of tests and then an interview and a meeting to discuss his care plan.

"Richard can barely stay awake for a few hours at a time," I say.

Dr. L assures us: "The testing will be four hours each day. Lots of breaks. At the end of these sessions, we'll have a clear understanding of Richard's neurocognitive and neurobehavioral functioning, including his strengths and weaknesses."

"Do you think he's had a brain injury?" I ask.

"The MRI taken in November appears normal, but a functional MRI was not taken. We can see increased signals, or 'motor tracks,' that can result in higher-level thinking problems, more apparent on the left than on the right. The tests will indicate where his cognitive difficulties are, and what the treatment plan needs to be."

These three days of tests are to include a sensory-perceptual examination, a tactile form-recognition test (matching geometric shapes to a board cutout), a finger-tapping test (quickly tapping dominant and nondominant hands), an aphasia examination (using written and spoken language to name pictures and perform simple math), a Rey Complex Figure Test (reproducing a line drawing by copying and by memory), a Hopkins Verbal Learning Test (recalling a twelve-item semantically categorized list), a Wechsler Memory Scale (testing spatial, symbolic, visual, logical, and auditory cognition, including working and delayed), a Brief Visuospatial Memory Test (storing and recalling visual memory and the spatial relationship of objects), and a Neurobehavioral Functioning Inventory (identifying problems with daily living), as well as tests to examine visual discrimination, judgment of line orientation, and executive functions.

I hear the names of the exams rattled off. What we want is the plan. Dr. L tells us we'll do the tests right away, but it will take a couple of weeks to pull together the results. Another round of waiting.

We take out the list we made when we first discovered that Richard had cancer, the list that always brings us back to ourselves, the list that has, since he died and came back, become *The List: Ten Things We Want to Do Before We Die*. There it is, at number five. Get to the Grand Canyon.

That week, I haul our camping gear out of storage, load the tent, sleeping bags, food, and water into the car, map the South Rim entry from southern California, reserve the campsite, make and freeze several meals we can eat at the canyon, pack oatmeal and brown sugar and ground coffee beans and Earl Grey tea into animal-proof boxes. We drive eight hours east, around the edge of the Mojave Desert, and into Arizona, our mouths becoming dry with the rising midday temperatures.

In the first week in May, the canyon holds midday heat, with evening temperatures near freezing. We are comfortable with these extremes, having learned to camp in the Canadian Rockies. We locate our site near Douglas fir, alligator juniper, desert bricklebush. We pitch our tent under the big tree. We sit at the picnic table and look at a map. We walk down the road until we arrive at the edge of the canyon.

One million arid acres stretch out in the afternoon sun. The mile-high crust, layers of umber, russet, charcoal, goldenrod, burnt sienna, and ochre, exposes two billion years of geologic history. We stand awe-smacked. We're the newest things on earth. Everything at the rim—all of the particles that big-banged themselves through the universe to be alive in just these forms—has been set in motion. Our lives are the vestiges of these events, events that seem to happen ceaselessly. As tired and grief-stricken as I am, there's still a part of me that knows that Richard's loss of memory, the death of his identity, his coming back as a new man, it all has its place in the order of things, or perhaps the chaos of things—just like these ancient, awesome rock formations.

But now, even though I have been stunned into a state of wonder by the Grand Canyon, I am also lonely. I don't know if I have a marriage, or if I will be alone with my thoughts for the rest of our lives.

Like the boy that he is, Richard gets too close to the drop-off at the South Rim, and I drag him back. The terror of nearly losing him can be scratched like the tender skin of the scar that winds up his middle. With him, I'm a young mother, all frightful imagining and smothering care.

We walk back to the campsite and make cups of tea on the camp stove. Richard climbs into his sleeping bag and naps while I write in my journal. Hours later, when he wakes, it's still light, and we watch a raven swoop onto our table, open a foil tea packet with her beak, pick out the bag, and break into the tea leaves. We smirk as we observe her open a matchbox and fling the matches to the ground.

"Now you're just showing off," I say to the bird.

Playing, laughing, even the organization of daily chores feels easy with this new Richard. On the road there's little tension inside him because there's nothing to do. He's simply living in current time, not fretting over the past or freaking out about the nonexistent future.

I watch him build a fire, the first one since the brain injury. Once he gets his hands on objects, he remembers. The paper crumples, the kindling is stacked near the bottom over a layer of tinder, bark, and dry needles. He organizes the logs by size so they can be fed to the fire in the correct order, small to large. After he arranges the classic log cabin shape, four walls around a central teepee, he digs in the waterproof bag for matches. When he takes them out he pauses, looks at the matches for a long time. Not seconds. A long minute. His hand seems disconnected from his brain. I open my mouth to ask if he wants help, and then I stop myself. I watch his fingers grasp the match and look at the wooden sticks, as if he can't recall what to do next. But he knows what to do, he simply can't decide to take the action. Suspension. Concentration. I watch his fingers take a few grazing stabs against the rough edge of the matchbox. Pause. Graze. Pause. Graze. And then he strikes a singular *sffft*; phosphorus and sulfur ignite. His fingers dance to hold the tiny timber of the match. He balances the flame and he lowers it to the tinder. He bites his lip. Releases the match. Watches the little flicker turn to heat. He purses his lips and blows air into the fire. The kindling catches. He kneels and feeds the logs, one by one, until the fire is hot and thick with gold light. He turns his flushed face toward me.

"What was that?" I ask.

He shrugs his shoulders. The big Whatever. He doesn't know.

"The match thing is quirky," I say. "Very Oliver Sacks."

"Yes," he says. "Strange."

This is just one of the curiosities of my husband's life now.

Later, in the tent, I listen to Richard's bearlike body snore, and I watch the curve of the stars fall into the scrape of rock, and I feel my body slowly rotating with the earth. I am one object of billions here.

# 15

# watershed

TWO WEEKS LATER we are seated on the smooth, cool couch of Dr. L's office while he offers us water and shuffles the papers in front of him and speaks in his calmest, most careful voice. He's making sure we understand. Where Dr. M simply read his data on Richard's cancer and surgery into his tape recorder and spoke a sharp, "Any questions?" at the end, Dr. L is all nurturance and tranquil authority.

"Your relationship is loving and mutually supportive," he says. "That's one of your strengths. Also, Richard is very bright and has a tremendous neuronal reserve. And he's in good health and is psychologically stable. These are critical to his success."

Richard and I hold hands across the couch. I sneak a look at my husband, whose face is, as usual, registering no emotion. I think these words are meant to soothe, but I can't catch my breath. After the tender setup comes the thorny truth.

"Richard, you've made remarkable progress under the care of your speech therapist. You've been learning compensatory strategies. The people who have administered the tests have found you to be extremely cooperative, and, frankly, you are the kind of person who succeeds through incredible effort."

I watch Richard blink back tears. His gentle vulnerability makes me warrior-like in my desire to protect him.

"Those strengths are going to serve you well. We do anticipate a positive outcome—however, the test results showed some areas of impairment."

I breathe for the first time since he began to speak. The word *impairment* sounds like a gong ringing inside the dim room.

"Richard, you have severely impaired tactual recognition skills. These are related to speed."

"What's tactual recognition used for?" I ask.

"The ability to perceive tactile, auditory, and visual stimuli. He had no errors with his left hand, and on some tests he shows up with a high average on the left side, but his right hand is severely impaired." I am not surprised, given the state of his right side following the brain injury. The doctor adds, "What's unusual is that his tactual recognition seems to be due to diminished sensory ability in his fingers, which makes it difficult for him to recognize geometric shapes with his hands."

I'm shocked to hear that Richard's ability to process what is happening with his hands has been limited. As a physical therapist, he depends upon this ability; it is his lifeblood. Richard shows no sign of registering concern for his future.

"Richard, your phonemic fluency skills are borderline. Your social skills are excellent, and we didn't find any significant deficits in word finding, verbal repetition, written spelling, or reading comprehension, but your semantic fluency is low. For example, you're at the twenty-fifth percentile in sentence repetition."

"Is it possible that the months he's been doing speech therapy have brought him to this level?" I ask, wanting to find something positive.

"It's possible. Though his visuoconstruction skills are at the severely impaired level. These are what we would call the executive skills."

"How low?" I ask.

"The fourth percentile in one trial. Up to about the eighteenth in another."

I wonder if I'm hearing accurately. This is a man who skipped a grade in elementary school, who nearly had a graduate degree, who, before the brain injury, was managing twenty physical therapy clinics and seeing ten patients a day. He was the fastest thinker I'd ever known. Richard squeezes my hand. I'm not sure if my husband is trying to reassure me, or is terrified by the doctor's words.

"Just a few more things to note. Low average in the following categories: visual learning and memory skills, simple and complex visual fluency skills, nonverbal problem-solving skills. These are significant neuropsychological deficits, ones that weren't present before the surgery. The best thing you have going for you, Richard, is that you were functioning at a high level for such a long period of time. Vocationally, you functioned at a high level. The brilliant mind you started out with is going to be of assistance in getting you back in the game. Like a lot of brain injury patients, you may find that is not the same game as it was before."

"What's his prognosis?"

"Postoperatively he has been unable to regain much in the way of his premorbid cognitive and behavioral capabilities. We would consider him to be permanently disabled."

Permanently. Disabled. The words crush against us. Our bodies hang like skinned carcasses. Permanently, as in forever. Disabled, as in unable to find his way back. I look at Richard's face, where I see confusion. He's not able to register disability as a part of his identity. I see where he wants to be, who he wants to become, what he cannot speak.

"So how do we get him back to permanently able?"

Richard nods his head.

"We begin with neuropsychological counseling, once a week for twelve months."

"I want to go back to work," Richard says.

"The goal for work is part-time. Modified. When you're ready to go back to work, you'll need to be closely supervised and in a structured environment. And not before the end of the year. We want you to see an occupational therapist. To help you create compensatory strategies. This will facilitate independence at home and at work."

Richard screws up his face as if he has eaten a sour lemon. He thinks occupational therapy is for the incapacitated, not for him. He considers occupational therapy, the practice of daily and work skills, to be facile bullshit. But he'll bust his ass to complete the protocol if he thinks those skills will bring him closer to being functional at work.

"You get good at the strategies and then you don't have to go to occupational therapy anymore, right, Dr. L?" I say.

"We're going to do everything we can to help you be successful," Dr. L answers, with the kind of confidence I want to crawl inside.

Compensatory strategies are used to help people with brain injuries recognize and make accommodation for their cognitive difficulties. On our next visit, I complain about Richard wanting to drive.

"Dr. L, he's clueless about what he can't do anymore."

The doctor takes me into his office while Richard meets with the occupational therapist.

"Richard has a reduced awareness of his deficits, which is typical in someone with a brain injury. In the rehabilitation process, the mind must become aware of what's missing, even when it doesn't recognize that anything is absent."

He's describing the same kind of denial my brain had to eliminate when I got sober.

"The tests we took also measured Richard's effort and motivation," Dr. L says.

"He's downright stubborn in his belief that he can get back to work," I say.

"No kidding," the doctor says. He tells me that Richard is remarkably motivated in comparison with other head-injured patients. I look out the window where the sunshine is glinting off the blacktop of the parking lot. I don't want the doctor to see my tears.

"He's so damned determined to relearn his career," I say. "He spends four hours every day reading his anatomy and physiology textbooks. Falling asleep and then waking up and doing it all over again."

Dr. L picks up the evaluation and reads a passage to me: "Qualitatively the patient worked hard throughout this evaluative effort. Responses to psychological measures did not suggest symptom exaggeration. If anything, the patient had a tendency to downplay his neurobehavioral complaints."

"He stopped driving not because he noticed that his reaction time is poor, but because I told him that he's placing other drivers at risk," I say.

"He has to do a driving test to ensure everyone's safety, but not until he's ready," Dr. L says.

"He wrote on his application to his disability company that he'll be back to work in two months."

The doctor and I smile at Richard's innocence. On the tests Dr. L administers, Richard perceives little in the way of neurocognitive difficulties, saying that he feels himself to be within normal range in memory, attention, communication ability, mood, and motor skills. I score those areas as problematic across the board.

But I tell Dr. L I think we have a bigger problem. Richard can't remember many events that happened before he went to the hospital, from childhood to a few months ago. And he's still struggling to hold on to things learned in the present.

"Though most people with a brain injury have their short-term memory affected," he tells me, "their long-term memory remains intact."

A phantom limb is a persistent memory of a part of the body, the sensation of a limb's presence for months or years after its loss. Richard has a phantom identity. His personality, history, self-image, orientation, gestures, expressions, and relationships have gone missing, and every day he wakes up without an intact sense of his former self. But there's no indication that Richard feels that he is without himself, or that he cares who his former self was. Only I seem to care about that man.

"Richard wants you to tell him what to do so he can get back to work," I tell the doctor.

"We'll talk about all of your goals and see if we can outline what's reasonable for him," Dr. L says, and he shakes my hand like we've made a terrific deal.

A railroad worker in the mid-nineteenth century, Phineas Gage, had an iron rail plunged through his skull, and when it was removed, his temperament shifted dramatically, from balanced to angry. (Unlike Phineas Gage, Richard didn't develop more aggressive tendencies, but rather became more passive. When I read stories of angry brain injury patients, I'm grateful that we haven't had to endure such bedevilment.) Gage became the subject of medical lore and books, and his case helped doctors understand the relationship between brain and personality functions.

Not located in just one focal region of the brain, like a language center or a spatial area, the personality is layered with all the aspects of our history. The personality is the narrative that we develop through which we regard and understand our changing world. The railroad worker's life was said to have been destroyed due to his uncharacteristically combative nature following the accident. His doctor, John Martyn Harlow, noted of Gage:

> A child in his intellectual capacity and manifestations, he has the animal passions of a strong man. Previous to his injury, although untrained in the schools, he possessed a well-balanced mind, and was looked upon by those who knew him as a shrewd, smart businessman, very energetic and persistent in executing all his plans of operation. In this regard his mind was radically changed, so decidedly that his friends and acquaintances said he was "no longer Gage."

After his injury, people were not interested in Gage, only his tale, a story he was quite uninterested in exploiting. He left for Chile, a place that did not know his past self, a place that could not keep him mired in relationship with what had been.

Richard, like Gage, has limited access to his past, and he's unable to project on the future a sense of who he might become. No history, no story of a future.

We, his family, are the ones who grieve his memory loss, but Richard may also be devastated by grief in his own way, in fear of his unrecognizable self. In what ways was he, like Gage, "no longer Richard"?

Gage became, like Freud's Anna O., one of the most famous patients in the history of medicine. Written into textbooks, fashioned into fiction, and referenced in cultural criticism, Gage was a figure of scientific and popular discourse, a kind of brain-rattled bogeyman. Over time, his narrative became so exaggerated that Gage was said to be a drunken, incompetent braggart who ran off to join Barnum's American Museum. In just a few years, Gage became a liar, gambler, bully, and abuser of women and children, though few proffering stories of his behavior had ever met the man.

In the aftermath of Gage's accident, a great neurological debate ensued between the scientists who believed that function could be located in specific areas of the brain, and those who resisted such notions. Dr. Harlow's story of Gage became distorted as it was used to uphold competing theories of the brain. Information brought to light in 2008 by psychologist Malcolm Macmillan reveals that instead of disintegrating into a raving madman, Gage improved over time, relearning social and personal skills enough to reenter the workforce (as a stagecoach driver, which would suggest a need for significant multitasking skills). But that did not serve the narrative that scientists of the former century had to uphold, as not to have their theories dismissed.

When I come across this story of Gage, it's instructive: I'm cautious about becoming the same kind of biased narrator of my husband's story. I don't want to make assumptions about what Richard has lost, or what he's going to become. But still, the words *permanent disability* keep cycling through my mind.

By the next counseling session with Dr. L I have a list of questions. I want to know how brain injury works, and why Richard has lost his memories of some things—our marriage history, major events in the children's lives—but not others: Hamlet's soliloquy and the Superman monologue.

"In a pressure drop or traumatic incident, the internal capsule in the middle part of the brain goes down first. This creates a watershed area, like water that goes into a floodplain. In the case of spotty impairments, one of these roots will be fine but others may not be intact," he says.

"Why does he seem to show such little emotion?"

"That's called a 'flat affect.' Richard's left internal capsule was affected, meaning the left lobe that moderates emotion."

"His speech therapist said it might not ever come back. But a brain injury survivor said that his emotional expression will certainly come back. What's the truth?"

"What you are hearing are people's opinions. Their pessimism and optimism. You won't know until about two years after the brain injury what's going to come back."

"We have to wait for the flood to recede."

"Kind of."

I think we're living our hurricane, tsunami, and deluge all at once.

Dr. L patiently explains that while Richard has a relatively coherent semantic memory, also known as the memory of facts—like recognizing his family and remembering who the president is—he has a nearly absent episodic memory, which is the working narrative of one's life, one's autobiography. His working memory, the thing that allows us to store and remember information in the short term (think of dual tasks like remembering to schedule a meeting while we leave a colleague's office and make our way to our desk), is quite impaired. Working memory measures our ability to acquire knowledge, rather than what we have already learned. In emerging research, it's considered more important than IQ in determining academic or entrepreneurial success. The hippocampus, that great wielder of mental maps and spatial orientation, seems to be functioning in Richard's ability to find his way around places and remember our faces, but flaws in his declarative memory (both semantic "facts" and episodic "experiences") make learning new material slow and plodding.

Author Priscilla Long describes memory in this way:

> Memory is reconstitutive. During memory, neurons from all over the brain, the ones that fired during the original experience, fire again. Neurons firing in the visual cortex re-create visions; neurons firing in the auditory cortex re-create thunder or opera. But these assemblies of neurons re-fire with less strength. And with fuzzy boundaries. Memory is an unreliable narrator. It's less like a scanned photo, more like a Civil War re-enactment.

And in Richard's situation, memory is more like a reenactment of something someone told him about in a crowded room one day, and expected him to visualize, hear, memorize, and understand days, weeks, months later.

In June, nine months after the anoxic insult, when it's clear that Richard isn't going back to work anytime soon, I write a letter to his CEO. Richard and I talk about what we want to say, then I compose it and he makes a few suggestions.

> First, we would like to thank you for your kindness during this very difficult time in our lives. . . .
>
> Following an evaluation with the doctor of the Neurobehavioral Clinic, it has become apparent that Richard is undergoing difficulties that compromise his ability to return to work. These include memory problems, impaired tactual recognition skills, expressive language difficulties, thought organization problems, and abstract reasoning difficulties. These areas range from severely to mildly impaired. Dr. L states that Richard is totally disabled, but that part of his disability might be temporary, and he is recommending occupational therapy and neuropsychological care on a group and individual basis for six to twelve months.
>
> The focus of the new treatment includes the development of a set of compensatory strategies to get him back to work on a modified basis. Richard is hopeful that when he is able to return to work, it can be in a structured and supportive environment. He would like to begin to integrate back into a Physiotherapy Associates clinic environment when he has been released by his doctors to do so. He also has set a personal goal of returning to a Clinic Director position within the next two years, should his therapies begin to correct his impairments.
>
> Of course you can imagine how difficult this is for Richard, who is almost completely motivated

> by healing others, devoting himself to his patients, and providing for his family. We pray for a complete return of his faculties, and will do everything within our power to get him the needed treatment to make that a reality. When it is appropriate, Richard would like to discuss the geographical areas that might be a good fit for his modified work needs, and to talk about integrating him into the environment. His work is perceived by him as a calling, and thus necessary to his life.

Shortly afterward, we received this letter from the CEO:

> Thank you for updating me about Richard's progress. I'm sorry to hear of his continuing struggle, and I join you in optimism about his eventual recovery. I know that Richard will continue to impress with his strength and courage; I know how frustrating his impairments must be today. Still, the future holds great promise for you, free of the cancer that threatened previously. You made the right choice, and Richard's story is one of victory and inspiration for all of us who love him.
>
> Of course, Physiotherapy Associates is diminished without his talent and presence, and I am confident that his return, when appropriate, will be as successful as he has always been on this team. I think he should focus on his personal recovery, and just say when he is ready.

We are being cut loose from every responsibility to which we have been tethered. We have two months left with our last child, and then she too will be gone. I take pictures of Dylan for the program of her senior voice recital. Beautiful images of her in our tiny backyard, her long straight hair and big eyes shining in the twilight. We design a handmade program and decide what refreshments to serve. Later, when Richard is sleeping, we sit in the hot tub under the canyon stars and talk about the changes that keep coming. It's not just the wounded person who changes after an injury. The whole web of relationships is transformed by the injured one. "One brain injury causing another," I say, and we smile, but we don't really know the meaning of this. Not yet.

# 16

# pathless

AFTER WE TELL Richard's boss he isn't coming back to work, his treatment program becomes his lifeline. Richard's days include performing a list of household tasks the occupational therapist has assigned him and reading his anatomy and physiology textbooks. He has a black-vinyl-covered day planner to organize his life. He sets an alarm for taking vitamins, talking to family, doing his homework. He learns to set goals so he can study in small segments without falling asleep. He learns to use the simplest tools he can: the microwave instead of the stove, for example. He starts a load of laundry at 1:00 PM and must write *Put clothes in dryer at 2:00 PM*, or else he will forget the clothing is there. He doesn't forget like you and I do. He forgets the clothing exists. He's learning the activities of daily living, sensory-perceptual skills, communication, and social skills.

*Patient has difficulty tracking tasks through to completion*, his occupational therapist reports. *Initiation and delayed thought-processing skills have been observed in treatment. . . . Compensatory strategies for these skill areas have been introduced to patient but at present he continues to require significant cuing to follow through with tasks.*

"Did you start your homework?" I ask.

Richard nods his head. Stares, wide-eyed.

"Eyes." The constant reminder to come into the culturally acceptable place of the adult.

Richard blinks. Goes back to the blank stare.

"What are you working on?"

"Grocery list."

"For what?"

"I don't know."

"What do you want to know?"

"What do we eat?"

"The assignment. What's the assignment?"

"Go to the store and buy our food."

"What do you want to make?"

"I don't know."

"Nothing?"

"I don't know what we eat."

"How about this. Get some rice and veggies, and then some chicken, and you can make a stir-fry."

"Okay." He writes *veggies*.

"What kind of veggies might you buy?" I ask.

"I don't know."

"What about a bag of frozen vegetables? Then you don't have to make too many decisions."

He writes *bag*.

"What else?" I ask.

He shrugs his shoulders. Stares with the big eyes.

"Fuck," I say under my breath, turning away. I pretend to pick up lint from the floor. Raise up. See him watching me.

"Eyes!" I say, impatiently. He blinks. "I said 'rice.'"

He looks at me, the question in his hovering pencil.

"Brown rice. Am I supposed to tell you where to find it?"

"No."

"This assignment is not going so well."

"No." He looks up.

"I'll drive you over. Do you think you can manage going into the store alone?"

He raises his shoulders.

"You're supposed to do this on your own, right?"

"Yes."

"You think you can?"

"I can do it."

After our trip to the store, Richard tries to make dinner by tossing frozen vegetables in a frying pan with soy sauce, but he burns the concoction when he has to stop and make the rice. He hitches up his track pants and looks at me like I'm the mother who's going to scold him.

"I'm sorry," he says.

He does everything asked of him. Mostly looking like he's trying to wake up from a really deep sleep.

*Good God*, I think. *How long is this going to take?*

"What else we got on that homework list?" I ask, hoping for something at which he can be successful.

When I get frustrated, I think of how humbling it must be to have to learn to be a human again. I make a new list.

THINGS WE NOW CALL HOMEWORK:

1. Write a plan for making a telephone call, so you can remember how to talk to the people you know and love.

2. Make a shopping list, and go to the grocery store on your own.

3. Work on eye contact. Learn to blink.

4. Go into a public place. See if you can be around people for an hour.

5. Find a support group.

6. Just fucking survive.

The children and I are aware that we're in the middle of a terrible event, but there's no way to describe what this loss feels like. We find ourselves with a man who is here and who is not here. We're not sure if the loss we suffer is real. As challenging as a diagnosis of "permanent disability" was to hear from Dr. L, it's provable through a methodology. I like my facts; they're a kind of truth based on a set of agreements. Yet people are unrealistically optimistic when they're with us. They say things like: "He'll be back in no time!" or "What an amazing recovery!" as if there's no sense that anyone has gone missing.

Ambiguous loss is considered by social scientists to be one of the most stressful kinds of loss owing to its nature: it is the loss that happens without possibility for closure. When my grandparents died, it was a stressful event, but our family was able to say good-bye, speak about what their lives meant to us, mourn the loss with our beloveds, and receive offerings of their treasured objects. We were able to move through our grief by connecting with family and friends who had lost their loved ones. We were collectively seen as the survivors, the grieving family, those suffering a loss.

With Richard having disappeared in a traumatic brain injury—or when any member of a family disappears through addiction, dementia, mental illness, kidnapping, genocide, holocaust, or other mysterious disappearance, whether common or catastrophic—the remaining family members are catapulted into an ambiguous, tenuous uncertainty. Pauline Boss, an expert on treating ambiguous loss, defines it as "any kind of loss with no clear information on the status of a missing person."

"In such uncharted territory," she says, "a family may become paralyzed, unable to grieve and heal." Wars and terrorism are particularly cruel in creating disappearance, and even though families mourn with symbolic rituals that help them cope, the disbelief that the loss is permanent can be so profound that hope for survival never diminishes. In psychological loss, there is no body to bury, not even the symbol of one, and the loss cannot be resolved with the usual rituals.

We will have to find some way to form an attachment to the Richard who is present. But first, we will have to find our own ways to mourn the man who died in the ICU that day.

Once Richard is diagnosed as "permanently disabled," our family begins the process of educating ourselves about what to expect from rehabilitation. While no other medical professional has been willing to discuss the caregiver and family's role in recovery, Dr. L makes it part of his program to offer guidance about how we can support Richard, including explaining what care will be tricky to manage.

"The family is usually more anxious than the brain-injured person, who may be unaware of his situation. You're going to become his primary motivator," Dr. L says, looking at me, watching me narrow my big eyes with seriousness. I stand straight, give the doc a nod of the head: *I've got this.*

I do not have this. I don't know that recovery might take years, or that in accepting this new role, I will lose my relationship with my husband as a partner and equal. In begging Richard to leave his comfortable room, coercing him to do his homework, and writing notes in preparation for doctors' visits, I become his motivator. I don't enjoy leaving the role of his lover to take on what feels like becoming his nurse, teacher, and mother. But I refuse to acknowledge my anger, even to myself. I'm determined to become the fiercest, most virtuous caregiver anyone has ever seen. I cry only when I'm away from the house. I watch our teenage daughter express all the anger I don't dare admit that I feel.

Richard has few of the aggressive behavioral issues of the brain-injured. He doesn't exhibit embarrassing compulsive behaviors like temper tantrums, but he's socially inappropriate and often forgets basic manners, something that never would have happened before thanks to his excessively polite Brit-Canadian education.

We're waiting in the silent anteroom of the doctor's office when he belches, a manly *rawwrrr* of a burp, and then sits quietly, his hands folded in his lap, not a suggestion of mischief.

"People commonly say 'excuse me' when that happens."

"Okay," he says.

"So?"

"What?"

"Say 'excuse me,' please."

"Excuse me, please." Calm, like he knows diddly about decorum.

I ask him to refrain from licking each of his fingers while eating meals. On one disastrous restaurant outing, he chomps a pie slice in three minutes, and then lifts the plate to lick it clean. Through gritted teeth, I mention that's something he should do only at home.

I'm waking up to a new reality: brain injury happens to families. Our son copes through absence; our daughter copes through anger; I bury all of my grief and become the "good woman," an extension of the nice girl I tried to look like I was when I was young. I decide to model myself after the mentors I'm in awe of, instead of being true to myself. I listen to their suggestions for how I might live my life. I adopt their language, enfold myself in their values. This is how I end up writing this letter to my friends:

> Richard has what is called brain trauma by Western medicine, but I call it a bit of enlightenment. There's been a space amid the cognitive rearranging for a new self to show up. . . . I most notice absence of the masculine, but when I attune to the new man before me, I see that he has the most natural yang-ness about him, it's just that it surfaces more slowly, gently, like a wave, watery yet powerful. I notice in myself that my personality is adjusting to being slowed down, to traveling more organically with changes as they appear rather than trying to always be out in front of them. I am being tested to let go of

my expectations of how things will be, to stay in the present moment.

This is me, full of shit. The one who wants to get it right, to sound more evolved than she is. If only I could cry, scream, pound, throw, hit, slap, smash, scrunch, crunch, piss, run away, tear things, knock, freak, shout: *Fuck you motherfucker!* Instead, I want to be grateful, righteous, spiritual. I want to be the best caregiver anyone has ever seen. The modest, slightly suffering partner, making a go of it. I don't like her. And I forgive her. She is only trying to survive. She can't yet risk saying what's true. She has to borrow the truth of others until she knows.

My calendar remains full of plans, meetings, assignments. On the outside, I look like I'm a normal, albeit driven, woman. But I'm hiding a dirty secret. A secret that makes me feel crazed.

I can no longer read.

From the time of Richard's surgery, and through this first year of his recovery, my mind cannot absorb the written words of others. I check books out of the library. Books sit open and unread on my lap. Books are stacked three feet high next to my side of the bed. I pretend to read. Not one word enters my brain. I watch Richard fall asleep over a chapter of his anatomy textbook and wonder if exhaustion is contagious. One day my friend Jennifer, a poet, comes to take me for some private time at our apartment complex's pool.

"I have to tell you something awful," I say. Jennifer is from Manhattan, and has more than a few hair-raising stories of her own.

"I'm not reading. I mean, nothing."

"That bad, huh?" Jenn says, raising an eyebrow on her freckled face.

"I mean, for fuck's sake, not even the words on containers."

"You read containers?"

"Shampoo, toothpaste, cans, recipes, even tampon boxes. I've been reading since I was four. Reading got me through a tornado that devastated our neighborhood when I was in first grade. Reading got me through a mother who has been on pills most of my life. Reading gave me a literature degree and bonded me to my friends and saved me from my melancholy. Books are my lifeline. What am I going to do?"

"The same thing happened to me after 9/11." Jennifer lost friends that day.

"Really?"

"Yeah. It's horrible for a while. You'll live to read again."

"Promise?"

"I'm sure of it."

It won't be during this year of doctors' appointments, therapy visits, and getting our daughter off to college. This year, instead of reading, I write half a novel, a story about a young woman living alone in a cave during World War II. While I'm writing this book, I think the story has nothing to do with my life.

After Richard has gone to sleep, I stay up and write. In addition to writing a novel, I'm writing screenplays. The year Richard was first diagnosed with cancer, I placed in the Nicholl Fellowship competition, and, feeling buoyed, I decided to keep writing for film. I visited the Writers Guild in Los Angeles to attend programs and meet other screenwriters. I booked myself into screenwriting conferences and pitched my work to producers. I wrote three screenplays. I entered and won two more contests. This year, I want to practice my skills diligently. But the commitment required to enter the field is all-encompassing. I can't give myself over to work that takes me out of the home for long hours when Richard needs constant care. Perhaps when he's better, I reason, I can return to film and writing books.

For the time being, I write in my journal, nothing purposeful, just feelings, impressions of what's happening around me. Late at night, when I stop doing things, the stars are stretched across the canyon in their fearless, formless realm. I hear Richard breathing. I walk to our bedroom and stand near him. The same beautiful legs. The long, wavy hair. Inside that mind, the same spaciousness as that which holds the stars. *Oh, yeah*, I think, *you imagine he is your sweet dream. You imagine he is your nightmare. You are, of course, correct. Your husband has nothing to do with it. In your inability to love him no matter how he shows up, you are looking at what you think of yourself. Husbands, wives, lovers, even the storyless like Richard—all a projection of the self.*

I keep waiting to find out how this is going to end, how we'll be a couple again. But a strong, steady voice inside me keeps saying: *This is it. The life that you're in now, the one in which you're chaotically alive, that's the one you've got, honey.*

"There's one thing about loss, Dad; it sure is making me resilient," I say over the phone to my father at our weekly check-in.

"You can tough this out," he says, meaning that he doesn't want more of my personal agony, that it's time to brave the situation with strength, not vulnerability.

The first song my father taught me was "Take Me Out to the Ballgame." Dad was a semipro baseball player, a coach, and an umpire. The eldest of his four children, who arrived in four years, I often spent time with him in the dirt of a ballpark. My father taught me many things: to find the best education I could afford, to question authority (as long as it wasn't his), to explore science as a means to truth.

At the time that Richard was trying to decide about this rigorous surgery, my father wrote to him: *Your title with me is son-in-law, but I look at you and love you as a son. The decisions I have had to make about my health have not been as complex and difficult as the one you have to make. Whatever your decision is, know that I support you.* Dad showed up at the hospital, and in weekly telephone calls, and, now, at the apartment, staying with Richard when I have work out of town. Throughout my childhood, Dad was often impatient with me, giving vent to his anger in blows to the top of my head with his knuckles. Richard didn't suffer the same fate with him. They're free to have a different relationship. Richard never had a father who showed up for him, and he was beloved by mine, as he was by every member of my family.

Before Richard got his cancer diagnosis, I was painstakingly private. My husband's illness pushed me to invite others into my heart, including the father whom I hadn't always experienced as an ally. This year, whenever Dad calls to ask if he can come stay with us, I let him come. I let him take Richard for walks along the beach and to doctors' appointments. Dad takes us out to dinner, usually meals that we couldn't afford. I know that I want to become, as W. P. Kinsella writes in *The Thrill of the Grass*, someone who "has fouled off all the curves that life has thrown at her." In the confusing aftermath of Richard's surgery, adversity is teaching me how to foul off the curves in a way that comfort never seems to do.

While Dad is with us, I tell him I'm considering consulting a lawyer who might help us determine if we have a case for medical malpractice. My friends, upon seeing how we were evaluating Richard's potential for a return to work, set up a meeting with a lawyer in Santa Monica.

"Collect the information," Dad says. "You can always decide later."

In July, we visit the lawyer, who informs us that we can file a legal suit only in the state in which the damage was done. The kind lawyer looks at Richard across the table and his expression suggests he is seeing his worst nightmare: a man who was once fluent and determined, now unable to access personal power. Richard sits in calm silence. I ask questions about the process, how long we have to decide. Thirty minutes later, we go out into the sunshine, buy a sandwich, sit in the street, and eat it, saying nothing.

When we get home I research medical malpractice teams. I want someone with trial experience, but also someone I can trust not to waste our time and energy. Barry Nace is a gruff, authoritative man with forty years of experience working for justice for the injured. I learn that Mr. Nace works with his sons and his wife, and that they believe in meticulous preparation and the art of oral advocacy. I imagine, as in my own family, he transferred these skills to his children while debating at the dinner table. I call Mr. Nace and explain that we are nearly a year from Richard's surgery, and that he's still struggling to communicate. Mr. Nace listens and tells me about medical malpractice cases in his state—they are complex, expensive, and hard to win in the Bush era. With the new tort reform, a climate of distrust of the individual has been created, and well-paid lobbyists work hard to strip the rights of citizens to sue big business. He tells me about corporate funding for "citizen action" groups against so-called "frivolous" lawsuits, groups that are demonizing the very people who have been wronged. He details how political spin is being used to make victims afraid to sue medical organizations for fear that they are contributing to an overburdened justice system and preventing good doctors from doing their jobs. If we are going to sue, Mr. Nace says, we have to be in for the torturous haul.

I hang up the phone and sit on the bed, breathing slowly. Richard is in the living room, doing his speech therapy exercises. His progress is barely perceptible. Still, I want to see how he does before we enter into a lawsuit. I want to forget about everything a lawsuit would require of me.

All that last summer together before the empty nest, we drive Richard to therapy, we attend Dylan's school events, we visit with Joshua, we walk on the beach, we make dinner, we clean up, we talk, we sit in silence. By July, Richard graduates from the first stage of occupational therapy and is excited to be eligible for a work trial as a physical therapist. Dr. L writes in his report: *Patient's family report him to be performing well in self-care. At home, he participates in homemaking tasks such as meal preparation, laundry, and cleaning. He has performed multistep grocery-shopping activities, having to shop at various stores. It is felt by his rehabilitative team that he is appropriate for a work reentry trial.*

By the end of the month, Richard begins a work reentry trial with a local physical therapy clinic. Dr. L sets him up with one of his colleagues who is willing to supervise

Richard's work and offer an evaluation of his physical therapy skills. Richard works two days a week for four hours each day, and comes home exhausted. I pick him up from the clinic, since he hasn't been cleared to drive on his own. He falls asleep in the car on the way home, then sleeps in our bedroom for the rest of the day. Richard reports to his occupational therapist that he's fully restored after forty-five minutes of a jolly good catnap when he returns from work. He can't stand the thought that he'd be kept from his work because he isn't recovering from his fatigue.

He's a kid. He doesn't know how to do things yet. He has to try a lot. He gets lost easily. He doesn't know who people are when he meets them the third or fourth or fifth time. If he doesn't write it down in his day planner, and then later his iPhone, it doesn't exist. Beginner's mind is supposed to be what we all yearn to achieve. But no one pays you for that (unless you start a business as a spiritual guru). I've never seen Richard try so hard and fail so often. He's unaffected. The stealth stubbornness he seems to have been born with is his greatest ally.

Soon, he's working three days a week and driving himself to and from work, having passed his driving test. All summer he has practiced and has discovered that he's able to work with supervision as a staff therapist. He has one final session before he's discharged from occupational therapy. But he's hiding the severity of his fatigue from his medical team. I know that there's no way Richard is ready to go back to work full-time.

The supervising physical therapist is honest in his appraisal of Richard's skills. He reports that Richard is having difficulty with initiation conversations and thought-processing skills, particularly in novel situations. The same kind of stuff that jams him up at home.

We talk to Dr. L about the plateau of Richard's progress.

"Should Richard return to active employment, he would be best with positions in which he works at a modified level," he says. "He must manage his residual fatigue and cognitive issues."

"I don't think it's a good idea to keep focused on just one aspect of your life," I add, but I can tell by the set of his jaw that Richard isn't going to give up his goal to get back to work. "Let's get Dylan off to school, and then see where we are, okay?"

Richard's hands clasp and squeeze around themselves obsessively in his lap, a self-pacifying gesture he falls into whenever he's feeling anxiety. He's afraid he won't make it back.

"I'm not giving up on you, I promise." I put my hand at the back of his neck. His hands calm. He breathes.

That summer, we shop for college gear. Dylan has received a scholarship in vocal studies to Indiana University Bloomington, near my family. In August, we will move our daughter into the dorm. I look at the color-coded calendar on my laptop. After we attend the Family Picnic and the Freshman Ceremony, I'll have to get on a plane and go back to our silent apartment. This place isn't home, but I don't know where home is any longer.

Each day, after Dylan goes to her summer job, I sit in her room at the apartment in Laguna. Sometimes I talk to my sister on the telephone, both of us sobbing over our girls, born within months of each other, now off to college.

"No one tells you that it's going to be like this," I say.

"You're going to miss talking to your girl," Christie says. "This is going to be a really quiet house without her."

I look at the framed family photos on her dresser. None of the photos are from after the brain injury.

"What are you doing for your anniversary?" my sister asks. I'd forgotten I had one. "Do something for the two of you," Christie says.

I say good-bye to my sister and walk to the living room. Richard's head hangs over a book, his mouth stretches downward at the corners, and his cheeks hang slack, his muscles drooping to his neck. I gasp to see him appear as if he has aged twenty years. I lean against the wall, wondering if he is alive. His eyes blink. His chest rises and falls.

"Richard!" I say, startling him. He looks up slowly, eyes fluttering fast, a dazed hummingbird. "You scared me. You look like you have a stroke face."

"I'm sorry, sweetness."

These months, he has been completely oblivious about how he appears to others. This man, whom I fell in love with for his beauty, grace, and magnetism, has eroded into a craggy, strange beast. I not only despise losing the beautiful man I adored, but also hate myself for being a woman who would care about such a thing as his physical beauty. I look at my face's reflection in the sliding door. I grit my teeth so hard that my jaw is like a boxer's. My body is lean, strong, capable. There's no softness to me, as there has been in the past. Ironically, I appear as I have always wished to be—angular, resolute, robust. The months of taking care of him while he recovered have made me this way. In the reflection, I see a sleek, raucous raven that wants to fly. I open the sliding door and look out toward the chaparral canyon.

"Yes," I say, and then I realize I have heard his unspoken question in the silence: *Are you going for a walk?*

He wants to come with me, but he will not ask. I breathe in the grassy bluffs, the dusty old cattle land, the salt from the coves below. When I turn back to him, his gaze is a child's, baby blue, all innocence and entreaty.

"Want to go?" I say.

"Want to go?" I ask my husband across the table at Mama's restaurant in San Francisco. It's two weeks before we take Dylan to school. Richard and I are on an impromptu weekend road trip to celebrate our wedding anniversary. We're staying at a bed-and-breakfast where Allen Ginsberg slept, visiting City Lights Bookstore, walking the winding road up to Coit Tower. I joined my San Francisco friends for an evening of writing, which turned into brunch with Maya, a willowy poet and chef whom I met at a writers' retreat. Now, she's telling me about her father's home in Brittany.

"I've been there, and it's beautiful," Maya says. "He has to come home and sort out some business and is looking for someone to take care of the house while he's gone. Maybe a couple of months."

The coffee nearly sloshes onto the saucer as I jump.

"Would you two be up for something like this?" she asks.

"Would we like to be caretakers of a four-hundred-year-old water mill?" I ask, the *hell yes* implied in my tone.

The French toast stops halfway to Richard's lips.

"We've got absolutely nothing holding us here," I say. "It's two months. We can do that, right?" I bypass Richard's startled expression across the table for my own romantic notions of what such an adventure promises. The Breton culture! The time to write! The cheese!

"Let me talk to my father and get back to you," Maya says. "I'm sure he'd love to have you stay."

I never wonder if we are going.

Mid-August, we fly across the country, visit my family, and settle Dylan into her dorm room. We find the organic grocery store and the campus bookstore. We go bowling in the Memorial Union. We visit the Lilly Library and Kinsey Institute exhibit. We hang out at the art museum and go for brunch in the Tudor Room. When we leave, even though we will see Dylan in one month, I cry all the way home. I cry for three weeks. I no longer know if there are limits to my grief.

We return home. I get back to my contract work for a couple of nonprofit organizations, and Richard returns to his therapy. Sometimes I go into Dylan's room and open her closet and look at the clothes. I call her every day. Soon after, she says to me in her firm, take-control voice, "Mom, don't call me for a while. I have to figure things out." And thereby sets me out to see what kind of relationship I have remaining with my husband. I know that the absence of our daughter and son at a time when we are trying to cope with the loss of Richard's identity is a shocking transition, but through my daughter's request, I realize that Richard and I have to learn we can rely on each other, not in our roles as parents but as people who can hear each other's truth. Our marriage has been full of large and small denials. Six years ago, we learned how to get honest. If we're going to find each other again, I have to see how our marriage really is, not just dwell in the relationship of the past.

I ask him on a date, to see if we can explore who we are. I pick a casual restaurant, one that won't challenge his naive etiquette and desire for fewer people. We're eating our burritos when I tell him how it felt to bond with my daughter when he couldn't talk.

"Do you remember the day she was born?" I ask, recalling the view of the mountains as I panted to slow down the too-fast delivery.

Richard shakes his head.

"Nothing? Not one fragment? The day Joshua was born? The day we got married?" I can barely breathe. It hasn't occurred to me that *everything* might remain wiped clean. I put down my fork and start to cry. A tray of frosty margaritas slides by, and I want to grab them and drink them until I'm gone too. Tears teem. I use the wadded napkin to dry my eyes. When I look up, Richard seems terrified. He's crying just watching me cry.

"It's like I've made the idea of Our Marriage from these messy, beautiful moments of our past. Like the time we went skinny-dipping on a deserted island on our honeymoon. Like taking Joshua to his DJ gigs. Like when you lived with Mimoo when you went back to school."

"She had dinner ready for me every night." He says it slow, like he's coming out of a dream.

"Really, baby? Did she make you her fried chicken?"

He gives the raised shoulder, the big Whatever sign. I realize that I'm trying to get him to believe in these stories, these beautiful symbols of who I think we are.

"Do you really think it's a good idea to go to France?" he asks.

"I think that it will give us a chance to get off this crazy ride we've been on for nearly a year. I'd like to write and I'd like you to get some rest."

"It's a long way to go."

We decide to ask Dr. L about it at our next meeting.

"His high motivation could be a problem for him." Dr. L is sitting in his leather chair and I'm sitting across from him on the couch, waiting for Richard to complete his final occupational therapy visit and join us. "Richard could go back to work too early and risk being vulnerable."

"You mean lose his job," I say.

"He lacks executive-thinking skills, and without the proper support, he's too fragile. What do you think about his energy?" the doctor says.

"I think he's overdoing it."

"We do too. He needs more time to restore his health. Brain injury patients need periods of deep rest because they deplete faster than most. This makes sense if you think about the energy it takes to learn new skills."

Richard appears at the door. Dr. L stands up to shake his hand and congratulate him on his "graduation" from the program.

"What's next?" Dr. L asks.

"There's an offer to go to France to live for a while," I say. "What do you think?"

"I think it could be an answer to a prayer," the doctor says.

Before we can leave California, Richard wants to finish his work trial. It's September, and I'm teaching at a conference in Seattle, then spending some much-needed time with Joshua. After I return, we'll visit Dylan in Bloomington for Freshman Family Weekend. We've already decided that if we're chosen to be caretakers for the home in Brittany, then we'll depart in November. The kids will be invited to spend Christmas with us.

Joshua and I haven't had a chance to be alone since his father's memory loss. In the time we've been attending to Richard's life, our son has become a man. He's working a full-time job at Microsoft, producing DJ gigs on weekends, and majoring in media and communications in college. It's a quick trip, but I stay the night at his Seattle apartment, teach the workshop, and have lunch with him before I fly out a few days later.

When I leave Seattle, I lean over to pick up my bag and realize it's not the men in the airport I'm smelling but myself, the aroma of aftershave, the scent of musk and longing, of sweat covered over with flowers, a perfume I can't place until I track it back to the parking lot at Madison and Sixteenth, where, upon my arrival, I hand Joshua the packages.

Joshua places the packages on the gravel lot and then he grabs me up, transferring his fragrance onto my sweater, my son lifting me into the air as I once swung him, my feet flying out in back, arms bigger than his father's, clasping so hard I exhale fast, trying to make myself lighter. He laughs and says something then, but I can't recall it because I'm thinking about how it would be to live in this city again, which is his city now. I've been thinking of what it means for Joshua, what it is to find yourself a stranger in your own life, to live years and years with the biting wit of your father and then suddenly to notice the complete absence of that bite. I'm wondering how it might feel to be the son of a man who's sustained a brain injury: to experience the loss of stories from your own childhood, the disappearance of your father's past. I'm thinking of his father's anger, how it took a toll on this child, and wondering if it was a relief or a restraint to have the story taken with the cut of a surgeon's knife. Where do the boy-regrets go? Do you speak of the wrongdoing of your father when he's not the same man who raised you? What reconciliation is possible, necessary?

My son is smiling down at me and I'm remembering how it was to have a strong husband, an exuberant man who could lift me high. Richard wouldn't think of doing such a thing now. He has no need to relate in many ways at all. I haven't noticed that I'm living without such delight, until I see my son.

We walk into Joshua's apartment above Madison Market. He makes me tea and we talk much of the night. He asks questions about his father's reality until I hear the sound of held tears in his throat. I reach my hand to his leg.

"Please cry. It's okay."

When he can speak, I'm surprised at the source of his sadness, though I ought not to be. "It's like being cut off from your history, when there's no way back to your father's people."

I tell my son a story I can recollect, of discovering I was pregnant with him, our first, the first grandchild on both sides, how we found out two weeks after his grandmother died, how she'd been driven over on the street while giving directions to a stranger. I told him how I was awakened one night a year later while he slept in the bassinet next to me, startled by his grandmother's shimmer at the foot of the bed, how she walked over and placed her hand on our baby boy, offering a sign of protection, a signal that she'd be there for this one, and how, when my fear grew stronger, his grandmother disappeared.

"That happened?" he asks.

I can't imagine that I haven't told him. Maybe these stories were told only to the boy-child, the one who used to believe in magic. Maybe I've forgotten that the man needs the stories, too, needs them as much as the food we'll send him when the demands of school and work intensify.

Or maybe the lost ought not to be reimagined. Perhaps the gift to this one would be the mutation of the mind that occurs when there is insight without the shadow of the past, enabling him to live in truth, what Krishnamurti called "a pathless land."

"I thought it happened," I say to my son, the ground under me shifting still, one radical brain change causing another, pushing me to reconsider, relinquish what I knew, once, to be true.

# 17
# pleasure

FOR THREE WINTER months we live in a village in Brittany, in a four-hundred-year-old water mill on an island surrounded by a fast-flowing river, guarded by a goose. It's quiet. So quiet that when Richard joins me after three weeks—after his work trial is completed—I have no need for him to speak. He's like the land: hushed, tranquil, calm.

While I wait for Richard to arrive, my friends come to Bretagne for their own reasons. Carole and her daughter Julia come to wander the Bronze Age megaliths near Carnac: menhirs, dolmens, passage graves. Wendy comes to paint and sit in Parisian bars. Grace comes to help me get settled, then sets out for her European tour. In the days we are together, we wander through forests, the sound of hunters' guns in the distance. The sly *renard* runs toward our picnic spot, seeking shelter. On meandering Sundays, we watch entire families search for chanterelles, their baskets weighted against their sides. We seek the legendary Brocéliande, the magical forest of Merlin and Vivien. We find the place called Merlin's tomb, and hang our wishes from its festooned tree. Having stayed past twilight, we walk out of the enchanted forests, barely able to detect our bodies in the dark.

When everyone goes home, Richard and I stay in the quiet. I write letters. Richard naps for hours each day. We go to the market every Saturday and eat an egg and sausage *galette* for breakfast, followed by a visit to the rotisserie man, the vegetable vendors, and the cheesemonger, who encourages me to learn French from him, a new phrase or two each week. I'm frustrated by my inability to remember the years of French I studied in high school. Not so Richard. He converses with neighbors and *boulangerie* owners with an unexpected ease.

"*Qu'est ce que vous recommandez?*" he asks the waiter, and then later, when our plates of *omelette fromage* and lard tart have been inhaled, "*Délicieux repas, monsieur.*"

We live in a new rhythm in this place, our days composed of rural pleasures: reading, building fires, retrieving the daily baguette, going to the village market, and creating food *à la française*. But we mostly sit in the cool stone house and barely speak. We don't visit the castles or study the architecture. Our minds are not closed to culture, but our animal nature has emerged. We walk, dream, eat, make love. We awake in the fog that comes with living in a millhouse surrounded by a fast-running river. I pad downstairs in my slip and a blanket while Richard sleeps, and I watch fishermen cast their lines from the banks. The men are so close I could open the window and hand them a *pain au chocolat*.

Crossing Brittany from east to west, the Canal de Nantes à Brest is a chain of canalized rivers: the Erdre, the

Isac, the Oust, the Blavet, the Hyère, and the Aulne. All of the social life of the town seems to happen along the water. At twilight, we stroll down the River Oust. We hardly speak anything of the future.

"Can you imagine what it was like when the Neanderthals lived here?"

He looks along the river where it bisects medieval chateaus. "Nomads."

"We can keep going, you know. Are you tired? I'm not tired."

"Sure, sweetness."

"Where did that come from? You never called me that before."

He raises his shoulders.

"Like it just got conjured out of whatever land you were in before you woke up. Do you remember whether you knew me when you woke up?"

"Yes."

"Did you?"

"Yes."

"I don't think you did. I think it was like imprinting. I was in the room, and you felt my love, and then as I was there, day after day, you bonded to me."

"Okay, sweetness."

"You're not sad, are you?"

"No."

"Well, honestly, Richard, I don't know what makes me 'me' either. I can't track who I am. But there's a lot of space between us. I remember who we were. And it doesn't look like we're going back there."

"Can we go back now?"

"Just a little bit farther? To that farm? Can you do that?"

He nods his head. His mutton-sized arms flop by his sides like he's only recently become bipedal. His head falls and he sighs.

I touch his back. "Five minutes."

His head lifts. The sun sets in a dusky mist along the bog. Bats fly. A Breton dog jumps through the marsh. I take Richard's hand, for he hasn't yet thought of taking mine. There's no need for him to initiate contact. He doesn't long for anything.

Before Christmas, we decide to visit Florence. We've never seen Italy, though we've long wished to experience *la dolce vita*. We take the night train that travels from Rennes to Paris to Florence. Richard sleeps the entire ride, and then much of each afternoon, but he is awake to the art at the Galleria dell'Accademia and the Uffizi, awake in a manner that I have never noticed in him before. He's immersed in the art, drawn to works that interest him, intent on studying pieces that move him, and able to articulate the impact of the exchange when I question him later, over dinner. He still cannot initiate conversation, but he responds to everything.

"What was your favorite work today?" I ask.

"I like those thirteenth-century paintings on wood, the gold, the Madonnas."

"Really. That seems kind of stylized for you."

"You can see that the bodies are moving from flat shapes to actually becoming fully human."

One day, we are wandering in the Duomo Museum when I'm drawn to a crucifix on the wall. As I come into the gallery, I see a woman sculpted from poplar, her feet gripping as she appears to walk toward her Jesus. It's the Magdalene, created by Donatello, her body ravaged, her eyes harrowing. I nearly fall to my knees in shock as a wave of sadness erupts. I'm sobbing, thankful that Richard and I are the only ones in the gallery. Richard turns to see if I'm okay, and then he leaves me alone. I squat close to Magdalene's feet, really looking at their tendons. Her legs and arms are lean, her eyes appear half mad, her lips parched, her teeth broken. Her hair hangs in ropes around her sinewy body. I stand eye to eye with this Mary. Subtle tones move through the wood, her hair gilded in radiant streaks, her muscles terra-cotta and umber.

When you look closely, you can see that she hasn't wasted away. She's fierce and unwavering. I'm not reacting to the Mary Magdalene of history, but to this woman I see before me, a woman who appears to have walked across the desert for her man. I see in her the impact of being bonded to someone you adore, someone no longer present. When I leave her, I find Richard a couple of rooms over. In his former self, he would have been perturbed at waiting for me to get on with things. Now he leaves me to my own ways. To be with him is to be peacefully separate. And not in a way that makes me want to throw myself into the Arno.

Later, when we walk the streets around the Duomo, I notice the Italians respond to Richard's openness. They point to him and invite him into their shops to offer him the end-of-day pastries. They enjoy his obvious appetite for their food. The *pensione* owner, also a physical therapist, upon hearing of Richard's brain injury, brings him treats and keeps the halls quiet for his daily naps. I'm jittery about getting lost in the maze of streets, and hesitant to speak the language, and flustered by not knowing the customs. Richard is not challenged in any of the ways that I seem to be. But he isn't being treated as if he's a big doofus either. People invite him not for what he's missing, but for what they see in him.

We stay for five days of gallery visits, afternoon naps, pistachio gelato, and leisurely dinners. On our last evening, we are seated at long wooden tables in a family trattoria. It's been over a year since his surgery, and he still mostly communicates with his eyes. We try to pronounce things on the menu. We ask for water "with gas." We're served polenta with three ragùs—mushroom, marinara, and sausage—triangles we lift to our mouths and cry over. Because we are in a room full of Italians, because we have finally made it to Italy, because we have spent decades wishing to be here, because we can speak with our eyes, we are right at home. In Italy, it is as if our rational, vernacular selves have evaporated, and we are living on tears and elation and lenity.

After we return to Brittany, our children arrive for Christmas, fresh from snowy roads, to simmering soup and platters of *sablés*, *galettes*, *gaufrettes*, and chocolate-dipped meringues. We play games in front of the fire and take the train to Paris and visit the Louvre and the Palais Garnier, and some of us drink too much wine or espresso and sleep late and argue about whether the French waiters want to be assholes or if their petulance just comes naturally.

When the children go back to college, I write and Richard naps. We read for hours each day. By January, he is negotiating the French roads as if their illogical curves are second nature to him. He reads more complex books. He begins to have more energy and invites me to take a stroll, or to help him learn to converse. He wants to learn what people expect from him in conversation. He begins to pick up body cues to orient his communication. He learns to pay attention. We take a final trip to Paris, to our favorite museum, Centre Pompidou. We sit in cafés and talk about art.

"Jesus, man, did you see that guillotine with the word *Chanel* written on it?"

"Did you see the women who came around the corner and freaked out?"

"Hilarious! I could have stayed in there forever. Except for the close-up of *Fuck Painting Number One.*"

"That seemed normal to me."

"It would."

"What do you think is the difference between pornography and art?"

"You're really asking?"

He nods. Butters a slice of bread and hands it to me.

"Baby."

"What?"

"That's the first time since the brain injury you've been curious about me."

"Huh."

We're counting the days until we have to return home, and we're confused about what "home" is anymore. We've happily lived out of suitcases rather than wardrobes. We've eaten what's local and fresh. All winter, reminded of the first night I arrived, when our host made a bread stuffing casserole topped with braised leeks, I've tried to make that dish until I got the seasoning just right. Cooking and trips to *la laverie* have become our social life. We've read from the home's library, we've played the homeowner's music, we've learned that pleasure doesn't come only from knowing what one wants. For months, I've been happy in the not knowing. Somehow the choices still get made.

By January, I have offers to house-sit in Galway, Ireland, and in Nice, France, and somewhere in Portugal. Rocky coves, cobblestone streets, sandy beaches. They want us to stay anywhere from three months to a year. I'm nervous about making a commitment, and thrilled to be offered such extraordinary adventures. I still can't decide where to be. I cry on the phone with my friend-the-therapist, because it's the first time in my life that I haven't had intuition about what to do next.

"It is like a black curtain has come down over the future. I can't see anything!" I wail.

She tells me the story of the manna from heaven, from the Bible's Exodus, about being in the wilderness and the food showing up, just when you need it.

"I don't understand how manna is going to happen," I moan.

"You don't have to understand," she says. "The answer arrives."

The answer does not arrive. Not within me, anyway. One morning, while the fishermen cast their lines in the river, I place my head in Richard's lap and I cry about not knowing.

"I want to be close to the kids again," he says. "I want to go back to the States."

The man without preferences knows what he wants. Our manna from heaven.

Within a few weeks, we have an offer to come live in a ranch house in a vineyard in San Luis Obispo, California, where I'll help a new bed-and-breakfast owner get on her feet. We pack our bags and thank our foreign place, one that's given me a chance not to know.

In the airport lounge where we wait to return to the United States, the first thing I notice is the loudness of the American voices. Some woman in a tracksuit who hasn't eaten red meat for a week shouts out her need for a rare steak.

A pair of American women discuss their children, in voices strident enough for us to hear about their GPAs, their summer programs. A belligerent man takes to smoking in the no-smoking zone, yelling at his wife: "Fuck off! Leave me alone! I told you I wasn't going to take it!" The change in tone is so abrasive that I start to do the breathing meditation that Pema Chödrön teaches. I'm breathing in his disgusting sadism, trying to transform this bile to loving calm. Shit. This is not working fast enough. The young bohemian couple across the room is transfixed and appalled by the way the man demeans his wife. People try to look the other way and can't. I want to heave my bag of books on his head.

There must be an injection of love in the room, I think. I throw my arms around my husband, kiss him in the way I've watched French couples kiss each other in museums, on the streets, in the train stations. I run my hands along Richard's hair, adoring him. Maybe because he's been living in France too, he kisses me back, heartily. In the airport we fill ourselves up with love, suffuse our hair and skin and words with sensuality. Not the shout-it-from-the-billboard kind of kissing, but the kind we saw in front of the frightening Rousseau painting at the Musée d'Orsay, the young man and woman turning their heads toward each other under *War*, their kiss an antidote, a communication of what could not be said, a politeness even, a way to hold the exposure to tragedy inside, among a roomful of visitors.

The kiss showed itself to us, consumed us, really, in our trips to Paris. In the Marais one Saturday night we had dinner at a communal table, our ears trying to pick up the patter of a barely known language in the conversation of the two men sitting next to us. We understood everything in the way the curly-headed one twirled the ring on the finger of the one with the sideways grin, then leaned over and kissed his palm. The next morning, rushing to find a café that served omelets, I stopped to watch the reflection in a *pâtisserie* window: a middle-aged woman wrapped her arm around another woman's head, leaned in, bit her lover's ear. I had been hungry for this, as it turned out. In another country I was satiated by the calm ease with which the gestures transpired, an effortlessness so transparent that it made me grieve for the loss of it on the streets of my own life.

The kissing in the airport calms me; I'm not sure what effect it has on the screaming man, but he stops the tirade. Ten hours later we are in a hotel room in Detroit, where we will wait for the next flight. My husband, he of the magnificent French kiss, turns on the television. From across the room I see him flip through ESPN and local news and stock-exchange rattle, and the world we created over there starts to slide away. All I can manage is: "I can't watch this crap. I can't do it. I'm going out." But Richard doesn't let me. He turns off the television and we banter back and forth a few minutes, and because we have been to many countries that have changed us, because we act as if the world we have agreed to let in is kind, we go back to trying to understand each other. We make a compromise, one that involves his need for a film in English, and my desire to soak in hot water. Later we eat pizza and a hamburger from the hotel restaurant. We ask, "What do you want to keep from over there?"

I want to keep turning toward the people I disagree with, learning to respect them through the exchange of ideas. I want to know when to kiss in silence, when to erupt in hearty dialogue. I tell my husband about how, on our last day at the Pompidou, I watched two men, one American and one French, get into a conflict about architecture as they exited a design exhibition.

"It's the functionality, the ability to work," said the American.

"But if there are no quality materials, then the design is a failure!" said the Frenchman.

And then the American hung back, holding his disagreement in his silence, unwilling to go out on the limb of conflict.

"We rely on the quality, *n'est-ce pas?*" said the Frenchman again, wanting the conversation to continue. Behind him a large color photograph of a Madonna concert glared, its circus aspects amplified by the image's giant stature. This is how our country is, I thought: we are big and bold, especially when the way is ours to take, when the performance is one that we control. We often cannot hear the question mark that entreats us into conversation; our discussion ends when the world's is just beginning. The American man nodded his head; that was enough. The Frenchman walked with him, explaining more.

Richard and I hold hands across the table and remember one of our last hikes along the canal. We try to hold in our memory the people milling in the charcuterie, the polite *bonsoir* we heard along the trail as other couples performed this daily ritual of the sunset stroll. We ache to remember the polite conversation, the peaceful gathering of such places, the way it has both civilized us and brought us to our wildish heart. That day, as we crossed the street toward the woods, a strange form came into my sight line. A flock of about a hundred birds moved across the sky from south to north, in a revolving wave that replicated the shape of a DNA strand.

"Oh my God!" I said, as I stared. "Have you ever seen anything like it?"

My husband, transfixed, shook his head. As the birds rotated within their shape they also flew across the sky, a spiral moving on an axis, each bird holding its position through flight and stasis. We speculated on what held them in this exact shape without the form disintegrating: perhaps their calls, perhaps their relationship to each other, perhaps a flutter of the wing. The birds disappeared behind the towers of a castle, and we stood for a moment to breathe, holding hands, trying to take in what we had witnessed. It was too much to speak of—we didn't have the meaning, and yet the birds were already inside us, shaping us, the fact that their form had happened, this magic at twilight.

Over the first American dinner my husband hands me the olives from his drink, keeps one for himself.

"What's necessary now?" I ask. "How do you want to live?"

He's ready to go back to work, but he also wants the quiet of rest, the spaciousness of naps, the inner sanctum of reading.

"What else?" I press.

He looks at me, open-eyed, wonder streaming through the jet lag. He tries to speak but cannot find the words. It's okay because when I kiss him later I will understand: he wants to remember that it happened; he wants to keep all the not-knowing that sits at the center of a mystery.

# 18
# friend

IN THE TIME we lived overseas, Richard coped with an ever-changing routine. In America, even though he still can't make jokes, he learns to laugh at others' witticisms. His aphasia—the loss of his ability to express himself—hasn't disappeared, but he can answer questions, understand irony, and respond to body language. Without facial cues, his conversations are a struggle, so telephone calls and email are a disaster. Dr. L thinks he'd become better at technology if he were in a place where he was motivated to learn, such as a setting where he was helping others. We ask the doctor if he thinks Richard is ready to look for a job, real work, work where they don't know anything about his brain injury. Within weeks, Richard has his answer. He's cleared to return to work as a staff physical therapist.

In the spring we move to San Luis Obispo so I can begin working as an innkeeper. We live a few miles away from the inn, in a little yellow ranch house in the middle of a postcard vineyard that is so fucking idyllic I can't stand it. Even in the swelter of summer, the place is gorgeous. This is the kind of place I am supposed to love: the fields are lush, the people are kind, there are beaches for days. My despondency is as incongruent with California as a neon Christmas tree at the seashore. The prettiness of the place is nauseating. Finding thousand-thread-count linens and luxurious towels for wealthy patrons is more vacuous than I could have ever imagined. On behalf of the inn, I spend days searching out trendy recipes to prepare for people so pampered by excess that they won't stand for a soupçon of oh-so-five-minutes-ago. The lack of meaning in my life is disorienting. In France, I found myself able to join the daily parade of villagers in the cobblestone streets; ordinary tasks felt like creative expression. In America, these same tasks feel trivial, materialistic, bourgeois. The period inn has been whitewashed. We track dirt and scuffs over its surface. Every day, I erase scrape marks from the day before. I decorate the innkeeper's little room with a bed and framed photographs taken by my friend Carole featuring *Castilleja*, their flowers shaped like saffron-and-rose-colored paintbrushes. Being surrounded by plant life makes me remember the fields of flowers I danced in as a teenager.

Richard interviews for a part-time staff position at a physical therapy office just a mile down the road from where we're living. I'm terrified that he's going to hurt a patient (or himself) by overreaching his physical or intellectual capacity. He's offered the position and wants to take the job without telling his employer he has a disability. I go along with this plan, mostly because he's scheduled for three days a week, which should offer plenty of recovery time.

One of the many effects of his identity change is that he's incorruptible. I know he'll disclose everything that happens at work. But Richard isn't able to communicate about his feelings yet. He has no language for what he's emotionally experiencing. Also, he has no way to say "no." Because the world exists to him in the present—he has little ability to access the past or plan for the future—requests that come toward him seem like the most urgent thing to do. He cannot differentiate priorities, nor can he remember commitments.

He neglects to wear his bike helmet because he forgets that his brain needs protecting. He tootles on his bike up the dirt road lined with lemon trees. I go running out of the ranch house into the vineyard screaming at him: "If you get hit without your helmet, you're screwed!" The peacocks jump down from the pepper trees, miffed at the insane shrill that has interrupted their idyllic nap. Richard forgets appointments—even when he writes them in his book—because he can't discern what's essential. We miss dinners and doctors and date nights. He lives as if he's stuck on "oblige."

One day I come home from work to discover he's entertaining the missionaries. I drop my bag at the door and hear a steady murmur coming from the living room.

". . . the conclusion of the system," I hear a male voice say.

"The end times," says the other man.

I walk into the living room where two stiff-shirted young men with Bibles stand. Richard smiles and waves from where he sits on the flowery couch, looking like beast-meets-shabby-chic, pamphlet in hand.

"Good afternoon, ma'am. We were just talking with your husband about . . ."

I'm fuming that they're trying to recruit my sweet, compliant man.

"Out," I say.

"There's nothing to fear . . ." says the other.

"Get out. Now."

The men pick up their things. Shake Richard's hand. I escort the black-tie boys to the door. They offer me a pamphlet.

"Too late. I'm one of the wicked," I say, as I close the door.

Richard looks up at me.

"We need to make an agreement about answering the door. If you're going to ask in the believers, you have to learn to say 'no thanks' first, okay?"

He nods. I want to test him.

"Will you clean the house and make dinner?" I ask.

"Okay . . ."

"Say 'no' to me," I say.

"I can do it, sweetness. I can help."

"Oh my God," I answer.

A few weeks after he begins at the physical therapy practice, Richard comes home flustered from work. It's rare to see him express an emotion, so I know something disturbing has occurred. I give him a cup of tea, and then we sit on the couch looking out to the fields of Cabernet grapevines growing beyond.

"What happened?" I ask.

"I burned a woman. I put some electrodes on her body. Her skin got fried."

"Is she okay?"

"She's upset. It's like a sunburn."

"Do you think the brain injury caused you to forget her?"

"I don't know."

"How did it happen?"

"It could have been the equipment. But it could have been me. I'm not sure. I meet with my boss in the morning."

"Are you okay?"

"I don't want to lose my job."

"You made your way to this point, right?"

"What if my license gets revoked?"

"You're getting ahead of yourself."

Richard turns on the television. Entertainment is his antidote to feeling difficult emotions, or being unable to communicate. He wants the excuse to be with himself; I want more conversation so I can understand him.

"How about we act out the meeting with the boss?"

"Why?"

"To help you get ready."

"Okay, sweetness."

I can't help remembering the letter that I wrote to Dr. L shortly after Richard took the job: *Richard's long-term memory is not improving very much. He cannot retain information over one or more days very well. Often if he reads a book, he forgets it shortly thereafter. Is there therapy or other support we could be providing?*

Dr. L wrote back quickly and asked us to continue to use the planner. He told me that it would be helpful to review key information on a regular basis with multiple opportunities for rehearsal, and to teach Richard some type of mnemonic to help him remember. This could be an acronym or a visual, but something he could study and rehearse to prompt him in tricky situations.

*Richard, this type of long-term memory issue probably will be with you for the immediate future*, wrote Dr. L, *and perhaps longer. I would really be creative about ways in which you can access information on your patients so that you are less apt to forget.*

Richard meets with his boss. He's relieved to learn that the woman's burn heals within a few days. Equipment is examined, and a loose wire is discovered. He gets to keep his job.

In the middle of a vineyard, unexpected events shape your life. One day the ranch and inn's owner, Cheri, a woman with long limbs and easy laughter, yells for me to come—there's an owl trapped in netting and someone needs to cut the animal loose. I see Cheri's stricken face. She can't stand suffering, and what she has witnessed is reflected in her horrified eyes and in her scattered speech. I run, following her sprint to the edge of the field, frightened about the scene I'm going to find.

Every night after dark I've been walking out to the porch to watch the owls hunt for field mice. Accustomed to the Richard's muteness, I can now stand for hours, watching the owls' velvet wings move in stealthy silence as they swoop from the tall coast oaks across the wide field to the edge of the vineyard. The owls gobble up hundreds of mice, as do the snakes that live near the barn and under our house, and making mice their teatime.

After we arrived, friends came to visit and found an owl dead on the road. We carried it to a tree trunk near the house, scattered flowers upon its body, gave it a memorial service. Burrowing owls, barn owls, grey owls, great horned owls—the region has so many owls that environmental groups organize night hikes to view them. The owls have become my companions, my allies, my closest friends. I read poetry about owls. I research their hunting habits. I learn how the owls have talons so muscular that they can crush their prey, and such strength that they can carry rabbits, raccoons, small dogs. In this place where my husband is often a stranger, and I can't find myself in relationship to humans, these owls are kindred. They're survivors.

Cheri comes to a stop. We're breathless at the dirt path where an owl struggles to free itself from a green polyethylene net used to block birds from the grapes. I drop to my knees. Each time the owl moves, the collapsible net squeezes its wings into a plastic straitjacket. The only way to prevent the animal from suffocating itself in the synthetic stranglehold is to hold it still. The owl lifts its wings and a string of netting cuts across its throat. Its eyes bulge. Cheri can't come closer and can't stand still.

"Get some help," I say. She runs toward the ranch manager, who's on a tractor in the field. I have no knife, but even a knife may not cut through this sturdy material. If I yell, I risk scaring the animal into choking itself, so I silently send a message to Cheri to bring back something to cut with. I lean close, but not too close. I want the animal to see me. The owl's view is vast, not nearsighted. I stare into its enormous eyes—golden, tubular, and still. Unable to move its head to grasp the surroundings, the owl has locked onto my eyes. I whisper to it, a few gentle words that turn into a kind of coo-murmur. My heart beats into my ears so that I can't hear my voice. The owl could take my fingers with one swipe of its beak, and its talons, which have poked through the net holes, could tear my skin open like a machete. I hold its wings. The owl flutters, chokes, submits.

The ranch manager, Hector, arrives with a knife. In the confusion of hands and pressure and conversation, the owl struggles. I watch the talons open and close, the beak hook toward me. Hector hands me the knife. I close my eyes, will my body to calm. I cannot speak. The owl pulses its feral stare into my sight. I look at Hector and I plead with my eyes: *I can't.*

He holds the owl firmly, waiting for me to free it. In my private antiphon, I do not crack. Cancer has made me like this. A woman who cares not for useless talk. Ground to the bone. Whittled.

I hold the knife steady with all of my will. The owl doesn't blink. Its beak screams silently. There is no fight left. My hands track along the netting. No wound. I must cause no wound. I look at Hector, who seems worried. I begin to saw at the net but it is unyielding. The knife's steel edge slips and enters the owl's pillowy, exposed breast. An image of my husband lying on the cold table, his arms bound open, his entire middle naked, his skin swabbed with mustard-colored disinfectant, his legs fixed in position, the surgical knife slicing down his middle from his heart to his pelvis, the blood pooling, the skin lifted, the organs scraped, his body eviscerated. Gutted. Like a wild animal. Like this wild animal. I can't breathe.

I trace my fingers along the owl's feathers. No wound. No blood. The blade has found only feathers. My body suddenly feels the desire to urinate with relief. I adjust the blade in my hand, tighten my grip. I slice along the net's rigid lines and in a few seconds it releases. We hold the owl like we are swaddling pure power with our hands, containing its impulse to escape until the net is cut entirely away. In a flash Hector raises the owl over his head and releases the bird to the sky. The owl flies. Wings stretch, lift, ascend. Soon it's away from our sight. I look around the field, wide-eyed, slow-blinking, shrewd. I stretch my arms into the wind. I walk back to the field and lie down, aching to fly.

The first time my husband and I went to hang out with the Sufis in the Canadian Rockies, in the late nineties, before the arrival of cancer, they gave us a name. In their tradition, a name is a way of recognizing a person's essential nature. And too, of calling those aspects out of the person, even if they are hidden or unrecognized. My friends were given the names Fazulanissa, meaning "princess of blessings," and Shanti, meaning "peace." The spiritual leader brought Richard and me together and said henceforth we would be known as Wali and Walia. (I whispered some joke about it being more like Wally and the Beav.) We learned that Wali meant "the friend" in Sufi parlance. To be as Wali and Walia was to be friends to each other and to all, in the same way the divine is the Friend. I was bemused, touched, and the feminist in me was more than a bit angry about my name being tied to my husband's. No one else in our community had received this joined condition. Even our children were given their own perfect, gemlike monikers. Years later, after the visitations of illness and death, after the brain injury that has taken Richard's memories of our life together, after our children have left, after we have been together and apart in strange and wonderful places around the globe, I want to see that we are joined as the Friend.

Rumi said:

> When someone asks what it means
> to "die for love," point
> here.

In the time we are living on the perfect ranch waiting for things to change, I want to point to myself, and say: "Walia. I am that one."

Instead I say: "I will never leave you, and I don't know if I can be your wife."

When I say this he's sitting on the bed that is not ours, but the one belonging to the ranch, and I'm kneeling on the hard floor in front of him. I've lost my temper about the thousandth thing he's forgotten this month—maybe it's a date that we're trying to have, maybe it's a memory I wish he shared, maybe it's some shit I wanted him to do. I can no longer pretend that I feel like his lover. Even though we have friends staying with us, I'm yelling, because every facade I've been holding up—the good wife, the nice girl, the nurse—is crumbling.

"I don't know what to do."

"I can't be the one to tell you what to do! If I get into that position, it makes me your caregiver, not your lover!"

He looks at me with innocent eyes.

"You really don't know what to do?" I ask.

He shakes his head.

"What if I help you find a therapist, someone who can help you figure out ways to commit to using your compensatory strategies?"

"Okay."

Richard begins the therapy. He starts to use his planner. The forgetting doesn't change.

"What do you talk about?" I ask, after one of his sessions.

"How to talk to you."

"How's that going?"

"Not very well."

"Do you want to go to the farmers' market?" I know that we don't have to talk if we're with other people.

"Okay."

I unpack my books and papers from our time in France; I throw away the novel I've been writing for four years. I crafted the book just like my mentor wanted me to, and then, halfway through, I realized that I had no interest in the story. The book's demise isn't my mentor's fault; I've been the one making her opinion more valuable than my own. I stop writing for a year. I wait for my husband to return.

It's taking me years to cultivate the kind of detachment I really need. To do so, I have to step back from the people who think they know what's right for us. I have to stop paying for workshops and just begin the daily work of building this new life. In order to observe my situation clearly, I have to risk saying good-bye to communities that make me feel accepted and loved, not because they're bad people, but because even their guidance has limits. I have to do this because right now, like Richard, I'm just trying to survive.

I go back to staring at the perfect vineyard, wondering if the owls are safe.

Though my environs are perfect, nothing feels calm. I walk the loop from the little yellow ranch house to the eucalyptus grove to the lemon trees, circumambulating with my grief. I talk on the phone with my therapist, my sisters, my minister friend, my daughter, my childhood friend. I pace the calls, a different person each day, because I'm afraid I'll poison them with my sorrow. I'm swimming through a toxic sludge of sadness. Every day on my walk, I cry. I mourn the loss of my former life, the graceful, beautiful man I was married to, and now I mourn the person I was with him: protected, desired, womanly. The sex is miserable, the forgetting is constant, our children are away until Christmas, my work is meaningless, and I'm grief-stricken about the unknowable future. Life is as silent as a Zen retreat, one where I'm on constant kitchen duty. In my surroundings of such ponderous luxury, I feel guilty for complaining about any of my problems.

Intellectually, I understand what's happening: I'm grieving the loss of the life I once knew. The past is no more, and because I'm no longer hoping for a radical change, or pretending things are otherwise, I'm what people call "depressed." Inside myself, it feels like I'm living in a black hole of waiting. I don't yet know that it's fine to wait to see what might show up. This is the *beat-beat-beat* before the chorus resounds. Entire civilizations have died out and new ones arisen, but I can't let go of the "us" that I knew once. And I can't fill up the emptiness with more craving. Look, there's never been "the one" to complete me. But I didn't know that losing what you hold on to could hurt like this.

Richard watches television, and I sit on the porch reading books about the brain. My shelves now include books by brain scientists like Michael Gazzaniga, who talks about how one's beliefs in one's story get created. The more research I do, the more my perception of my solid self slides.

Good God, I think, you're making this up. You live in this life, and at the same time you assign meaning to it. Unlike your spouse over there watching a reality show, you amass masses of forethought, made available by the left hemisphere of the brain, which monitors all the other parts of the brain's network and deciphers their actions in order to create an acceptable sense of a unified self. Brain researchers say there is a part of the left hemisphere whose job it is to make things appear logical, to form the input we receive into stories, stories composed to feed our hungry self-image, stories that rewrite themselves to become what we now believe to be the truth.

The things that shape us, the moments that make us up, may not be possible to authenticate. But our brains create them. The "interpreter" part of the brain can impose order on information that doesn't make sense, seeking patterns, finding relationships, making personal mythology of the mysterious, irrational, and instinctive.

"Any time our left brain is confronted with information that does not jibe with our self-image, knowledge, or conceptual framework," Gazzaniga says, "our left-hemisphere interpreter creates a belief to enable all incoming information to make sense and mesh with our ongoing idea of ourself. The interpreter seeks patterns, order, and causal relationships." Our brains can even be stimulated to create religious experiences: when we receive information that doesn't jibe with the brain structures that give rise to self-awareness and understanding, one of our possible reactions is to categorize it as a sensed presence, as God.

Those times you call magical, miracles, numinous: any certainty of their otherworldly nature comes from the effect they had on you, how they moved you toward some state you really couldn't have anticipated.

My husband, in the life we had before, called me his "spiritual scout." I was responsible for being investigatory, grazing on the offerings, gorging at the godly feast, and then coming home and reporting on it. Viatic rogue to his vicarious aide-de-camp, I was his personal mythology; he was mine. This is how we ended up making our story about ourselves. It allowed us to wake up in the morning, imagine who we were, remember our past, and go about our day inhabiting these roles. Even though we create the narrative, this interpreted version is not who we are. Did Richard already know this?

I sit on the side porch, reading my brain books, looking out to the fields of flowers, dry and brittle from the summer blaze, the bees lilting for some succulent nectar.

"We think we're willing our own choices from one defined mind, like a queen bee ruling over all. But the human brain has no such sovereign ruler," I say to the bees.

In the nine months we live in the vineyard, I want Richard to track me, to remember my longings and history and requests, but *I* cannot track me. I see that Richard isn't scared of our situation. The sadness he occasionally feels is because he's concerned about my suffering. I'm the one who is terrified of losing my identity. Especially the "us" that I think I remember. While I'm making dinner, crying to my friends, listening to my husband snore, I slowly wake up to the truth that I have no idea what makes me "me." And the thing about truth is that it dismantles even as it inhabits.

Something astonishing is happening to me in my aloneness. I'm losing my religion. There's a long list of beliefs being stripped away: suffering, betrayal, hope, loyalty, freedom, success, failure. Ideas based on the desire for a future, or despair about the past. The ideas don't all leave at once. And sometimes an idea shifts so strongly, I never return to believing that concept. One day God is an external force, a childlike sense of all that is beneficent. And then God is a higher power, the grace that offers an explanation for what can't be deciphered. Later, God is a shaman, a dreamer, a force that suffuses the natural world. Finally, there is no God. God is a way of belonging to the club that believes in God. And what's left inside me that needs to belong is disappearing. I'm not angry with God about what's happened. My faith in something outside of me, something that can save me, has disappeared. In truth, my belief in needing to be saved from my situation is exactly what is sloughing away. And with that loss, the spiritual-scout self is going too.

Life after cancer eats what isn't true, our outworn notions, the ideas we hold on to because we want to do life "right," which mostly means what other people want us to do. But the body doesn't die. The body changes form, goes on to be dust or food or firmaments. That personality, though, that story we grow attached to: dead, dead, dead.

"I can't stand it," I say to Christie over the telephone. "I don't know how I'm going to stay with him." I'm walking the grove of the vineyard where we've been living for six months now. "This should be Eden: we've found work, we live in a sweet house, and after years of the grey, we're living in sunny California, for God's sake. But Christie, I feel alone!" An owl gazes at me from the eucalyptus trees.

"Sometimes I think it would have been easier for you if he had died," Christie says.

She's speaking a thought I've been too ashamed to admit.

"The way that it is, there's no funeral, no support. No one knows that you lost him."

I fall on my knees on the stone road. The owl turns its square, spotted head. My lungs fill, as if I have been holding my breath since the night in the hospital when I watched Richard leave.

One week, I call all my friends and family, and everyone says some version of the same thing: "Move back to Seattle. This place is where you can be supported. Richard's okay. You helped make him that way. You're not okay. You need help now."

Movement has long been my ally. In 1968, when my father took a job in the Blue Mountains of Ontario, Canada, I lost my former identity as an American. I arrived at my first day of third grade in a foreign country dressed in a plaid wool jumper my grandmother had sewn, my sisters and I dressed alike from our lace socks to our grosgrain hair ribbons. I tromped through several feet of billowy white, freedom cascading through me like the November snowstorm. In Canada, we had wilder land to roam. We met first-generation families with strange brogues and unfamiliar ways. And we developed an entirely new relationship with nature. I lived as often as possible in the trees. I was out of range of my parents' view for hours upon hours. I entered into my own rich imagined world. Later, Richard and I were constantly on the move. In Canada: Waterloo, Toronto, Banff. In America: Louisville, Memphis, Seattle, Laguna Beach, San Luis Obispo. Some of these moves were about escape, an attempt to cover my tracks. Every move was a chance for reinvention, a chance to get on the road, a chance to become someone else.

We've never gone back to someplace we've lived before. We've always moved on. But I'm having trouble living with the new Richard. In Seattle, there will be artists and writers whom I can join in conversation. There will be reading. There will be weirdness. There will be too many gloomy days, and a ridiculous number of fleece coats and politically correct opinions, but it'll feel like home.

"What do you think?" I ask Richard. "Can we go back?"

"I'm not sure I can get a job," he says.

"Call the company," I say, handing him the phone.

Five minutes later, he has a meeting scheduled with his old company's regional director. Six weeks later, we return.

We're neither homesick for a former geography nor nostalgic for a former community. We already know that you can't go home again. What we long for has been erased. Gone are the memories that once held us together, gone is the history that made us "us," gone are the ways we communicated with each other, gone is the mythos of our affair. Gone, baby, gone is the oasis of our (imagined) identity. Still, we need smart people and a city that feels kind.

We move back to Seattle. Dylan gives us a present of these calligraphed words: *When I say I am going home, I mean I am going to where you are.* The poem is framed on our wall. But every time I read this sentence, I cannot find this home. Home is disappearing along with the character I once called "me."

# 19

# heat

WHEN WE WERE teenagers, he was the one who awakened my sexuality. Now we are middle-aged, and I have been given his virginity. It's as if thirty years of sexual exploration have been wiped clean.

Long after the brain injury, when I'm sure he has forgotten all that transpired in those early erotic days, he dredges up his first memory of pleasing me.

"I remember that look you gave me the first time," he says, soon after we move back to Seattle. We're nestled in our bed, in an alcove with a window angled above us. We watch the birds momentarily come into view as clouds swirl past the rectangle.

"You do?" I say.

"When I asked if I could explore . . ."

"Everywhere. Oh my God. You remember?"

"You said, 'Please!'" he says, like he's won the jackpot.

In my mind I see the way that I looked at him then: keen, ardent, craving.

"Why did you remember that now?" I ask.

"It was the sweetest thing I ever heard," he answers.

I am not erased.

I realize I could respond with irony, some joke about Richard not usually remembering things sweet or sad, yesterday or forever ago. I have become accustomed to his memories that come and go, memories that aren't ensnared in a belief. I don't want to hold on to the romance of his words, words so very few these days, words that are pure and true, words based on a fleeting memory. There's a part of me that wishes to defend my heart, to make sure I don't allow this small miracle to open me. But that woman of dry wit and caustic mockery died en route from the cancer hospital.

In that moment, even though he has mostly forgotten our sexual history, I decide I can risk wanting him as a complex, intimate partner. I want a companion who relishes play, a lecherous husband who strips off social correctness like underthings to be cast off. Our sex was once a creative commons, a place for *libre* learning, freewheeling, edupunk, DIY, no-rights-reserved action. It doesn't matter that we're not that couple anymore. In the here and now, there's innocence and impartiality and spaciousness and silence and emptiness.

On one of our first Saturdays in our new home, Richard eats cereal at the table and looks out the window, which overlooks giant evergreens.

"Do you like me?" he says.

"You're a late start on Monday and Wednesday, right?" I say, not looking up from the calendar on the computer.

He pours himself another bowl of raisin bran.

"If you eat like you're twenty, your body is going to show it," I snark.

He chews. Keeps looking at me. "I like how you go after what you want," he says.

"Even when I hurt you?"

"Yes. I like everything about you," he says.

"No you don't."

"I do."

"My need to control? The insane obsessions?"

He nods.

"The freak who yells at a man with a brain injury because he forgot something?"

"Especially her."

"Why?"

"You're not giving up on me," he says.

His honesty makes me breathe as if I've been living on half-air.

"I'm trying to get to know you," I say.

"Me too. I'm trying to get to know me."

"Do you mean you can't remember . . ."

"That guy," he says, with a nod backward.

"The man I want you to be," I say in a near whisper. For some reason, it hadn't occurred to me that Richard would have to develop a relationship with the one he was before in order to begin enacting that man. For the first time, I wonder what he'd be like if I never asked him to become that man again. And then the thought is so terrifying in its essential emptiness that I push it away, where it will stay sequestered for years.

"I was a good lover once," he says.

"More than once."

"Teach me."

The first time we told the story of forgetting sex to a neurologist, he said he'd never heard of such a thing.

"Does the equipment work?" the doctor asked.

We nodded.

"Well, you'll figure it out then."

We'd been happily libidinous through our entire marriage and rarely skipped sex, with short breaks after the births of our children and when we traveled apart. Unlike so many couples we knew, we'd stayed adventurous, made sex a priority, and challenged each other to move out of our comfort zones. But also, sex had been a way of relating to each other when we really hadn't understood each other intellectually or emotionally. Sex had kept us together.

Years ago, in therapy, we'd learned new strategies for connecting through conflict. We had since become, in marital strategist John Gottman's parlance, masters at repairing our relationship, moving quickly through discord to forgiveness. Sex was a way of celebrating our fondness and admiration for each other. We stopped holding resentments. We became motivated to please one another. We were, as sex columnist Dan Savage says, "good, giving, and game." After our early marital conflicts, we'd become close again, and we found new ways to turn on, explore, indulge, conduct post-coitums, fantasize, fetishize, freakify, relish, practice, appreciate. We made concessions for each other's sexual wishes and found ourselves enjoying aspects of ourselves that were beyond our familial and cultural understanding. Before cancer arrived, we'd hit our groove; we were kids who'd discovered the delicious treats at the adult candy store.

Finding out that some ruthless god had hit the reset button on my husband's sexual history was a cruel joke. I haven't shared my despair over what I've lost with Richard, because I'm worried that my grief will harm him. I cry on daily walks. I talk to my therapist friend. I've asked Dr. L what he thinks about Richard losing his sexual history.

"Memories tied to primitive areas of the brain, such as sexuality, can be selectively damaged," Dr. L said.

When I've risked telling a few women friends, they've tended to react nonchalantly—they laugh. ("That's like riding a bike, right?" or "So, did you tell him how much he just loooooved tipping the velvet?") The men I've told have mostly been stunned.

I'm not laughing. I'm not standing around waiting. I'm going to become a one-woman sex-education crash course. Or die trying.

"What do you want to try first?" he asks, all innocence and excitement.

"Field trip," I say.

"Where?"

"Babeland."

We go to Seattle's egalitarian erotic emporium, the same place I took my daughter when she wanted to buy her first sex toy. I watch him wade wide-eyed through dildos, double dildos, vibrators, cock rings, condoms, lubricants, handcuffs, collars, blindfolds, harnesses, slings, rope, strap-ons, edible body paint, massage oil, sex games, instructional books, porn movies, and the orgasm-in-a-box. We scoop up toys to take home. Sexual exploration becomes like summer vacation. There are few rules. The children are in college. We stay up late, playing.

At first I think the teenage sex will dissipate, that the fast intercourse, few words, and all-boy appetite will be replaced by the experienced sexuality the two of us shared before the cancer treatment. But it still isn't possible for him to ask for what he wants, or conduct a conversation, or remember the ways my body responds. And that's not even critical, because we're still in survival mode, trying to help him relearn his career, and settle into a new house, and help our children negotiate adulthood. Because Richard experiences both long-term and short-term memory loss, remembering sex is arduous, even when he is motivated to learn. The brain changes have made his desire immense. He artlessly reaches for me, his man-hands grasp my breasts before an exchange of words, glances, clinches. Even though I'm angry at what's happened to us, I cannot ignore his longing.

I show him simple things—kissing, touching, the mechanics of moving the body. Flirting will come much later, when he has grown a sense of self-awareness. I demonstrate affection: compliments, rapport, embraces, caresses, calls, catcalls, the French kiss. Every suggestion, forgotten. Every action, forgotten. In order to adopt the behavior, he must be reminded. Not dozens of times. Thousands of times. I must learn to respond with compassion rather than anger. This one lesson—to deliver the sweetness that is now his favorite name for me—takes me five years to learn. Two thousand days. So whose brain is injured?

Sex is paradoxically the most frustrating and the most meaningful way for me to learn how to detach from the desire for results. I'm constantly reminding myself—there's nowhere to go. This is it. But Richard seems to be able to focus on learning sex with all kinds of patience.

"How's it going?" I ask him, after an unsatisfying session.

"Being a good sex partner is challenging."

"Right?"

"I could please you before. Most of the time."

"Yeah, but . . ."

"It isn't for lack of effort," he says, reporting.

"I know, baby. But you last more than a minute these days. That's good, right?"

"I'm horned up all the time," he says. "But I don't ask for more because you like to talk first, and I can't."

"Jeez, it's like you hit the reset button on the whole aging thing. So, what's the deal with doing the same motions over and over?"

"You say, 'This doesn't feel good.'"

"Like when you used to stare at people without blinking."

He reflects. I've learned enough of his process to be patient with the time it takes him to go from thinking to speaking. "I'm only able to think of myself. I can't remember to think about what you feel at all."

"If we slow down, you'll get it."

And we slow down every gesture, we stop and start again, we practice asking for what we want. For the first five years after the brain injury, he doesn't even think of seduction. To seduce means that you have available the skills of humor, teasing, tension, flirtation. But allurement isn't necessary for me anymore, because I'm reacting in ways I could never have imagined.

My body starts to respond differently than it ever has. My entire core heats up. I become a furnace. Even when my hands and feet are cool to the touch, I'm burning. My sexual appetite becomes ravenous. I covet every male between the ages of sixteen and sixty-six, and quite a few women too. When my friend Judith calls to ask how it's going, I say, "Well, I didn't lick the barista today." I flirt with my male friends. I notice what men I am attracted to, what men I avoid. I gaze longingly at the surfer dudes and businessmen and construction workers. This is serious. My body is eroticizing itself at the exact time that I have been least sexually fulfilled.

Some friends say it is a midlife crisis. Some say it is an expression of grief. A few spiritual friends say it's kundalini energy. I've heard of this energy expressing spontaneously in yogis and others who "awaken," and I even experienced it in a meditation room years ago, a moment that manifested as a bodily tremor, an aspen in a mountain gust. But there's nothing enlightened about this feeling. I wonder if Richard's horny teenager mojo is contagious.

Turning up the heat on my sexuality at the same time that he's more desirous—and less adept—is a strange brew. We're fleshly fools. I have what many women would enjoy—a new man, a fresh man, an unencumbered man. What I learn from teaching Richard about intimacy is that I only *think* him to be absent. His touch and gaze and presence are with me. Every time we are together.

Our first year back in Seattle, Richard and I go on dates again. This has been our tradition, Saturday night out, just the two of us, which we have done since we found our way back to each other. In the past, we've had exquisitely simple dates, like the time we bought ice-cream cones and sat by the river, telling each other our dreams. And we've had outrageously fun dates at concerts, at the theater, and on backpacking trips. Now, post brain injury, our identity as the couple who can pull off those kinds of easy conversations is over.

Richard prepares questions for each date, so he has something to talk about. Without the preparation, conversation is impossible. One evening we pick a fancy Tom Douglas restaurant and make reservations. I wear a beautiful dress and take time with my hair. I help him pick out a sweater and jeans. We sit in silence through most of the main course. He orders their famous doughnuts for dessert, and they come in a white paper bag, warm from the oven, ready to toss in the sugar. He spills their powder over the table. Then he licks his fingers and slides them across the sugar. Licking, sliding, into the mouth. I glare at him. He's too shameless to notice.

He isn't deliberately ignoring me. Part of what I'm learning is how the brain-injured can be unresponsive to emotions. Weeks later, when my father nearly dies of a stroke and the doctors find a brain tumor, I sit on the stairs, sobbing. I raise my head.

"Dad had a stroke! They found a brain tumor! They don't know if he's going to recover!"

"Oh," Richard responds.

I know that I must change some of my ways to accommodate my new man's artlessness, and sometimes I fall short.

At dinner, I grind my teeth and spit my words through a frozen jaw: "If you lick your fingers in the restaurant, I'm not going out with you."

In the wake of Richard's passivity, I have become assertive and in control. I manage our financial affairs, parental decisions, medical services, family relationships, and everything that was previously shared by the two of us. I'm one tenacious bitch, not unlike my paternal grandmother, Frances, who had ten children and kept intact her marriage, family, and a large farm. But who I have become in Richard's silence surprises me. I'm increasingly uninterested in what others think. If a medical professional is unresponsive to our concerns, I fire that person and move Richard to another provider. I drive aggressively on the highways. I take my place. I learn to reject what isn't true. I leave friendships that aren't meaningful. I become more adept in examining my flaws, asking mentors and my children to help me see my shortcomings. I'm leaving behind a persona, the "nice girl," who was, once upon a time, a useful inner chick who allowed me to slide unscathed past a raging father, offensive bosses, and misogynist teachers, all while looking pretty in pink.

Once I was shy, compliant, and in the shadow of my tall, brilliant, authoritative husband. I remember a visit to a book festival long before the cancer arrived, an event that nearly cost us our marriage when Richard, despite my objections, confronted a respected author in front of an audience of a few hundred people, on a subject Richard knew nothing about: contemporary poetry. I ran from that room ashamed and furious, and straight to the therapist's office, where I spent months trying to get clear about the kind of woman I wanted to be: feminist and forgiving. Post brain injury, Richard remembers nothing of the incident, and sits silent in audiences, and has not one thing in his nature that causes him to be combative or commanding. He's opinionless.

Because Richard is an entirely new man, I realize that I don't have to bring our shared history to our experiment. I don't even have to presume that I know anything about his satiation. In truth, what astounds me about my new man is that he doesn't have many preferences. What is the experience of pleasure when we are not habituated to a certain response? What do I have to learn from reconsidering my favorites and prejudices?

As part of Richard having no preferences, he's not sure about his sexual identity. Does he like certain acts and not others? What kinds of sex make him feel pleasure? What are his limits? Is he attracted to both women and men? (He likes women, he finds.) Is he getting enough sex? (Usually, not.)

"Tonight's date-night subject is sex," I say.

"I'm on it."

And later over Pagliacci pizza and then at Cupcake Royale, the conversation continues.

"What kinds of experiences are sexual anyway? Why is intercourse considered sex and not punching down the yeasty dough of this pizza?" I ask.

"What do people mean when they talk about sex?" he says, really curious.

"What are your erotic desires?" I volley back.

"I get to be with you. That you accept me as I am. And you?"

"This is our marriage. We get to do it the way we want."

Later, I write what we say about our sex life in my journal.

TWENTY WAYS SEX HELPS OUR RELATIONSHIP:

1. Burns enough calories to rationalize cupcakes or pie or ice cream.

2. Reunites us after a time away from each other.

3. During vacation, fits perfectly between museum-going and a late dinner.

4. When the children were young, relieved the stress of parenting.

5. Solves disputes. Do over!

6. An orgasm keeps me from killing him when I have to clean the toilet again. (It keeps him from killing me when the dishwasher isn't loaded uniformly.)

7. When we are very good, we feel sexy for days afterward.

8. Communicates the unknown.

9. Hides the unknown. At least until the pillow talk.

10. Dirty, taboo-busting, throw-me-against-the-wall sex erases our tired old ideas about marriage, aging, and retirement planning.

11. Helps us be vulnerable enough to share (or fear) that fantasy, and how much we are willing to do (or hide) to make sure it is realized (or never happens).

12. Let's face it, sex after babies, surgeries, failed exercise programs, and eating your way through Italy is the best arrogance-buster you can find.

13. Cultivates a sense of humor. Especially when you break the bed trying that new position. [That's the moment I knew I would marry him, when he was as graceful in calamity as he was in the thrall.]

14. Better than coffee or Tylenol for relieving a headache.

15. Induces a good nap.

16. Shows us that we belong together.

17. Keeps us curious about the ways we can become better lovers as we change minds, bodies, cultures,

commitments. Even about what we mean when we say "better" at loving.

18. Allows us to forgive each other for all the ways we ignore, defend, withhold, criticize, stonewall, insult, and make wrong.

19. Makes visible to the other the joy of our love and marriage.

And as Richard says, after the brain injury:

20. Sex allows me to express myself nonverbally with passion in a way that I would like to be able to express verbally but can't.

Amen, man.

Even after a few decent dates, I'm still so attached to the return of my husband's definitive self. I miss the Richard who knew what he wanted to eat, how he wanted to exercise, where he wanted to go, when he wanted to arrive, who he'd be when he got there. Even when we were young, he was a man with a persuasive magnetism. As he matured, he asserted a strong sense of what he wanted to create. After his brain injury, even though he's working his way into new relationships, he isn't sure about much.

"What movie do you want to see?" I ask.

"What do you want to see, sweetness?" he responds.

He returns the question to me on matters related to our social, intellectual, emotional, financial, and spiritual lives. He's even more open-minded about food, trying things he refused to eat most of our marriage. He's emotionally calm (especially when I became frustrated) and seems to have few desires other than simple physical ones: food, sex, and warmth. I see his new, unattached self as young. I yearn for the forceful, masculine one I remember. It seems like we've traded places, like I have become the decision maker. I'm slow to find acceptance of the new man. Very slow.

When I tell my therapist friend about these changes she says, "The Great Way is not difficult for the man without attachment to preferences." I've read this line in the *Tao Te Ching* and admired the idea there, but I do not appreciate the newfound lack of attachment in my husband. I want to be married to one who is defined.

For years after the injury, Richard is without the ability to express a "no," even if he has a preference. And I enjoy the excessive control I hold in our relationship. Getting things done is so much more streamlined when there isn't anyone to fight. But the belief in productivity is slipping in me too. I used to check things off a list as a primary route to happiness. Now, I stare at the ceiling with a book open on my lap, pretending I'm reading. I'm silent, and raging against silence. If Richard is to become a companion, I think, he has to learn to say "no" to me.

I realize how easy it would be to get my way with Richard. This new husband would be so easy to manipulate. I try altering my history a couple of times, to see what I can get away with. When some story about my drinking comes up, I minimize how devastating my alcoholism was on our family. But the feeling I'm left with makes me want to hurt my body again. Then, I understand one of the values of his lack of preferences, his boylike innocence, his ongoing forgetting. He's not invested in representing me or us in any particular manner. He has no unfinished business. I wonder: What would it be like to live life that cleanly?

One Saturday, he's asked to hike with two doctors, men who refer patients to him in his physical therapy practice, men who also share an interest in the mountains. I'm overjoyed that Richard is choosing a social connection instead of sitting alone reading and watching television, which is his usual weekend. We agree to meet for our date at twilight. When the agreed-upon time arrives, there is no message by phone or text. When he finally walks in the door, hours past our reservation for dinner, I bombard him with my anger. He's apologetic, sweet, and devastated by my reaction. Five minutes into my tirade, I start screaming, "I'm not angry with you! I'm angry with the brain injury!" This thought has never occurred to me before, that I am allowed to be furious with his condition—not him, but what happened to us. And why not be angry at this incident? Richard didn't do anything to bring the brain injury upon himself, any more than he willed himself to get cancer. I shout like a crazy woman. He joins in. Then we're both standing in the kitchen, screaming and stomping and shaking our pissed-off selves until we're depleted. Later, I make grilled cheese sandwiches while he showers, and we sit talking about what happened out there on the mountain. Turns out the men made plans to take a more arduous route, and even though Richard knew the hike would take much more time than he'd allotted, he couldn't negotiate his way out of the deal.

"You can't say 'no,' still," I say.

"Not really."

"Would you be willing to try an experiment?" I ask.

He raises his shoulders. The big Whatever.

"Let me find someone who can show you how to say 'no.' Obviously I'm failing at it, but there've got to be some resources out there. Right?"

Richard shrugs his shoulders.

"Okay?"

He nods.

"I want the word," I say.

"Yes, I'll try," he says.

In a week, we are in the office of therapist and boundary teacher Jovanna Casey, a redheaded pixie with bright eyes and an adventuresome appetite for life.

"Say 'no.' And push me across the room," she says. "Go on, I can take it."

Richard puts his soft palm, the size of a grizzly paw, on Jovanna's shoulder and gives her a paltry shove.

"No."

"I'm keeping you from something you want!" Jovanna yells. "Push me!"

Richard tries again, this time with two palms and a voice slightly louder. Jovanna doesn't move an inch.

Jovanna takes his hands, looks into his eyes, and says, "You can't hurt me. I'm a strong woman. Push!"

Richard closes his eyes and moves Jovanna a foot across the carpet.

"Think of something you really want," Jovanna says.

Richard has his desire in about ten seconds. He opens his eyes, looks at Jovanna's scowl as she snarls: "That thing you want. You can't have it. I'm keeping you from having it. How about that?"

Richard lays his hands against her shoulders and pushes her across the room, shouting, "Noooooo!" He's not faking it. He's mowing this woman down. Crazily, a zing goes into my belly at the sight of him taking charge. Some memory of the physical attraction that drew me to him when he slammed a basketball, killed a tennis serve, threw me down on the bed. How post-feminist of me, I think.

Despite my desire to be more evolved, there's a wave of grief that rises up after I see him get his wild man on. The two of them mistake my tears for happiness. I'm thrilled for Richard, and for me. Now that he can declare what he wants and what he doesn't want, I have a chance to leave the caregiver role that I have assigned myself. But getting even a taste of the guy I fell in love with, the competitive, strong warrior, makes me miss that one with all my heart. I decide I have to hide my despair from him, or risk hurting his recovery.

From my girlhood, I have imagined myself powerful. At thirteen, I fought with my father on the steps of the Catholic church my family attended for the right to make my own religious choices. I paid for my education, managed our joint finances after marriage, took jobs so beyond my skill level that they were frightening. If you'd asked me how I defined myself, I would have told you I was a feminist. I celebrated my sexuality as a means to empowerment. I gave up the phallocentric writing that was the mainstay of my literature degree, and instead read what I missed: women's stories. My women friends expressed themselves however they damn well pleased, in being mamas, matriarchs, and, sometimes, in taking apart the patriarchal-industrial complex. The guy friends I hung out with treated me like an artist who mostly made up her mind about things and then did them. Before the departure of my formerly assertive, definitive, and physically and mentally strong husband, if you'd asked me whether I had an egalitarian marriage, I would have assured you that we treated each other as equals, and that our marriage was generous and thoughtful, a meeting of matched minds. When the qualities that I identified in my husband as masculine left, autonomy was thrust upon me. Beauty, power, strength, decisiveness, and even freedom had been situated not within myself, but in who I thought he was. Those projections came flying back, like Huginn and Muninn, those trickster ravens of thought and memory. As much as I'm aware of the deficits in Richard's brain, I'm also increasingly aware of my own shortfalls. In my young marriage and long relationship, I wasn't as self-reliant as I imagined myself to be.

Soon after we arrive back in Seattle, our college-graduate children uproot. Our son makes his home all the way across the country and our daughter chooses to live in Europe. We stay where we are for a change, and regard another new year, not from the perspective of mother and father, just as ourselves. We work, eat, and sit at home in silence. Silence that I'm not one bit grateful for. But it's the kind of silence that leads me to ask questions of myself: *What are you? When did you begin? Where are you going? How do you define your values, beliefs, truths?*

In Richard, now years after the brain injury, I have a chance to observe someone who has no answers to these questions. He does not exist in memory, even to himself. He constantly forgets information, narrative, instructions, agreements, history, attachments, associations, requests, niceties, traditions, experiences. He doesn't always forget and he doesn't never remember. He is habitual and he is random. There is no method to understanding how the forgetting works. Even without a steady self, he has no issues related to lack of self-esteem. There is very little self to require esteem.

I begin to notice all the times that I am not awake to a solid notion of myself: when I'm driving, while my mind is on a problem, when I'm immersed in a deep sleep, when I become lost to the world during orgasm, when I stop seeing the room around me while I am writing this text. In these moments, my own life vanishes. Even my assured stories about our past are only shots in the dark, a way to bring a family tale to life. I think of birthday photographs from my childhood, and, of course, I cannot register my history in its entirety. Prompted by a specific photograph, I tell my story about what happened on that day—how I loved chocolate cake, for example—and I may not reveal that my sister was crying, my mother was pregnant, or that way back when, chocolate was not my favorite cake, I only wish it were so. I fill in the details of the narrative with a sense of how my family was then, or my sister adds her anecdote, or my joke about the event lightens the original mood. Then this story becomes "mine."

When Richard begins to make his memories, I realize I'm constructing them through a collective rather than an individual reference, that the stories I'm telling him are an amalgamation of my memories and the ones he shared with me before the brain injury. When his mind begins to hold on to a story, he delights in telling "his" version of things to friends, colleagues, and his patients. As I listen to his tales, I can identify the elements that came from a variety of people. I can hear when a sentence comes from the recordings that Richard made with his sister and brother so his children would have their paternal history. The humorous ending to one of his stories comes from my attempt to make him laugh when I shared what he had done to amuse me, oh so long ago. He even picks up our language cues and voice pacing and punch lines.

The collective recollecting becomes a way by which Richard remembers himself. His posture, ungainly and awkward following the surgery, becomes more conscious and graceful as he learns his story. His gaze softens and responds like a sensitive human's rather than a scared animal's. He isn't "coming back," as people often like to say. That former Richard no longer exists. But I see that Richard is building a container of a narrative to help him move about the world. And with these memories come fear, regret, and the desire for forgiveness.

Richard isn't experiencing grief for a lost self; grief pours only from us who knew him before. Richard sees himself as helpless to find that former being. He forgives his helplessness. He learns the stories because to form a history is to make us happy. He cares not for the worst or the best moments of his life—they are the same to him. I learn that the specific narrative does not matter. The genuineness of him, the presence of him as he is—what some people call awareness—is unadulterated. For the first time in my life, I begin to love someone for his essence, not for what he can offer me, or reflect onto me, or leave with me. It occurs to me that I might have watched my husband become himself, my desires for him notwithstanding. By waiting in the silence these circumstances have made for us, I've come to see him not as mine but as something altogether curious and wonderful. Sometimes it's sweet. Sometimes it's sexy. Other times, it's just damn hard work. In this way, as it turns out, ours is not much different from any other marriage.

# 20
# lover

AFTER NEARLY THREE years of clumsy, repetitive, rudimentary sex, I ask Richard if I can take a lover.

"Why do you want to do that, sweetness?" he says.

He's working full-time, coming home, falling asleep watching television. He can't figure out how to have a conversation when he's depleted from managing troublesome health-care paperwork. For months, we haven't shared more words than what keeps our household efficient. I'm scared to tell him that I'm hurting. He's come so far in making it back to his work. How can I insist on my desires at such a time? But if I'm not honest with him, I'm worried that I'll become his caregiver forever, that I'll be locked into a maternal relationship rather than ensconced in a mature and erotic one.

I turn off the television, which is blaring some sports event. "Our sex isn't satisfying to me," I say. "I know you're trying. I'm not even sure this is about you."

"What's it about?" he says.

"Baby, it's like your brain injury has started to take apart my way of seeing myself. Like I'm not confined by who I was in the past."

He stares at me.

"You know?" I ask.

"I think so . . ."

"I don't want to leave you. I want to be your wife in every way. But something's missing, some kind of intimacy we had before, and I'm not sure it's going to be recovered."

"What do you want?" he asks.

"I don't know." I'm terrified of his innocent question, its purity and scope. *What the hell do I want?* "Let's keep talking about this," I say, running to wipe down a kitchen counter.

Much of my childhood was oriented to Catholicism, which has a history of denying women's sexuality and keeping wives powerless. I stopped going to church in my teens, but my extended family is rooted in traditional family values. Would I lose the love of friends and family if I forthrightly stepped outside my marriage? If our children knew, could this choice damage their intimate relationships? I worry about what others would think of me, if they ever discovered this secret fantasy I harbor. But Richard's acceptance of his brain changes and his passionate appetites embolden me to claim what I am hungry for. I don't feel selfish, because I am involving my husband in the ongoing conversation. I want to finally tell the truth, without the need for approval. I want to risk disappointing others. My social structures led me to believe that there was an authority that could protect me. All that conditioned thinking is proving false. What Richard's loss of history is showing me is the absolute unpredictability of life. No one knows anything. No one knows what's right for me.

My curiosity about intimacy, touch, sex is consuming. Every day I meditate in the Zen style I learned long ago, watching the questions arise. Why do I ache to be touched (in certain, specific ways)? Who is *this* doing the longing? What's longing made of? What's in another that isn't in myself?

Because I'm not clear that Richard, as a man without preferences, can find a "no," we talk about the possibility of a lover for most of a year. We find a romantic cabin in the woods, and drive there listening to a Dan Savage podcast that articulates a case for holding marriage together with occasional trysts. We make a fire and sit by the flames asking each other questions. We talk about what preserves closeness in our relationship. And how we'll keep all of our stability while inviting in variety. And how we feel about taking away any distinguishing aspect of our union, our specialness, and if that might fundamentally change us. Despite the changes in the last few years, we feel bonded to each other. He knows I'm not leaving. I know he's a new man, up for most anything. But then there are all the things we don't know, all the things we have not tried. We don't really know what we're getting into.

One day he says, "If a lover is something that you think will make you happy, then of course, sweetness."

When he has spent a year able to say "no" to me—*I don't want to go to the theater*; *I don't want to do that chore*; *I don't want to get my hair cut*—I trust that Richard is strong enough to allow me to act.

First, we conduct research about marriage, affairs, and open relationships of all kinds. We read *Sex at Dawn: How We Mate, Why We Stray, and What It Means for*

*Modern Relationships*. We check out videos and books by Drs. John and Julie Gottman, on making marriage work. Even though we're not sure we're interested in having an open relationship, we read books by people who have done this. We find scientific articles on the human species that report we did not evolve in monogamous nuclear families but rather in small, intimate groups where individuals had several ongoing sexual relationships. We discover that men and women in monogamous relationships don't talk about their desires openly. Married people, regardless of gender, cheat at about the same rate: almost half of us find ways to step out at least once. If you count kissing, sexual webcamming, and online sex, infidelity is nearly the norm in America. Three-quarters of men say they would have an affair if they knew they could never be caught. Still, open marriages, whether polyamorous, or swinging, or somewhere in between, make up less than 5 percent of the married population.

I invite Richard to an educational meeting about polyamory. It's at a sex-positive club that looks like the Legion on games night, if bingo had been replaced with, say, mud wrestling. Wood paneling, cheap flooring, ordinary couples. We ask a few questions of the presenter, then leave, wondering if an open relationship is truly what we desire. The scene feels tawdry; the people seem sincere but oddly like Mike and Marcia Brady, grown up. I'd expected something more Amsterdam burlesque, less *That '70s Show*.

"I don't want someone else," he says.

"If I do, it's not some random dude."

But random is the first thing that happens anyway.

I think about the parts that are missing in our sexual life, what a lover would fix. I open up the personals section of the alternative weekly. I'm trying to find the best dessert—something sinfully tempting. I work up a plan with Richard: I'll interview the potential partner, and if the new man works, I'll set up a date to meet him.

Surprisingly, the first man I contact sets up a time. We agree to have a drink by Lake Washington. This guy is short, skinny, talkative, stained with paint from his art—he's all the things my husband is not. We walk the docks around the night-lit water and then sit out on the deck of his houseboat, talking about the tech industry and art and music. He drinks vodka straight from a jam jar and speaks about himself. The chosen man is melancholy, in that pathetic manner of newly jilted lovers. When it begins to rain, we go inside where he tells me his sad story. His blond head hangs like an angsty, lumberjacked grunge boy's. I drink water and tell him my story of a husband who's forgotten his life. He's startled by my words, and tries to cover by arranging his hair, apologizing for the state of his houseboat. I make him promise that he isn't going to sleep with me out of pity. He nods, serious. We talk about the rules for our encounter, all the things I've promised myself: safe sex, what I want, what isn't going to happen. He picks up varnish cans, shoves his clothes into the corner, pulls me onto his bed.

When we have sex, I feel like a body, a stand-in, a repository for his past. I've moved from a lover with no memories to a lover with nothing but memories. Still, when he says that he'll call, I do not know he is lying. After months with no contact, I ask him to lunch. In a cold café overlooking Lake Washington, I tell him that rejection is one thing, but disappearing on a woman who is trying to survive the death of her partner is another matter. He buys me a sandwich. He doesn't squirm or look away. He holds me when we say good-bye.

I cry afterward, thinking I'll never find someone with the kind of exuberance my husband and I used to share. I start to hate myself for having stepped outside my marriage. The only consolation that I have is my honesty with Richard.

For months, I sit on the couch with my husband while he watches television, and I stare into the screen, and I pretend that I feel close with him. I decide that I've gone about this all the wrong way. Like a good writer, I think that I simply haven't done enough research. I need to find a man who's as sensual as I am, someone who knows about the pleasure of sex as well as its sacredness. Because Richard would find it easier, I think this would be a wonderful time to be attracted to a woman, but I'm not. I crave the masculine because it's precisely Richard's dominant maleness that's gone missing. I've been wired for his testosterone; now his power has vanished.

No man appears. Not one.

So I think about food. A lot. I make desserts that could elicit marriage proposals. I study cooking shows. I cook for people at retreats. I join an online forum about food. I talk to chefs. Their voices are direct and actionable and delicious. I crave their minds, their language, their foodie style of intellectual competitiveness. Their cocksure authority. I devour the polarity of the masculine and feminine back-and-forth. I meet a man at an online food forum. He loves food as much as I do. We write letters for months. The chef arrives on my doorstep. Hawaiian, with a wide chest and thick arms and tattooed legs. He's softhearted, with few traces of bitterness, and he has friends who are artists and performers, open-minded people. I introduce him to my husband. The chef soon discovers that he's really, really monogamous. We become friends who see each other once in a while, sharing recipes and anything but small talk. We like each other, but we don't hang out, trying to tempt fate.

A week after I say good-bye to the chef, Richard and I are having tea with my therapist friend.

"What's it like to have a brain injury?" she asks Richard.

Miraculously, my husband can find the words. "She wants me to be that man I was before. And I don't know him. I want to be a good lover to her. I want to be there for her in all ways," he says.

Richard cries. Like he cries every day since he's come home. He's still a stranger to me in his emotional expressions. When he cries, I become stalwart. It's as if I'm becoming a man. I hear my husband's words like a train coming in the distance, about to roll over my inert body. Sadly, I'm stony-faced. I'm in despair over what was, and unable to tell the truth about my loss. I haven't finished grieving the death of my relationship. I don't know who I'm married to. Except this: the love is genuine.

My therapist friend and I attend a workshop on relationships at a nondescript hotel with grey walls, greyer skies. A dozen couples in the room are in the process of divorcing. The rest of us are trying to sort out our relationship baggage. I think my friend has invited me to be of support to her. We write pages and pages of our beliefs about the opposite sex. We analyze former romantic relationships by asking each other questions. Some couples stand up and talk about their problems. Everyone listens, hard.

When we go for lunch, we walk across the wide lawn, and I ask my friend: "If I'm going to be responsible for my happiness, I'm going to have to come to terms with my beliefs about intimacy. But I don't know what makes me happy. Is it selfish to want to be more adventurous in our marriage?"

"Ask yourself if it's possible to be anything other than self-centered," she says.

"What?"

"You're doing life for you. Because you want to feel good, even when you give. Perhaps marriages work when each person helps the other to be selfish."

I decide to give myself an experiment I've never dared—Doing What I Want. Selfishly. Shamelessly. Every moment of every day (or only when I want to do the experiment). The experiment starts as a project for a day, and then becomes a week, and then it goes on and on. I do what I want for most of a year.

I sit in silence until I register a want. And then I get up and satisfy that want. There's a lot of lying on the couch. Even more time searching through the pantry for snacks. At first, it looks like a stoner's weekend. All the ice cream and salted peanuts I can eat. Then come the foods from my childhood I'd avoided overdoing because they might make me fat: Kraft Dinner, mashed potatoes, barbecue. The foods I'd rarely give myself because they represented luxury: a great steak, a decorated bakery cake, some fancy cheese. I let myself read books (even when I think I'm supposed to be producing something). I sit in the kitchen and stare out the window. I take long walks at the park when I feel like moving, sometimes twice in one day. I take a ferry to an island and walk in the woods in the rain. But much of the time, I really want to write. I close the door to my home office and write in the voice that's my own, not the one of a teacher, or of the successful author I admire. In this year, I don't help other people much because it turns out

I'm doing those things to get noticed, to be seen as a good wife, a good mother, a good friend. I stop talking to people unless I want their company. I don't keep commitments that I no longer want to do. I give up several community groups that I stayed in out of loyalty. My calendar develops white space. I learn that "no" is a complete sentence. I give up the compulsion of doing more, having more, seeking more. I stop buying shit just to feel good about myself. I'm no longer busy, and so I can't use the excuse of being busy.

I learn that I like sex, and that I'm happy with my nature, even though it seems that compared to other middle-aged women, I might have a high libido. I flirt with my husband, sending him sexy love letters that end in a bloody fine afternoon shag. Armed with a dream and a trusty vibrator, I find my inner Betty Dodson, and make a study of fantasies I've never allowed myself. All inside my own mind (maybe with a little help from Tim Curry videos). There are orgasms before breakfast and during dessert. The shame I've carried about my body ever since I came down from hanging out in trees is gone.

Once, at a party in college, I flirted with a man in front of a group of my friends and he called me a slut. I didn't hear his comment, but my girlfriends, disgusted by his cruelty, got me out of that sexist house. Much of my life, I've found it considerably safer to orient as societally appropriate. And then I married before I'd had the chance to explore what my erotic life was to me. In my Doing What I Want experiment, I understand myself as the woman I am (rather than what a misogynist culture would like me to feel conflicted about, which includes powerful, liberating sexual urges). In this year of giving up others' expectations and living for my own desires, I don't believe that my erotic imagination and choices are wrong. Left to my devices, I like what I like.

In this year, Richard and I, happily empty-nested, take days when we don't get out of bed. We plan getaways. We take meals at the table instead of in front of the television. We enroll in a tantric workshop, hoping we might learn how to re-experience each other, the way we did when we dated. In sex-positive Seattle, there's a whole category for tantra on Yelp. I pick a woman who specializes in personal development, Buddhist-lite, the orgasmic bliss-centered practices of late capitalism. If I'm going to have tantra, I want some serious business.

In the workshop we sit on stiff chairs in a dark room while we practice how to kiss. The red-haired instructor calls herself a "modern tantra master" and sits cozied up in yoga pants and a curve-skimming sweater.

"Allow your partner to show you how he or she wants to be kissed. You be the receiver. Pay attention," the instructor says.

I look about the room at the couples of every age seated around us. The twenty of us here are calm, dignified, curious. I'm excited to show my husband how I want to be kissed, to practice slowing things down between us. I watch his face for a long time, come close, pause. I want to show him how I like to be teased. He smiles. We kiss, our heads tilted, our fingers holding on. Now it's his turn. He holds my shoulders in his hands. Hands slide across my back. He pulls me close. He kisses me with no theatrics, completely guileless. My kiss seems like a silent screen kiss in comparison to his frank foreplay. My heart skips. Could he be secretly good at this? Maybe I haven't been paying attention to the man I live with. We make a deal to do more kissing.

That night, we begin a new ritual. Every night when he comes home, I meet him at the door, and we have one of those kisses. Before the news of the day, we kiss. In that year, I fall in love with the new Richard, the silent Richard, the sentimental Richard. Just as he is.

What I have lived through Richard's loss of identity allows me to question everything that heretofore seemed incontrovertible. Somewhere in the year or so of Doing What I Want, I recognize that no one knows my marriage better than I, because I am the one who made up my marriage in my imagination. Of course, Richard said "I do" to our union too. Twice. But *my* marriage is entirely the one from my perspective. There's no Best Marriage Award for doing relationships right. There's no one living my exact circumstance of being married to someone who has forgotten sex. I get to find my exquisite truth. I have been living in the fear of others' disapproval of my choices my entire life. I can no longer take on what I imagine others want for me (because I risk talking about my pain to few people, these discussions usually happen inside my mind). My constructed reality has been driven by the illusion of isolation, the belief that my thoughts are my currency, that I own them, that they are me. I don't want another identity, as the monogamous one or the not-monogamous one. In the year of Doing What I Want, I've discovered that I can trust myself. And that my wants shift constantly. And that you can't always get what you want, as Mick said.

What hasn't shifted are two seemingly contradictory pieces of our relationship: our sexual life is improving through my acceptance of its limitations, and I want the presence of another man. I reintroduce this possibility to my husband. He ponders. He asks questions. He tells me what he wants. He no longer wants to be out of the room. He wants to be a part of everything.

I tell Richard stories about our sexuality. I tell him about the time that I was with a woman a decade ago, how she came to bed with both of us a time or two.

"Before the brain injury?" he asks.

"All of my kissing used to be with girls when I was little. I met you when I was a teenager, and just never had the chance to be with a woman. And then I did."

"Huh," he says.

"You were cool with it."

He smiles. This is the easiest thing for him to imagine.

I fill him in on the story as we've told it to each other in the past, conscious that this has been our private knowing, that I can alter any of the details, that I can try to protect him. I don't.

"You liked her," I say. "But we didn't want to share our life with someone else. I realize I may be making a mistake in asking for a lover," I add. "I promise you that I don't know the ending to this."

He looks at me with forgiving eyes.

We talk about how we don't want a sexual partner to negatively impact our relationship, health, or careers. How we have to keep this private, only for us. We want to be thoughtful about how we invite another into our life. It isn't just a bed, it's our entire intimate life we'll be sharing. We make up our own rules. We each have veto power. Friendship first. Risks eliminated, or at least moderated.

I don't want to be the only one inviting honesty in our relationship. So I ask him: "What would you be into if you knew I'd say 'yes'?" He tells me a couple of his kinks, none of which involve anyone but me, and we begin exploring. Richard, as it turns out, is the most monogamous straight man I've ever met. But his identity changes lead me to ask questions of our erotic life that I'd never consider had we stayed that same couple. Our honesty in asking, and our joy in discovery, are saving our marriage. This transition isn't about preserving our monogamy but about discovering our fidelity. We want to define our commitment, one that's about staying together through all of the changes, including the sexual ones. Sexual exclusivity matters less to us than preserving what's core to our union: friendship, touch, humor, adventure, abundance, and sovereignty. And inviting a lover into our lives doesn't mean a stranger has carte blanche. We will make choices as a couple first. There will be no secrets. If something is too edgy for one, no one goes forward.

In the Catholic-sponsored Engaged Encounters we'd taken part in before we were married, we'd met other engaged couples who strayed and stayed together, but no one had the nerve to ask how the long-married panel members coped with wanting variety after being together for decades. Dan Savage uses the term *monogamish* to describe the unions of freewheeling couples who want experimentation with their longevity.

"No labels. We don't have to define ourselves by who we sleep with. It's the twenty-first century, right?" I say to my friend Judith, mostly to convince myself that I'm on the right track.

"There's no natural state of marriage," says Judith who, at the time of our talk, is hoping her own long-term union with a woman will be officially recognized and given some of the legal benefits of straight marriage. "Not every partnership requires monogamy, but they all do rely on integrity. You're arriving in your integrity by making sure Richard is on the same page."

I'm not interested in what anyone other than Richard thinks. I'm not taking a stance against society. I'm simply concerned with us.

A few months later, I introduce myself to a writer, ask him on a date. Evan is like Celtic poetry, a lanky man with sensitive eyes and a chronic illness. He's one of those meditators whose engagement with their spiritual practice has penetrated their entire lives. Even though he knows I'm married, when my wide-shouldered husband greets him at the door, he jumps. We leave the house to talk at a restaurant nearby. We bond over our stories of suffering, the joylessness that will undo us in the end. I'm charmed by his expert conversational skills, his easy compassion. Best of all, unlike other men I've considered, he lives out of town, so we won't run into each other. Later that night, we kiss. I tell him there are only certain ways I want to be with him, that any relationship with me has to be structured so it works with a long-term marriage. This guy's been married. He no longer wants matrimony. He gets us, he thinks.

"We want holy sex," I say. "Not just screwing. The kind with intention and intensity. We want you to come to bed with us."

I do not tell him that I want him to teach my husband how to make love to me. (It's not that I'm embarrassed to ask for his help. I don't speak this desire because I don't yet know that this is what I want; I don't yet know that learning is possible in such circumstances.) The writer stays the night, sleeping alone. He watches us in the morning, observing our small kindnesses, listening to our language. By the time breakfast is finished, he has decided to become a lover.

We explore. We play. We write long, poetic letters to each other nearly every day. For a while, this feels like freedom. For all of us. We like each other. My husband and Evan become friends. As predictable as projection, I fall in love with Evan. I fall in love with all of us, with the sexy soirees, with the effortless communication, with the three of us walking together under streetlights laughing about our unusual alliance. I'm living a tantric party, an unabashed adventure, a dream that I've wondered about since I read *The Harrad Experiment* at sixteen. The three of us make meals together, and eat them by candlelight, and talk, long hours of talk. There are moments when Evan shows Richard how I respond. We laugh over the strangeness of our situation. We fall asleep talking, and wake up holding each other.

Except this isn't all romance. It feels dangerous, and sometimes difficult. There are times my husband doesn't want me to hang out with Evan, and I go anyway. There are times that Evan asks me to go to his place outside Seattle, and I refuse, knowing Richard wishes not to be alone. Richard and I talk for months about a beach vacation that I want to take with Evan.

"Why do you want to go?" he asks.

"Because I like adventure."

"And you don't get that with me," he says, sad to be left behind.

"I love our life, baby. I can stay home. This doesn't have to happen if you're not ready for it."

"I can't get in the way of your happiness."

And so I pack, and make arrangements, and Richard drives us to the airport, and we all say good-bye.

When we get to the gate, Evan turns to me and says, "I'm sorry that he's hurting so much."

"He'll be fine," I answer, confident that nothing can cause a rift between Richard and me.

"He was crying in the car," Evan says, surprised by my nonchalance.

"No, he wasn't."

"Yeah. He was. I saw his tears in the rearview mirror."

I was too busy going over home matters and discussing how we were going to stay in touch to notice Richard's reaction.

"Oh my God. Shit. I gotta call."

I walk up and down the airport hallways as I talk with Richard, ready to call off the trip.

"I'm okay," Richard insists. "I had a moment."

"A moment that's going to haunt us the rest of our lives?"

"I don't think so."

"This isn't worth it. I can't leave with him if you're not okay."

"Go."

"Really?"

"Make me a promise."

"What?"

"Don't have too much fun?"

I laugh. "I'll call you every day."

Every morning on that trip I sit on the patio in the sunlight, talking to Richard while Evan sleeps into the afternoon. There is little pleasure in being without my husband. The truth is that we have made a life together, and even a beautiful beach destination can't take away the sadness I feel in causing him pain.

While I enjoy the exploration, Richard isn't interested in being with another woman. Clearly, if he had his way, I wouldn't be choosing this route. My husband is saying "yes" to this arrangement because he wants my happiness. I'm alternately guilt-ridden and amazed by his love.

As we go along, we make up the constitution of our country of three. Evan takes other lovers. I take a vacation with each man. We decide it's not safe to come out to our families and friends. We're private to the world and transparent to each other. We experience jealousy and joy. We joke, we misunderstand, we argue, we break up, we leave, we reunite. I never feel shame for what I am doing; neither does my husband.

Somehow, Richard becomes an insightful lover, more expert than he has ever been, all while staying as tender as he really is. My sexual renaissance includes rearranging my thinking about the masculine and the feminine, and my role as the submissive one in my marriage. Richard's gentle-giant spirit offers me room to become less defined by roles, sexual and otherwise. I sense all the ways that I limit my power, and soon I am tracking what pleases me, learning my relationship with my sensual nature.

One day, Evan and I talk about the events that led us to break up for a time, during which he refused to speak with me. I wanted a relationship with someone who had fewer partners; he didn't want to change.

"You had a part in that too," I say.

"What do you mean?"

"I was honest about my problems with your other lovers the last time we separated."

"You were jealous."

"That too. What I'm saying is that I think *both* people in a relationship have a responsibility for its failure."

The conversation drops. I think I was speaking a truism, until he shows up at my door weeks later.

"I never would have reconnected with you if I didn't feel like you had genuine regret for your mistakes," he says.

"I had regret. That's why I apologized."

"You have zero ability for self-examination. None!"

"Look, I'm not saying I wasn't wrong. Maybe you also didn't want to stay for your own reasons."

"We broke up because you weren't being honest about how you felt. And now you're further injuring me by not taking responsibility for that moment."

"I'm trying to . . ."

"You're being false!"

"How do you know what my truth is?"

"I can perceive falseness in others."

He goes on making his case, yelling, criticizing, blaming, until I get so scared of him I grab my shoes, put them on, and go to sit on the front porch until he can calm down. I've never seen him like this, out of control, full of resentment. By the time I come back into the house, I know we won't resolve this.

Richard and I have developed a tolerance for each other's views that allows me to ask bold, even stupid questions. But we've had decades of practice to learn how to withstand conflicts, including holding differing perceptions. I know that I can't expect that in other, less primary relationships in my life. In this moment, I no longer believe I must agree with Evan about the past, or anything. I've discovered that the only person I can betray is myself. I can betray myself by being dishonest with him in order to make him feel better, or I can tell the truth as I see it. When I stop expecting Evan to be something that I want, I can see that I made him into my romantic ideal. But it's myself I desire, the one who creates and risks and loves. When Evan leaves for the second time, there's nothing missing in my marriage; there's nothing missing in me.

"Did I go overboard in doing what I want?" I ask my friend Jack after Evan leaves.

"You have done nothing wrong. Your heart knows everything," Jack responds.

"Lovers don't have to be bound to our stories of each other. I get that. But Evan thinks I'm suffering from self-delusion, that I lack presence."

"If you suddenly couldn't write and were stricken to a hospital bed and no one could visit for a few weeks due to a quarantine, it wouldn't change the reality of what you are. It would simply change 'the story of what Sonya is doing.' This unchanging reality of what you are is the simple presence listening to this sentence."

"I'm this presence regardless of the details of my life," I respond.

"When we were kids, we played tag in the park. Before each game, we would designate a tree to be "Home Base." This is where anyone could go when they got tired of running around, being chased. The simple presence that listens to this sentence is that Home Base. When the game of being someone gets tiring, how wonderful that the default resting place is our true, easy nature. The good news is that the less we leave it, the less chasing and being chased we experience. No right or wrong to playing games. Just nice to know where the real rest is," Jack says.

The next summer, I take a month away from everything and everyone. I return to my beloved Canadian Rockies. I hike every day. I devote myself to a particular range of mountains, one-hundred-million-year-old thrust faults, often with unique, dramatic dipping sedimentary layers. I sense that these particular mountains are essential to my understanding of my own nature. I make a commitment to return to them each year. I hide in the bushes. I roll in the dirt. I lick leaves. I play with sticks and flowers and rocks. I lie naked in the sun. I stay out in the dark. I slide into the stars. I become the moon.

On a day I'm far into the backcountry, in the Slate Range, near Skoki Mountain, after a month of day hikes across rivers, hauling up switchbacks, scrambling over scree slopes, and walking onto ledges I'd previously considered death-defying, I look over the limitless range of mountains. There is no one for miles. The wind slices toward my body, and I feel the sensation of my "self" dropping away from the edges of my physical form and extending, farther and farther. I'm no longer observing the mountains: I've become indistinguishable from them. For hours I hike within that sensibility. Identity dissolves, and I haven't been sent into disarray. Is this what Richard feels like every moment? I find myself a part of something previously unknowable, a state I haven't ever imagined. This experience is outside of my ironic sensibility, and truthfully it is outside of the sentimental one and the tragic one too.

This state feels like _________. (There is no word.) I feel undomesticated, unalterable by a culture. I'm excited to discover what it might be like to live from this place, as fresh as a brain-injured man, as untethered to a past or a future as this breath.

What this state erodes is irony. Like much of my post-modernish generation, I often prefer to view the world and myself through the cultural filter of an ironic view. Over these years of Richard's recuperation, while adapting to burgeoning social networks and media options, I have turned toward a kind of passive form of self-involvement, adopting an unquestioned Facebooking, HBO-sized, Twitterish cool. But Richard's childlike innocence is in sharp contrast to any contained, controlled self-image.

Richard's silence makes me ask: How much of my existence has been about looking without seeing, about reporting without knowing anything? How much have I lived in existential angst, without questioning its tyranny? The reflection of my wounded husband onto my "I"-ness has become part of this cage. Without that reference, I wonder, who would I be?

I wonder who I am. I wonder who he is. I wonder who we are.

I wonder if who I am is who he is.

I wonder if I am anything at all.

For most of a year, Richard listens to the same song by Alexi Murdoch every morning. It's called "Wait," a Nick Drake–like, sparse-guitar-strummed, hauntingly hushed ballad. One day Richard comes upstairs crying and thanks me for waiting for him.

"You waited for me when I was silent and couldn't leave the room."

Sometimes things are mysterious in our relationships, and then we get to see our beloved, and it cracks the heart wide open.

The thing is, I learn so much from this man. I love that he thinks that I waited for him, when all this time, I've been the one slow to understand his mind.

> And if I stumble, and if I stall
> And if I slip now, and if I should fall
> And if I can't be all that I could be
> Will you? Will you wait for me?

Months after the end of our erotic reeducation Richard and I are lying in bed, in the afterglow.

"Would you say our sex life is fulfilling?" I ask him.

"Yeah. Wouldn't you?"

"It is now. What do you think changed?"

"I don't know. I don't know who I was as a lover before."

"I think you're more adept. It doesn't take you a thousand times to learn something," I say.

"True. But I also know what it is to be injured. Perhaps that makes me more sensitive," he says. He pulls the covers over my body.

When we wake, he will make me a cup of tea and I will start dinner. We will spend hours in silence that's no longer uneasy. I will realize that the experiment of Doing What I Want has ended because nothing is unspeakable, nothing has been left outside our home. Everything that we want to bring to our lives happens, or not. But it isn't because we're afraid to come to terms with our desires.

Years after the night Richard died to his former self, we are seated on stools at the Tractor Tavern, surrounded by beers, beards, plaids, braids, boys. I call him Buddha Bear, his secret label, his bedtime name. His hands reach for my bottom. Squeeze. A gesture hidden and overt, the perfect flirt. We lean into each other, starry with the song and the dusk and the delight of this time.

If I silence the obsessive longing that parades like a madcap clown in my mind, Richard is the perfect man for me. My husband shows me that the fundamental nature of being here—on earth, in love, within the sexual experience—is joyful. As long as I know that in the midst of having anything, I don't get to keep it. Enjoying the ephemeral. This is the best definition of sex that I can imagine.

# 21

# wondering

AFTER LIVING THREE years with the brain injury, Richard still expends enormous energy learning to manage his own physical therapy clinic. I take over all other responsibilities so he can be free to rest in the evenings and on the weekends. We enlist a brain injury counselor to help us set up strategies to make social interaction easier. Richard learns how to use "cheat sheets" to preplan conversation topics, how to finesse a day timer to keep track of relationship commitments, and how to initiate conversations. In role-playing sessions, he explores how to initiate sex, understand nonverbal cues, address relationship conflict, and deal with our children's responses to his brain injury. I attend every session so I can become his memory when he forgets. While he learns tools to aid his memory, I'm witnessing his acceptance of his condition. He attempts, falters, tries again. It isn't easy, but he doesn't fight going to the sessions.

When the summer comes, we stop going to counseling in favor of hiking and playing. When we evaluate his progress in the autumn, we decide to look for a brain rehab program that will give us new information on the current state of his disability, as well as provide community support from other people who have experienced a brain injury. Richard doesn't want to be with other brain-injury survivors. He wants to imagine that his injury will go away of its own accord, and on many days, he's effective at faking his way through.

"He looks great!" people say when they run into him on the street.

Managing the clinic is boosting his confidence. Without a solid program to push him past this comfortable plateau in his development, he's going to stay right where he is. That's going to result in unsatisfying personal relationships.

Much of the research on brain injury says that most improvement happens within the first year after the injury. If people move into rehabilitation programs early and find adequate care, they can be functional and contributing members of society. Even our neuropsychologist, Dr. L, said that much of the radical improvement would occur within the first two years. Patients do not "recover" in the sense of returning to their previous lives. Many of Richard's deficits were likely to remain, and my work would be in accepting him as he is.

Still, I've read "The Median Isn't the Message," scientist Stephen Jay Gould's excellent essay on the problems of cancer statistics. Gould took a rational approach to unpacking the polarities inherent in either ignoring the stats or depending on them so wholly that they seem like a death sentence. He approached his own cancer recovery by analyzing median statistics and their variation from the viewpoint of an evolutionary biologist. What he discovered was that certain factors, including an accurate understanding of the death data, as well as personal characteristics like an optimistic personality, increased his statistical likelihood of survival. We're inspired. Just because brain-injury patients land in plateauland doesn't mean that Richard has to. We haven't seen any evidence of permanent stasis. Travel, adventure, body-based therapy, art, and God knows the novel erotic situations I keep throwing at him have helped him make important leaps in functional gain.

Richard doesn't need talk therapy (although I find myself opening up more to friends for counsel and support). Richard's problems are not psychological—they are related to executive function and cognitive difficulties. We contact the University of Washington Medical Center to be referred into the brain injury program. First up, a neuropsychological evaluation for him, and an interview with each of us by Dr. P. We want to know where to start again.

Richard's tests give us a new baseline measurement. What's strong in Richard: effort, involvement, immediate recall, immediate working memory, performing with structure, problem solving, and deductive reasoning. What's severely to moderately impaired: language skills, complex verbal memory (especially spontaneous recall), formal naming, verbal fluency, right-hand sensory discrimination, auditory memory. He is found to have a flat affect, and difficulty with initiation, planning, and carrying out activities. His range, speed, and level of independence with complex information skills are all diminished. He's not depressed. The good news: everything that was an asset before rehab has become stronger. The bad news: the weaknesses have not improved. Richard is using the compensation strategies he has learned to their maximum.

Dr. P writes:

> People with his profile are stoic, conscientious, and tend not to complain much of difficulty. At times of added stress, they're vulnerable to some intensification of cognitive, and physical or behavioral difficulties, which can lead to aggravation of memory, fatigue, and overall social withdrawal. Richard's mild, moderate, or severe areas of neurocognitive and neurobehavioral difficulty are quite consistent with hypoxic injury, and not psychiatric in pattern or nature. At the same time, this man's profound degree of change in overall function and life circumstances, and a personality that tends to minimize or compartmentalize, may be complicating his optimal levels of adjustment.

When Richard hears the recommended treatment program, he blinks away tears. We find out several weeks later, when we read their report, that the University of Washington doctors thought his reaction to his evaluation was sadness about his impairment. When we talk on the phone with Dr. P, I ask to clarify his reaction.

"I asked him why he cried in the office," I tell her. "He wasn't sad. He told me that the reaction that you saw that day is relief. He's relieved that you can help him." There's silence on the other end.

"We will help Richard," Dr. P says.

One week later, he's signed up for cognitive rehab, group therapy, individual therapy, and consults with the lead neurologist.

Just a few months earlier, when we neared the three-year deadline for filing a legal case against the hospital for causing Richard's brain injury, I called our sister-in-law, a lawyer. I wanted to hear what we might be in for if we file a medical malpractice lawsuit. I sat in the dark stairway of our home listening to her tell me how our life will be taken apart, how the justice system can ruin relationships, how there's no guarantee that years of our life won't be wasted in the enormous effort.

"If we do this," I tell Richard, "we're going to have to refuse to let it take over our lives. That means we talk about it only when necessary, we don't get involved in learning about the system, we do what they ask us to do and no more."

"Will you do the work of the case so I can focus on working at my clinic?" he asks.

"Yes," I say, not realizing how many hours of preparation, interviews, and tests it's going to take to be involved in a lawsuit.

When we call Mr. Nace to tell him of our decision to go forward with a lawsuit, he advises that the case will be filed immediately to observe the statute of limitations. We tell him we are clear in our motivations: even though it terrifies us to enter an adversarial system, we wish to be compensated for what was lost when Richard's brain injury diminished his capacities. But we want something else too. We want patients entering the hospital to receive the blood they require, for there never to be a competition for plasma. If it takes legal action for patients to receive uncompromised, life-giving care, then we're willing to be the ones to set things in motion.

"Tricky business," says Mr. Nace. "We're not in control of those kinds of outcomes. A malpractice lawsuit tells the hospital that they're responsible for providing good-quality care, but gives the doctor and the staff the freedom to determine how to do that."

"We can't influence them to change?"

"It could very well be that when the depositions are completed, we have a clear idea of why things happened as they did that night. And once the cause is established, their policies may have to change. But we cannot make it a condition."

We tell our lawyers that we don't want to hear about details of the case unless our attention is essential. We don't want to read depositions; we want as little involvement in the legal functions as the system allows, so we can focus on Richard's healing. Mr. Nace assigns his son Christopher to our case. They begin the vast accrual of information.

Now, everything that we have undergone is open for scrutiny. Once the hospital corporation brings in its high-powered legal team, we're requested to surrender every piece of material that could potentially be relevant to the case. We must send the lawyers every aspect of our history: medical records from his doctors; any paper that mentions his treatment or hospital stay; lists of expenses and bills; every calendar entry since his surgery; every piece of paper and every item of electronic information that mentions the doctor or hospital; all our records related to any therapy or psychiatric visits in our twenty-three-year marriage, including the private notes our therapists wrote about us; every letter written about Richard's treatment, including those private letters sent to and from family, friends, and our community. In the end, I have to hand over copies of all of my journals and notes, including everything I wrote during our stay at the hospital, and for the first years of his treatment.

I learn from friends that in Canada and many other nations, only the specific events of the patient care are admissible in medical malpractice cases. In America, legislation has limited the power of medical malpractice lawsuits; patients are considered to be escalating "frivolous" suits, thus we're subject to greater restrictions than citizens of most other countries. In order to conduct this case and keep our wits about us, we'll have to adapt to becoming more vulnerable than we've ever had to be. And that includes handing over the most intimate details of our lives to a team of lawyers who want to find ways to expose our family.

I read the private letters and journal notes, and cry. I absorb the particulars of those terrible initial months. We go over the five-inch-thick volume of the hospital record to learn the specifics of the course of events on the evening Richard lost consciousness. Until this time, we haven't had much energy to isolate precisely what happened. Every fact of the hours Richard spent in spasms, bleeding, and in restraints on the table in the ICU, every scream, plea, and breakdown as I fought for his life, is written into that record. The surgeon told me that I couldn't come to the ICU the evening after Richard bled out, due to hospital policy. I read his written orders to the staff denying me access to the ICU. Every request for information about Richard's memory problems, every note on my discussions with the nursing staff about his strange mental state, every complaint about his lack of cognitive recovery is noted in the hospital record, in black and white.

One day I come to the kitchen to see Richard sobbing with his head in his hands, the hospital record open on his lap.

"What is it?" I ask.

His finger points to a line in the record. "Wife present at bedside. Every day. Every time they take the notes."

Richard shows me how we might make it through handing our private lives to strangers to judge. We've got nothing to hide. Even our mistakes have been so very human. But I'm not naive enough to believe that the legal world works in this way. The case has its own terms of engagement. We listen to what the lawyers make of us, but we do not allow it to disturb our peace.

We enter one of the most challenging times of our married life: balancing Richard's part-time rehabilitation and part-time work with my responsibilities—the court case, household and family obligations, and the launch of a career as a business coach and writer.

We meet with the team at the University of Washington Medical Center's Brain Injury Rehabilitation Program. Four doctors, a counselor, and a team manager sit in a light-filled boardroom. The doctors and rehab counselor outline a program for Richard. He'll begin with an eight-week cognitive group to help him understand brain injury, and individual rehab psychology to provide support in managing the alterations the brain injury has made in his life. He's also strategizing with the rehab counselor about his new tasks as director of a clinic: marketing to doctors, managing staff, and conducting planning and financial projections.

"The rehab team would like to add in speech and group psychotherapy," the counselor says.

"I'm not ready yet," Richard says.

"He's not trying to avoid the therapy," I say. "It's just that he's absolutely committed to his new role at work, and doesn't want to compromise his job."

"These treatments are not expected to restore lost neurocognitive or neurobehavioral functions," Dr. P tells Richard, "but the use of strategies and new techniques can allow you to function in more effective ways. Actual performance may improve somewhat even if underlying brain functions don't undergo any dramatic further improvement."

We nod our heads. There are no guarantees.

"Why did he end up with both short-term and long-term memory loss?" I ask.

"We think that he may have had a significant response to waking up without his former identity," she says. "Post-traumatic stress disorder can suppress long-term memories, and leave him temporarily or permanently without his history."

"PTSD?" I ask, not able to recognize how this could possibly happen.

"Richard could have been so defined by his former personality that the shock of who he had become after the brain injury caused his memories to disappear."

It's unfathomable that PTSD could have such an impact on his brain that he'd forget his entire past. It becomes a possible story to explain things, but it doesn't actually help us change our situation.

Once a week, Richard goes to a cognitive group program. They study the effects of brain injury, including the deficits that injury to each lobe is apt to cause. He learns about activities to stimulate attention and strategies for reducing distractions. We discover there are times and environments in which Richard can focus (in quiet, with structured routine, at the beginning of the day) and moments in which concentration will prove to be impossible (when fatigued, when he is obsessed by having to get this one thing done). Time management is not an issue for Richard, but his fatigue is constant and overwhelming. His sleep requirements after the brain injury increased dramatically, but rest is even more necessary after he returns to work. When he hits his limit of endurance, he practically falls asleep at the dinner table, just like our children used to do. I learn not to ask for communication at the end of the day, and to do all of our family-related conversations in the morning. Richard also learns to take notes, manage social settings, plan projects, schedule his life and work. He identifies his greatest fears: having to speak to more than one person at a time, and being overly dependent on me. Over the weeks that he takes the class, he becomes more attuned to his deficits. With the help of the instructor, he recognizes that he withdraws because he's afraid of being alone. He resists asking for help. For his homework, he interviews me about changes I see in him that he does not see in himself. I'm way too excited at the chance to weigh in on his personal defects.

We sit in the kitchen. He takes notes while I tell him how it is to be with him.

"You drive way too fast for your brain's slower reaction time."

"I'm a very good driver. A very, very good driver," he says, trying his best Rainman.

I don't smile. "Terrible sense of humor. Put that down," I tease.

"No."

"Okay, here's one. Since the brain injury, you have an enhanced capacity for empathy."

"I do."

"You're obsessive. And occasionally inappropriate."

"How?"

"Grabbing me in front of the kids."

He's blinking twenty times faster than normal.

"And you have some strange physical responses. You went from this flat affect to a fast eye-blink whenever you're emotional."

"Anything else?"

"Obsessive hand-wringing, repetitive touch, social phobias, inability to form friendships, difficulty with technology."

"You didn't have to think."

"I mean, these are things that I notice all the time. What's on your list there?" I point to the form where he's filled in the responses with his strange scratchy handwriting.

"My goals. From before the injury."

"You remember?"

"Climb Mount Rainier. Be promoted to regional manager. Play competitive tennis."

"Baby . . ."

"It's okay."

"What about now? Are you making any new goals?"

He looks at his list. "Stay active. Eat healthy. Keep a balance between work and home life."

To accomplish these goals, he'll have to keep saying "no." As for me, I'm going to have to free myself from the notion that he's going to stop forgetting, or that he's going to find former parts of himself. He's not a warrior. He's more like a mama bear who has been hibernating in the long winter, dazedly awakening to his brood.

I'm curious about Richard's mind, and the ways his changes affect who I think I am. We live as pluralities, all these selves that try to unify under one autobiographical narrative. I'm the high school student and the parent; the nice girl and the unkempt lover; the wild woman and the caregiver. As Whitman said, "I contain multitudes," each self-concept operating from a past or present sense of "I." But there's another self too, the "possible self," the one that represents the notion of who we'd like to become, the things we might do, even who we are afraid to become.

Because Richard's past has so fully disappeared, he also has no reference for what he might be in the future. He is rootless and visionless. If he could have pulled on his old personality and history like a worn coat, he would have. Just to make us happy. But he seems to require a do-over. And because I feel somehow responsible for his reinvention, I have a chance to ask questions that would never have occurred to me: What does it mean to have an identity? Is there an enduring self when the narrative is released? Is there something beyond who we think we are?

We have weekly telephone calls with Joshua and Dylan, which work because these conversations are structured and time-limited. But when they have days or weeks to be with their father, what they're struggling with becomes apparent. It's sorrow over the loss, and confusion over what their family is now. In stressful situations, our daughter is more naturally angry; our son is given to withdrawal. Because in the past I've been the emotional center of the family, their concerns and complaints often come to me. Now that they see their father has become sweet, gentle, and unencumbered by his past, our adult children want to get closer to him. They want to define what their new relationship will be.

It takes me years after the brain injury to begin to speak with Richard about the angry man he used to be, about the cycle of addiction and rage that we kept enacting in our family out of habits learned from our parents. One day, as we walk at Green Lake Park near our home, I tell him about the violence in his past.

"Joshua was insistent upon making his own choices, even if they were destructive. He was skipping school, taking drugs, and physically pushing us around."

"That must have been hard on a man who spent most of his life trying to control his environment," he says. That man. The one he no longer knows.

"Your temper got the best of you. You hurt him," I say, and describe in detail the fights he had with his son.

"How could I have hurt my own child?" Richard asks, tears blocking his view. I pull him to the grass, wait for him to stop crying.

"What do you remember about the violence in your childhood?" I ask him.

"My alcoholic stepfathers spanked me. My uncle beat me with a brush when I didn't bring him his pain pills from the pharmacy. I can recall instances of being hit by others, but not ones of being the hitter."

Richard had a chance to clean up some of his past years ago, when we went to therapy. But he hadn't really come to the importance of vocalizing his part in perpetuating violence before the cancer wiped out his life. For months we walk the park, preparing for Joshua's winter visit.

When they sit in the kitchen together after breakfast, Richard says, "I am so sad that I hurt you. I can't remember those things, but I can be with you as the father that I am now."

Joshua says, "Dad, that man doesn't exist. There is nothing more necessary."

In this new relationship, Joshua and Richard play tennis together and talk about sports and laugh over our son's fine quips. Dylan likes to ask her father questions and go for a beer at the pub and watch movies and talk about ideas. They say this new father feels closer to them than the time-starved, demanding one they knew before.

"Why did you never come to the hospital?" I ask Joshua before he leaves after that visit.

"Losing my dad was the most terrifying thing I could imagine. I couldn't go to any place where that seemed possible."

But there are challenges that come with the power shift in the family. Joshua initially sees his father as being too eager to accommodate my requests—"That poor bastard," Joshua remarks when I ask Richard to do errands for us. Until his dad reassures him, Joshua doesn't understand that Richard's motivated by generosity, that he knows he has a wife who copes with stress by becoming a "control enthusiast," and that he is doing what he wants to do too. When an early essay from this book is published in the *Southern Review*, and I begin blogging about our experiences, Dylan expresses her resentment over the story being in my control. When a memoirist writes about her family, people get pissed. Dylan sends me a letter, written in the form of an essay, shocking at first, that describes her fate:

> My mother is a writer by profession. My father's story has been lost. And so I moved from resenting my father for his lost memories to resenting my mother for her only tactic in also grieving this loss: filling it up with her memories. She was rewriting his story. And I wanted in. In fact, my retaliation was so stealthy that I didn't even know it was happening. My mother and I have a wonderful relationship. And excluding a short time in my early teens where I felt the need to reject her stupid ideals in order to prove my independence, we've always been close. And so when my parents started their blog, I was the person behind the scenes, reaping the benefits. But then when the stories started to come out, I felt a tension in my jaw, a balling of my fist. "What is all of this romantic

> bullshit?!" I screamed inside my own head. In the most cunning of ways, I began to attack my mother's writing.

The words of my child make me aware that I am molding Richard's story as I wish, and that words have impact. I want to be uncompromisingly honest, but this is not my story alone. I have to take into account that all memory is radically subjective and that, when we raise questions about ownership, the story becomes even more complicated. Recent research supports this assertion. Memory can insert things from the present into recollections of the past. It can make us think we fell in love at first sight, when, in truth, we're projecting current feelings into our history. Our memories do not archive events like film footage; we reframe and edit events to create a story to fit our current world. The hippocampus, that untrustworthy film editor, makes the memories we wish to see. Shaping a story is unavoidable.

Later, Dylan will tell me that her essay was written in "classic late-teen sensationalism" to address a deeper awareness: years after Richard's brain injury, she was still coming to terms with the guilt and loss she felt for having left home, and for never really knowing her father at all. She wanted her perspective noted in the family lore.

But perhaps my daughter was right—my stories have had the tinge of "romantic bullshit." There are parts I find dear because of the ways Richard is altered: his innocence and newness, his empathy for the human experience, his crying over anecdotes of people lost and found again. In the early years of the brain injury, romanticizing our story was safer than confronting reality. I needed to capture the potential mystery and excitement of our relationship so I might hold on to its promise. But being with Richard also dashes my idealizations, for the ways that I suppress and disregard my emotional reality reveal themselves in being with a man who cares nothing for making himself something for others.

His brain injury, even though it brings challenges for coping in life and diminished potential for career success, also has an iron imperative: you must wander to find yourself. In that wandering, I lose my religion. I find a silent, steady undercurrent below thoughts, beliefs, concepts. And all of those thoughts—how much I love the former man, how I'll never be in that relationship again—are of the past and the future. What Richard's brain injury provides is an entry to an immaculately fresh present moment. Perhaps the former husband and father disappeared so we can find our way toward this. Perhaps his memory loss—the loss of his association with the past—is not simply trauma, but rather his genius, the daemon enacted upon him.

On a family vacation long after the brain injury, I ask our son, "What's your favorite thing about us?"

"Mum, you see families that are troubled and you see families that are healthy. Rarely do you get to see a family that goes from fucked up to amazing. We got to live inside that remarkable experience."

He's right. We are all of these things.

Alongside the progress Richard makes with his physical therapy practice, and our acceptance of the brain injury, is the truth that Richard has problems that are not being resolved. He still has trouble initiating and maintaining relationships; he struggles to communicate verbally; he has challenges with intimacy of all kinds. Recovery from brain injury is marked by fragility, vulnerability, instability. Without a coherent identity and the purpose, interdependence, and self-management to balance the disruption of the self, the brain-injured enter a liminal state, seeing themselves as neither "me" nor "not me." Richard struggles to find balance between life and work, and even though he improved dramatically in the first few years, he has no access to the executive-thinking skills that were the basis of his former career and the financial support of our family.

For the medical malpractice lawsuit, the effects of the brain injury on Richard, as well as their cause, must be documented and proven. Richard and I fly to the state where the case will be tried, to have him examined by psychologists and neuropsychologists, and to be deposed by lawyers. Our doctors, nurses, lab technicians, hospital staff, therapists, rehab specialists, financial planners, relatives, and children are also deposed. The case will take nearly three years. We don't worry as much about exposing our private lives to strangers who might use the information against us, but we do fear that we will be castigated for bringing the lawsuit. We know the sequence of events that led to Richard being refused blood, and the toll that mismanagement of his care took on his health and life. Now we have to convince ourselves that we are rightful in taking the health-care corporation to court. Because the lawsuit will be grueling, we need to know we are being responsible and acting with integrity.

We learn from our research that the hype about medical malpractice suits is, according to Tom Baker's *The Medical Malpractice Myth*, "urban legend mixed with the occasional true story, supported by selective references to academic studies"; that, including legal fees, insurance costs, and settlement payouts, the cost of medical malpractice suits comes to less than one-half of 1 percent of American health-care spending. Neither are the cases frivolous: 90 percent of all cases show evidence of wrongdoing, courts efficiently throw out baseless cases, and jury awards are not going up. A rise in medical mistakes, not frivolous lawsuits, has been found to be at the basis of increased medical malpractice in the health-care field. In fact, it can be said that the increase in lawsuits has pointed out specific problems in how medical injuries occur. According to Baker, "Lawsuits are the reason that we know what we know about medical mistakes."

Someone has to shoulder the ongoing responsibility for a brain injury, and it's often the patient and the family. We feel the consequences of Richard's injury ought to be shared by the hospital. We could never have caused this event, and we did everything we could to prevent it, even screaming for an intervention to be made on his behalf when the nursing and resident staff were unresponsive. We expect that the surgeon will be absolved in the case, because he could not have prevented the injury. The nick on Richard's stomach happened in the surgery, but the actual cause of the brain injury was the bleeding that remained unaddressed for hours. The surgeon revealed—both to my sister and me in person and in his deposition before the lawyers—that he ought to have been called in the first moments of the catastrophe that evening, not when Richard was near death. It is clear to us that the ICU staff made the mistake, and that the hospital is accountable for failing to do what their own policies indicate is the right thing.

We are compelled through our sense of responsibility to Richard's health, our children's needs, and our awareness of the American values of justice and safety to follow through with the lawsuit. The hospital corporation's lawyers will do everything in their power to discredit us.

One court stenographer, three barristers, Richard, me, and a lot of coffee in a steely, lawyerish meeting room. My husband is being deposed. Many hours, many questions, each one becoming more personal. Whenever Richard cries, the men cringe. The lawyers are best at being adversarial, not at looking at what went wrong in a situation and addressing what needs changing. Oppositional stances do not feel true to us. There's been no experience in our life where a process oriented to combat has had more relevance than one oriented to cooperation. We're out of our league, trying to understand why the corporation's legal team wants information on the state of our marriage, the times we've been to therapy, why we didn't follow conventional Western medicine and instead chose alternative methods to complement Richard's care.

Three months later, when the first phase of the rehab program at University of Washington is completed, and we have made our second trip to do interviews for the case, I write to our lawyer and ask him what his thoughts are about Richard taking a break from all of the rehab activity.

Chris writes us back in his usual plain talk. *The reality is that Richard is working very hard with his therapy while also trying to continue working. If he needs a breather, no one is going to fault him for that. And, again, I can't emphasize enough that you and Richard should be doing what you need to for you guys, not for the litigation.*

That summer, Richard and I make a list of the things we'd like to do if we are awarded a settlement: pay off our mortgage, zero out the kids' student loans, take a small vacation, give to our favorite charities. Other than our home, we have no debt. We have medical insurance and we are oh-so-thankfully healthy. We have each other. We place the list of wishes in the box in which we keep all of our lists, and we forget about the legal case. A few weeks later, I learn that my father is dying. I leave home to be with my mother and father, to set up hospice and help coordinate his ongoing care. Richard meets me there to say good-bye to the man he knew as a father. When my sister comes to stay, Richard and I fly to Banff to hike the wilderness and restore ourselves. By the end of the summer, my father is dead.

After grieving, memorializing, and reconnecting with our family, we're called to a court-ordered mediation, a part of the process we'd expected. It's six years after the surgery and we're clearer than ever about what matters in our lives: authenticity, kindness, love. There isn't any possibility of losing anything. Still, I'm scared. I want to settle rather than have our lives raked over in a weeks-long court case.

I call my therapist friend, who says, "The justice system also works for wayward, bohemian people who live in liberal Seattle."

"Huh?" I say.

"Justice. She works for you too."

"You think?"

And then my friend, who has been a whistleblower in a landmark case, listens while I tell her how I'm feeling optimistic about the judgment, except when I am freaking out about how ridiculous it is to put ourselves through this process, and how sad I am that Richard has to revisit the terror of the hospital, and how I want to come across the table and slap the face of the smartass city lawyer deposing me. Richard and I pack our suitcases, and by the New Year, we sit across a table in a lawyer's office waiting for the whole mad dance to end.

Our lawyer, Chris, introduces us to Eddie, our mediator, who has come out of retirement for this gig. Eddie has silver hair and spectacles and animated gestures that, over the course of the day, escalate from a finger point to a stadium wave.

"He looks like the Planters peanut guy," Richard says, and we smile.

Our lawyer tells us that we will not sit across the table from the opposing lawyers and be interrogated. That part is over. Instead Eddie travels back and forth between two groups: us—two long-married, jet-lagged, less-than-loquacious people and their lawyer; and them—three lawyers, one hospital CEO, one parent company representative of the hospital CEO, one risk-assessment expert, their legal assistants, and several consultants by telephone. Eddie says this is likely to take all day.

He starts the process by giving us some ridiculous number that wouldn't cover the expenses of the legal process, which Chris rejects, threatens to walk away from, and then the gauntlet goes down. In an odd display of what can only be called professional bullshitting, Eddie rushes into our room every fifteen minutes or so, throwing down some piece of "evidence" intended to impugn our characters and prove we are unworthy of any of their hard-earned corporate profits.

"Do you realize you used sketchy alternative medicine to heal him?"

"In the progressive parts of the country, this is called 'complementary medicine.' And we also followed the advice of our neuropsychologist," I retort.

"Not to the letter," Eddie responds.

"Does anyone?"

"People who care about their spouses do. He wasn't treated for months during this period," Eddie says, pointing to the calendar.

I pull my laptop from my bag, open my calendar, read off Richard's therapy appointments, homework assignments, practice sessions.

"Did you make these available to the defense?"

"Every single piece of information," I say.

"Do you realize that a jury in this part of the USA is going to be composed of Republican grandmothers? They'll never understand you," he surmises.

"The justice system also stands for wayward, bohemian people from liberal Seattle," I say.

For most of the day, the mediation goes on like this, cajoling, catastrophizing, smearing, shaming, scorning, nitpicking, demanding, whining. For hours. Until the CEO of the corporation that owns the corporation that owns the hospital calls. Eddie listens to her speak over the phone and reports the message to us.

"She says the surgeon saved his life!"

"We know," we answer.

"For most people, that's enough," Eddie says.

Richard and I look at each other. My husband has said little all day, and now he blinks back tears of gratitude for being given his life. I look closely at Eddie. My gaze says: *You really want to put this gentle, beautiful one on the stand?*

On the whole, it's amusing to parse how we might be judged. I calculate the day's salaries the corporations have paid to those present in the adjoining room (whom we see when we go for coffee breaks), and start to welcome the obvious game of verbal barrage. I'm thankful to have been surrounded in my life by cancer survivors, peace activists, ecofeminists, same-sex-marriage advocates, and rebel artists, people who have taught me about power and its uses. The strange thing about Richard losing his former identity as an eloquent, dashing, smartest-man-in-the-room guy is that now, all of his former personality can be seen for what it was: window dressing. Not wonder.

The other side starts throwing numbers around. Chris asks to take a break and tells us the choice is ours. His firm is willing to go to trial, and if we wish to walk away, there will be no difficult feelings. Everyone leaves us alone. Richard and I sit in silence. I can't find an answer inside about whether we ought to settle. It's like being in France again and not knowing where home is. I have no intuition. Richard looks at me with big eyes and says nothing. I go to the bathroom and call my friend Judith to ask her what she thinks. Her words go into me, but they do not hold. I sit on the floor of the bathroom and talk to my dead father.

"Hey, I know it's a little soon to be involving you down here again, but I need your help. Can you knock some heads together and get this done?" I say to the walls.

When I come back to the office, Richard and Chris are sitting together.

"Have you made a decision?" Chris asks.

"I don't know what to do," I tell him. I'm scared that I'm going to do nothing and regret it for the rest of my life.

Eddie bounces in the door, his tie askew, and yells out a number. "Final offer!"

Richard looks up at him, and says, "Tell him if they can get to $___, we've got a deal."

I look at my man a long, long time. Not only are these words the most he's said all day, this is also the first time he's made a strong decision since the brain injury. I start laughing, which makes Chris look at me like I've gone a little crazy.

"You okay with this deal, Sonya?" he asks.

"Looks like he's ready to settle," I say.

Less than five minutes later we have a typed, notarized contract to sign, and we're shaking hands and preparing to go home.

In the taxi on the way back to the hotel, I ask Richard, "How were you able to be so definitive?"

He shrugs his shoulders.

I get it. The big mystery. That's what we're living in.

Nearly ten years after Richard was diagnosed with pseudomyxoma peritonei, we learn through the *Washington Post* that the experimental treatment that saved his life is now considered the standard of care for long-term survival. A decade later, the cell pathology is still often misdiagnosed and the treatment methods are misunderstood. No one knows the cancer's cause. Far too many people suffer early deaths from not receiving a diagnosis, or not being referred to a PMP specialist. This disease is not curable, but it is treatable. People are living years and years. Richard's yearly CT scans come back free of disease. His death is as certain and unpredictable as my own.

When we return to Seattle after the settlement, we start living like he's cancer-free. We've been married for thirty years and we decide to have a blind date. We meet at the art museum downtown to enact the roles of two people who have not known each other. Richard is waiting for me when I arrive. At first glance, I'm relieved that I'm attracted to him, like the pretending has begun some way of seeing that I was incapable of when he was a slurping ape over a cereal bowl at breakfast.

We walk around the exhibit, watching each other. I'm pretty sure he's checking out my curves. I observe what art tends to captivate him. When we sit down to dinner in the restaurant, he orders for us. He looks at me directly. He has fine manners. He leans across the table.

"What are you drawn to in a partner?" he asks.

This brain-injured man, the one who forgot our life, the one with few desires, the one whom I have been teaching to become a lover again, is teaching me what it is to imagine with all your heart. Everything he wanted to keep—identity, objects, status, strength, allies, the past, and the future—has been lost. Dying for a time in surgery showed him that lives are impermanent too. He has taken me into his irrefutable truth: nothing I am in any moment will remain.

Like most of us, I have had many false selves that evolved out of desperate refusals to meet *this, this right here, right now as it is*. Sufferer, sweetheart, scapegoat, spiritual scout. My husband's willingness to meet the conditions of his life has altered our family and loved ones. It has freed us from the tyranny of our story. The man I have known for decades, who is also the man I have never known, reaches across the table to take my hand.

"What do you love about your life?" he asks.

The story of the family we created once—with all of its rage, shame, mistakes—flashes through my body, and then I remember there is nothing to prove with him, or with others, or here. I won't know who I'll be until I give up seeking who I will be. I take his hand. For the first time I answer his words with silence.

But this is what I'm thinking. We are all storytellers. We remember. Or we think we remember. Every day we wake up and we create a story about who we are. We create ourselves from the remnants of our past, a past that exists as we imagine it to be. Before we raise our heads from the pillow, we fix our beliefs in our memory, and we construct our remembered roles—child, parent, lover, worker—and we thrust our expectant bodies out of bed.

But neither history nor our memories are reliable. Our minds influence not only the probable future but also the remembered past. Our very biology makes this so. Our stories do not emerge exactly the way that they happened. They are pieces, collages, mosaics, found objects, assemblages. Montaigne said, "Painting myself for others, I have painted my inward self with colors clearer than my original ones. I have no more made my book than my book has made me." Turns out, the only thing reliable about the past is our insistence that it was so, a drunk claiming he can drive.

This story that Richard and I created together has been read (in part) by our children. Over the years, I've listened to dozens of therapists and medical professionals and healers tell me their opinion about what happened. We've sat with friends and family who have their own experience and ideas about what happened in our lives. I've read a hundred books on memory and identity, and followed the works of brain scientists plumbing this territory. I've interviewed many people—teachers and therapists and mystics—who specialize in the thought-created narratives we tell about ourselves. I've had conversations with my husband that encourage me to look more deeply at what I think I know.

"What do you remember about your time in the hospital?" I ask my husband, years after the surgery.

"I remember waking up," he says, then pauses. "Wait. That's a lie. I've been told that I woke up and, like many aspects of my life, it became my story."

"When did you come to?"

"I'm walking down the hallway with you. I look over, and you're there."

"That was ten days after you were awake, talking with me."

"Yeah. That's how it is."

The tale you have read here has been crafted by my memories, and also by my asking Richard to sit in silence with a question until some memory emerged. Even then, many of these vignettes are my recollections. I'm the one who writes things down. Sometimes I read the story to Richard to see if I have imagined correctly. The thing is, how would I know if I hadn't imagined accurately? The man wants to agree with me. That's how his love extends. His actual memory comes and goes. So does mine. So does yours. We are all making this up, even though the narrative form pretends that our life events are cohesive and understandable. Our stories are at best mash-ups: they point to things; they are not the thing.

After the settlement of the medical malpractice case, we take out our box of lists and do everything we said we were going to do. We give away money, pay off the house, put some funds in a savings account for travel.

"Is there anything left to do? Anyone left to forgive?" a friend asks Richard.

"One of the things that weighs on me is trying to remember my childhood. I've always identified with my mother before the brain injury. Didn't know my father at all."

Richard's military father and bohemian mother divorced when he was a toddler. His parents never saw each other again. Once, when Richard was eighteen, his father dropped by the house on his way across Canada with his new, younger family. Richard was home alone. They stayed to use the bathroom, and then they were gone.

"What's there to do?" I ask.

"I think I need to forgive my father for not staying in our lives," Richard says.

Other than Christmas and birthday cards with five-dollar bills tucked inside, Richard's father never tried to get in touch with him. We'd always wondered how he could separate himself from his family. After fifty years of silence, Richard works up the courage to call his father. He's a ferry ride away, in Victoria, British Columbia, but he doesn't want to meet his son.

"I'm not good company," Richard's father says. "I don't want you and your wife to go out of your way."

Richard insists that we visit.

We take the ferry to Victoria, planning to camp for the night at a city park. But first we arrive at his father's tidy suburban home.

"How you doing?" I ask Richard when we park out front.

"Apprehensive," Richard says. "I have no memory of this man, and no relationship with him. So I'm not sure why."

We're surprised at the man who opens the door. He is five foot eight to Richard's six foot four. He offers a shy smile and invites us into his house. When Richard hugs him, his father steps back. Then he leads us into his traditional living room, which is dark and lonely. We ask questions about the family. He shows us pictures of his parents, tells us about his Mexican mother and German father. He cries when he speaks about the death of his second wife, who passed two years ago. He tells us of the many regrets he's had about his life.

"What about your marriage to my mother?" Richard asks.

"The marriage was a mistake. We were not well suited as a couple," he says, looking sad.

Richard looks across to me, takes a deep breath. He's going to ask the question he's been wanting to for years: "Why did you divorce?"

The reply is one we never expected.

"There was a question as to whether all three of you children were mine," the man says.

Richard and I are stunned. Our host goes to find some letters from the family. I walk across the room to the couch where Richard has been sitting, and I kiss the top of his head. We talk about trival things for another fifteen minutes, and then we leave.

We drive across town, set up our tent, make a fire, then sit at our campsite eating s'mores and wondering what to do with the information. Clearly Richard's younger brother is his father's child because they look alike. It's Richard and his sister who don't look like the paternal side.

Months later, Richard is ready to talk with his sister about that day.

"Richard, I've been holding this secret for decades," she says, over the phone, a country away. "Mum revealed it before she died. She didn't mean to, it just came out. You aren't his."

Richard cries, looks out toward the bamboo lining the yard.

"Does anyone know who my father is?"

"Not a word from anyone. It could be one of Dad's friends . . ."

When Richard puts down the phone, we walk over to Green Lake, the park near our home, and watch the ducklings form a trail behind their mother.

"Damn, baby, life keeps sliding the rug right out from under you."

"You know, I'm okay."

"Are you going to try and find him?"

"I've never associated myself with having a father. My mother raised me, taught me how to make my way in the world. I don't need any more than that."

The regretful man who never raised him, who knows Richard isn't his child, keeps sending the Christmas cards. Signed *Dad*.

Later that year, Richard says, "Let's go somewhere for your fiftieth birthday."

Because we've made it through the brain injury and all of its tricky requirements, I want to do something frightening, to be taken over by something bigger than I am. Richard's recovery has been a shared fire-walk, but I want a trip that will shred my psychic comfort by making me rethink everything I think I know about who I am.

"I've always wanted to go to India," I say, terrified. Would I lose my mind in India? And would I want to live in that shocking emptiness? I'm drawn to and daunted by the thought of journeying to the land of Kali and Saraswati and Mirabai. A Google search later, we discover that the world's largest act of faith, the Kumbh Mela, is happening within two days of my birthday. We can't find any compelling reason to say no.

This year, the Kumbh Mela will take place in Haridwar, where the River Ganga enters the plains from the Himalayas. The Kumbh Mela (Festival of the Pot of Nectar) is the largest human gathering in the world. We've heard estimates of eighty million people attending over four months, with half that number present at the festival's pinnacle. The religious festival draws devotees, sadhus, rishiks, yogis, and tourists from almost every corner of the world. We will be present for the opening *snans* (or baths).

Hindus believe that the waters of the Ganges turn into nectar on the auspicious occasion of Kumbh Mela. And that a holy dip in the divine waters of Ganga eliminates all the evil and past sins from an individual's life. Bathing at Har ki Pauri Ghat during the festival is said to purify the inner self. I don't know if any of these things are true. The last few years have only made me leery of the notion of self-realization. What is exciting about the Kumbh Mela is the chance to be taken on a strange journey, to give up thinking, and instead to experience.

On the day before we are to take the bath at the Kumbh Mela, we discover that the town's security situation has changed. Our guide, Parikshit Joshi, drives us around the site so we can see what we are in for. The main ghat will be inundated with sadhus and temple leaders, who bring their devotees by the thousands. We'll be hiking toward Ashti Parvath Ghat, directly south and across the Ganges River from where the sadhus will immerse themselves before dawn the morning of January 14, the first bath of the months-long festival. Because of the need for high security in the region, twenty thousand members of the Indian military, state police, and Rapid Action Force have been brought in to suppress potential riots and terrorist threats. We soon learn that plans may change hour to hour, and that we won't know until the day of the events what our approach to the site might be.

Mr. Joshi points to the long, fenced, narrow bridges and tells me that if the procession becomes too crowded, security will herd people onto the bridges and then lock the gates, sometimes for hours, until the bathers at the ghats move toward their homes and tents. My husband takes my hand. I have been claustrophobic for years. I avoid elevators, crowds, and locked rooms.

"Think you can do it?" Richard asks. I close my eyes and listen for an inner voice I have learned to trust. Could I overcome my fear if I got locked on a bridge? I look to the man sitting next to me, whom I have been loving for three decades. Something beyond our intellectual understanding has brought us to the Kumbh Mela, and I want to complete the ritual, to understand something about why we have come. I nod, feeling safe, thinking that neither of these men will allow us into a foolhardy situation. When our guide asks us when we'd like to go, our first impulse tells us to get to the Kumbh Mela at the beginning. We must get a quick sleep so we can leave the hotel at four in the morning, to be at the ghats when the sadhus are in attendance, likely one of the busiest times of the festival.

Pilgrims walk many days to get here, often with bare feet or worn sandals. The weather is unseasonably cold in Haridwar, four degrees Celsius at night, and so this is not an easy journey. Many families save for years to come for a bath in their beloved Mother Ganga.

In the hours before dawn, we walk through the dark. No vehicles or bicycles are allowed, only those travelers on foot, and we walk down alleys so black that I cannot see the ground. People emerge from alleys and buildings; people come from everywhere, chanting, moving quickly in the blackness, no lamps or lanterns. Although I have prepared myself for what it might be like to be noticed as Westerners—we've had a few days of acclimating to being the new ones in town—I have no idea to what degree those effects will be amplified at the Kumbh Mela. According to our guide, people coming from rural areas may not have seen many Westerners except in the media. As far as I can tell, I am the only Western woman among the millions who have come this morning.

When we arrive at the ghat, we look at the roiling water. We take off our jackets. Richard removes his pants and shirt, strips to his underwear, as the other men do. I become aware of the people around us, watching us while they make their own preparations. I walk down the stone steps into the freezing river just as I see my husband's body fall below the churning waters. He holds on to the iron rail to keep himself from floating away, for the current is strong. I drop my hands into the river and pour the stream over my head, my skirt flowing around me like a blood-red pool in the steel-grey water. A statue of the destroyer god Shiva glows in the distance and lights the heads of other bathers, who are falling, rising, jumping, bowing, shivering, stilling.

I splash a river salutation. In my mind: *Ganges! Ganges!* as the loudspeaker blares instructions in Hindi. Over my body flow the ashes of the dead. Where we stand in the river is the place of last night's puja, a ceremony with fire and flowers that was chanted by a young man and a priest as they performed the last rites, then set the relative's ashes into the water. I think I am swimming through souls. And then I wonder if I believe in the soul anymore. But there's a beauty in being here, like what Mirabai has written:

> I came for the sake of love-devotion;
> seeing the world, I wept.

We towel off, and then we walk around the great display of humanity milling upon makeshift bridges, the loudspeakers blasting instructions, everyone still in the shadows. My hair and skirt are wet from the dip, and my feet are bright red from the cold. Around my shoulders I clench a saffron shawl for warmth. Before we leave the ghats, I ask for a moment to offer my gratitude for everything we have been through together, for Richard surviving the cancer and its challenging treatment, for the brain injury that separated us from who we thought we were, for our children who have learned to be transparent and safe too, for always being taken care of, especially when we were frightened.

I'm not thanking any God, because all of my gods are falling away. Just as I've learned that love doesn't count on anyone's participation, I no longer need any other to be at home here. No husband, no lover, no children, no God, no Buddha, no mama, no Mother Nature, no Jesus, no Mary and Joseph, no Allah, no Rama, no Krishna. No teachers. No gurus. No Byron Katie, no Eckhart Tolle, no modern-day masters, not even Science. There's no one coming to save me. I'm alone with the experience of my life. I bend toward the river and lift the water to my head, my lips, my heart.

To forget is not to fail. Forgetting is memory's raison d'être. "My dreams are like your vigils," says the man in Jorge Luis Borges's "Funes, the Memorious," who has acquired the gift and burden of never forgetting. The man dies of congestion from holding on to useless details. To know what is worth keeping, we have to be willing to let go of what is irrelevant; for us, it's the myth that we need anything to be different in order to be at peace.

My husband isn't "the one," as people like to say in their love stories. Although I've spent my life as his scout—seeking answers through romance, religion, expansive substances, spiritual practices, nature, sex, therapy, words—this life as it is happening, this story beyond my control, keeps killing my ideas about it. Not only am I tired of wanting understanding, but also I'm exhausted in my search. This exhaustion makes me pause.

We stop expecting to be happy. We do things we enjoy. I give up the role of the caregiver; he is not the survivor. I stop trying to fix him, or me. I stop trying to "wake up." When I examine myself honestly, I see that the desire for "awakening" is a desire to transcend reality and separate myself from others who are not "awakened."

Somewhere along the way, we have gone from railing against disease to accepting it. In our acceptance of his condition, we do not ignore his care. We have the best doctor and treatment possible for this orphan ailment. Every year, Richard gets rigorous checkups. We eat nutritious foods, exercise regularly, and limit our stress. But we stop fighting cancer. We stop using the language of commercial cancer: the battle, the fight, the struggle. We realize that humans tend to heal when they're at peace, rather than at war. His calm is life-giving, to him and to those of us caring for him. There is no race for the cure. Reality is the cure.

I am no longer hopeful that the old Richard will return. The evolution of his illness has taken my hope, and not in a manner that is without joy. I no longer want to be someone who imagines a better future, someone yearning for things to be different, someone who hopes her way into missing what perfection is, right here, in her face.

My husband's memories continue to return. Not whole or instantly, as in some Hollywood version, but slowly, through the stories we tell him over and over; through images, and sounds, and tastes, history is woven back into consciousness. Even with the help of what seems like a hundred therapists, some memories hold, while others drop like useless stitches. Our family accepts what has been released by his mind: the ability to multitask, much of the past, the desire to communicate. And we adore what returns: the loving man, the generous man, the man who can fulfill his work as a healer. In our reconstruction of his life we learn about remembrance: it is communal and powerful. And it is also solitary and ephemeral.

Our stories do not include prognosis; we stay rooted in love, we feel more than report. Our lives are rich in folklore and secrets. We refuse stories that don't include the hot of tears on the cheek, the song of a street protest, the scream of a child's nightmare, the slick of saliva on skin, the smell of jasmine or sex or apples or sickness, the plain diaphanousness of ghosts, the jolt of a question harkened. We have not kept genealogies, archives, first editions; our stories are passed down in festivals and barbecues, in ordinary objects like blankets, Bibles, ice-cream buckets. There are no memorials to birthing, grieving, getting by. There are no markers to dreams or inspiration or forgiveness, for unlike battles, they occur in the most unlikely places.

Still, we love.

We awake.

We forget.

We begin.

There is no "we" here. I cannot ever know if I experience Richard for who he is to himself. I can only know my interpretation. The work in my life is to come to a brave self-awareness. Even when I love him, even when I adore my memories of him, even when I cherish my idea of a future with him, I am only in relationship with myself. This self who does not really remember, but instead imposes a narrative line upon gaps, images, sensations. I began this journey as the woman who wondered who the man was who arrived fresh from death, swaddled in gentleness and empathy and silence. Now I wonder who I am. I wonder without the desire to know. I wonder at the beauty of *this*. This wondrous life.

# epilogue

WE THINK WE have seen everything. Until one midnight when the light comes into our bedroom and fills everything with a blaze of lightning and snow and cosmic latte. As the bedroom goes dark we say, "Did you see that?" at exactly the same time. All the things the light could have been—a hall bulb exploding, a plane landing, a UFO peeping, a neighbor teasing, a wire shorting, the moon eclipsing—are discussed and eliminated. We can imagine little else being the source of the light, and so we close our eyes and we sleep.

Four months later, the light shows up in our bedroom again. The room is saturated in brilliance for mere blinks of an eye. By then, sick of finding logic in cancer and identities and death, we grow tired of imagining reasons for the light too. We say, "Wow, that was something!" and "Must be a mystery." We go around as if we aren't the kind of people who have seen this light. We stop insisting it happened just like this.

# acknowledgments

THIS STORY WOULD not exist without my husband, Richard, for he gave me the privilege of creating us on the page. Nor would I be the woman I am without his undying love. He was a collaborator, writing impressions of his experiences and reading every version of this work (usually with tears in his eyes). He was my patron and my inspiration, providing physical and emotional sustenance for our entire family. We did this together.

Whenever people asked how the revision process was going, I told them I was working with my "dream" editor, Tony Perez of Tin House Books. Ours was a collaborative endeavor that included my longed-for literary conversation and his ability to gently persuade me to deepen difficult scenes. I remain in awe of his ability to refine my sentences and to win me over to the serial comma. That the world still has room for literary icons like Tin House gives me hope for the future of books.

Anne Horowitz is a detail-driven copy editor who made me more thoughtful of my word choices and vastly improved my sentences. I'm so thankful for her influence on this text.

Waverly Fitzgerald was an early editor of this book, and she has become a friend whose rigor and advice I value enormously. I can't thank her enough for leading me in the right direction.

Priscilla Long has been my mentor for the past six years. Without her input on discipline, grammar, sentences—all the ways she encourages virtuoso writing in her classes and in her book, *The Writer's Portable Mentor*—I couldn't have done the hard work.

Researcher Renee Bellinger contributed her expertise to the Notes section. We are fellow caregivers of spouses with PMP, and her loving attention extended beyond source- and fact-checking to real compassion and understanding of what it means to live with a rare cancer.

Of course, very little of this would have happened without the faith of Victoria Skurnick of Levine Greenberg Rostan Literary Agency. Victoria helped me see this work as a book about relationship, and educated me about the publishing world, and I'm so happy for her guidance, and the fine work of Lindsey Edgecomb too.

Nanci McCloskey and Meg Cassidy of Tin House's marketing team helped me get this book to its readers, and their thoughtful consideration of its themes helped me give opportunities for others, especially those wounded by cancer, brain injury, and PTSD, to have their stories heard. Thank you.

I have so much gratitude for the early readers of this book, for their encouragement, evaluation, and support. Thank you Sheila Belanger, Jack Saturday, Carole Harmon, and Anne Douglas. Warren Etheredge did the equivalent of treading water endlessly while waiting for me to jump from a very high cliff. And Laurie Wagner of Wild Writing held my hand when I was skittish about including all of me in this book. Oh my God, I thank you forever for your friendship.

The women in my writing groups were fearless and thorough in helping me tell an honest story. Debra Carlson and I shared our thoughts about writing, children, relationships, and wishes for over a decade, and I appreciate her compassion for the roller coaster that was this book coming into existence. Lisa Whipple asks the kinds of direct questions you want from a writing colleague and a wisecracking friend, and her terrific editing improved many scenes. The writers of the Advanced Short Forms Seminar offered the kind of grace, warmth, and critique essential to my development. Likewise Melissa Layer, June Blue Spruce, Angela Mercy, Nan Macy, and Katie Nelson were advocates in a writing group that kept me company during years of writing.

Excerpts from this memoir have appeared in various literary magazines. *Brevity*'s "Ceiling or Sky? Female Nonfictions after the VIDA Count" brought my work to the attention of people who wouldn't have found me otherwise, including George E. Miller of *The Prentice Hall Reader*. Thanks to Dinty Moore, Dr. Miller, and guest editors Barrie Jean Borich, Susanne Antonetta, and Joy Castro. Your support was instrumental in helping me launch a career.

I'd also like to extend my gratitude to Bret Lott, who selected an early excerpt from this story for the *Southern Review*. Your letter gave me the strength to continue when the writing felt like a madness.

Fish Publishing honored an excerpt from this book in its international memoir competition, judged by David Shields, and I'm happy for the recognition at a time when the form of the book was changing.

I'm lucky to live in a city in which essayists and memoirists specialize in some of the same territory covered in this book. Suzanne Morrison spent hours talking through ideas and sharing her relationship to the personal story form. Likewise, Claire Dederer, Nicole Hardy, and Brian McGuigan lent their time and expertise.

Seattle's writing community luckily includes the magnificent Hugo House, which funds a writer-in-residence. Ryan Boudinot saw an early essay and told me he thought I could make this a book. Peter Mountford introduced me to Tin House and ensured that I had what I needed to negotiate a changing publishing world. I love his books; even more so his generous nature that extends to the writing community everywhere. We're lucky to have him in Seattle.

For Artist Trust, which gave me a grant to complete the early stage of this work, much appreciation. It gave me time from the day job to get the momentum going.

For a writer, Seattle is the luckiest place to live because its public library makes available research assistants twenty-four hours a day, seven days a week. All the researchers at Ask a Librarian (who prefer not to be named), I appreciate your resources.

I'm indebted to everyone who has supported my work: the audiences at Cheap Beer & Prose, readers of my essays, and you, reader, who have completed this work through your engagement.

The writing here began in a journal that I scrawled in at the hospital, to try to make sense of what was happening. In the decade that followed, so many people provided emotional and material support to us, offering everything from the comfort of their homes to their research acumen. For a few years, we counted on the generosity of friends, family, and strangers. To you who kept us fed, sheltered, healthy, and sane, our deep gratitude.

To all the doctors—and in twelve years there's been a number of you—and to the skilled nurses, therapists, healers, and health-care workers who supported us in the surgeries and treatments, thank you. To the surgeon we can't name for legal reasons, thank you for Richard's life. We'd like to especially acknowledge Dr. Lechuga of the Neurobehavioral Clinic and Dr. Mary Pepping, since retired from the University of Washington Medical Center's Brain Injury Rehabilitation Program. Without their patience, education, and expertise in rehab medicine, Richard wouldn't have had a chance to be useful, and we wouldn't have understood our situation. Healers Deena Metzger and Valerie Wolf were pivotal for support and understanding in the early stages of the brain injury. Included in this group are Chris Nace and his family, who became our friends as they helped us argue a hospital's error through a challenging legal process, which hopefully changed policies for future patients. Thanks for your wisdom.

Thank you to cancer survivors, people with TBI, PTSD, and those enduring challenges with memory, and their families. Many of you inspired us along the way, and we're so grateful for your care.

Sometimes you don't know where to go, and you count on the ones you've known forever to make a way. My childhood friend Wendy Richardson never turned away from us; she introduced us to Suzi Bliss, who gave us a place to live and a way for me to make a meaningful contribution. Poet Maya Stein introduced me to her father, David, who offered us an ancient water mill in France, a place so magical that our time there was transcendent in experience and in memory. Lifelong friends the Harmon Hutchings family,

Carole, Julia, and Sebastian, provided their apartment for two retreats in the mountains, where I was able to find the solitude I needed to confront some challenging self-reflections. We couldn't have flourished without such wise allies and friends.

After I moved to Seattle, I made friends with Trey Gunn, and once a week, usually with barbecue, we talked in my kitchen about creativity, art, and trying to make money. He's the best kind of friend, who supported this work by making me braver.

Pamela Grace has the kind of wit and depth that help you cut through your own nonsense. She's been a confidante, a writing colleague, and someone who reminded me that I have no reputation to manage. I can't thank her enough for helping me develop the tools to create an enduring relationship.

Judith Laxer is a gardener of the spirit, the kind of friend who tracked me when my husband couldn't. She read manuscripts, asked great questions, and listened to rants and tears when called upon. I adore her.

Our families were there for us in some dark days in and out of the hospital. My father died during the writing of this book, but he was proud of the essays published along the way and encouraged me to keep going. Thanks to my mother, our siblings Christie, Shelley, Joe, Russ, Robyn, and our entire extended clan.

Our children were shaped by these years and, being artists themselves, have asked the kinds of questions that helped us understand our story in fresh ways. Joshua and Dylan, it's our joy to spend this wondrous, wild era with you.

# notes

## PART ONE

### 1: waking

*5 in the hospital lobby* The name of the hospital is not mentioned according to the terms of a 2009 settlement that prevents us from naming the parties.

*6 rare disease* A rare or orphan disease has different definitions in different cultures. In America, it means a disease that afflicts one in 1,500 people; in Europe, one in 2,000. Richard's rare cancer, at the time of its discovery, afflicted about one in a million people. Global Genes estimates that three hundred million people worldwide have a rare disease. Statistics are available through the National Institutes of Health, Office of Rare Diseases Research.

*6 the warrior Boudica* Boudica was the queen of a Celtic tribe circa AD 60 who led an uprising against the Roman Empire. Though she was nearly forgotten by the Middle Ages, Shakespeare's contemporaries resurrected her image, and she has been referenced in songs, plays, poems, books, films, and yes, even video games, since then.

*6 pseudomyxoma peritonei (PMP)* Although the first case of PMP was diagnosed in 1842, it is still routinely misdiagnosed. Most medical definitions state that PMP is characterized by mucinous ascites resulting from rupture of a mucin-producing neoplasm, typically originating in the appendix. The cancer rarely spreads through the lymph glands or the blood.

Everyone untreated dies, usually from bowel obstruction. At the time of Richard's surgery, the pathology and best treatment were widely debated. An overview of this debate can be found in Eric Nakakura, "Pseudomyxoma Peritonei: More Questions Than Answers," *Journal of Clinical Oncology* 30, no. 20 (July 2012): 2429–30, doi: 10.1200/JCO.2012.42.3764.

7 *cytoreduction with hyperthermic intraperitoneal chemotherapy (HIPEC)* Also called hyperthermic chemoperfusion, this process involves a chemotherapy bath of a chemical solution heated to 107–109 degrees Fahrenheit and delivered into the abdominal cavity, where it penetrates the diseased tissue directly. HIPEC was called the "gold standard" for PMP patients as early as 2009, but in 2003, little data had been collected on the treatment. See Terence C. Chua et al., "Early- and Long-Term Outcome Data of Patients with Pseudomyxoma Peritonei from Appendiceal Origin Treated by a Strategy of Cytoreductive Surgery and Hyperthermic Intraperitoneal Chemotherapy," *Journal of Clinical Oncology* 30, no. 20 (May 2012): 2449–56, doi: 10.1200/JCO.2011.39.7166.

7 *MOAS, for Mother of All Surgeries* This term was coined by the spouse of an appendix cancer patient. "Glossary of Terms," *Pseudomyxoma Survivor*, http://www.pseudomyxomasurvivor.org/glossary.html.

8 *five-year survival rate* My numbers here are based on a 1994 study of debulking and systemic/intraperitoneal chemotherapy, one of the few papers available to us at the time: D. B. Gough et al., "Pseudomyxoma Peritonei. Long-Term Patient Survival with an Aggressive Regional Approach," *Annals of Surgery* 219, no. 2 (February 1994): 112–19, http://www.ncbi.nlm.nih.gov/pmc/articles/PMC1243112/.

Estimates of survival rates in 2003 varied widely, since research was scarce. One report said, "Overall survival at 1 and 3 years was 61% and 33%, respectively. With median follow-up of 52 months, median overall survival was 16 months" (Perry Shen et al., "Factors Predicting Survival after Intraperitoneal Hyperthermic Chemotherapy with Mitomycin C after Cytoreductive Surgery for Patients with Peritoneal Carcinomatosis," *Archives of Surgery* 138, no. 1 (January 2003): 26–33, doi: 10.1001/archsurg.138.1.26).

Morbidity rates were also analyzed in Z. Güner et al., "Cytoreductive Surgery and Intraperitoneal Chemotherapy for Pseudomyxoma Peritonei," *International Journal of Colorectal Disease* 20, no. 2 (March 2005): 155–60, http://www.ncbi.nlm.nih.gov/pubmed/15503065.

More recently, survival rates have been analyzed as follows: "Favorable results with combined modality treatment have been achieved for patients with benign disease (DPAM) and complete cytoreduction, with 5- and 10-year survival rates of approximately 75%–100% and 68%, respectively. However, patients with malignant disease (PMCA) or intermediate disease (PMCA-I) showed a significantly worse prognosis, with 5- and 10-year survival rates, respectively, of 50% and 21% for PMCA-I and 14% and 3% for PMCA. Patients with DPAM seem to benefit most from this approach. However, it remains controversial whether patients with PMCA benefit from this aggressive treatment. Moreover, completeness of cytoreduction has additional prognostic value and is strongly associated with extent of disease. Patients with extensive PMP are prone to incomplete cytoreduction and a complicated recovery." (Thomas Winder and Heinz-Josef Lenz, "Mucinous Adenocarcinomas with Intra-Abdominal Dessemination: A Review of Current Therapy," *Oncologist* 15, no. 8 (July 2010): 836–44, doi: 10.1634/theoncologist.2010-0052.)

9 *Richard's physical therapy company* Richard worked for Physiotherapy Associates, owned in 2003 by Stryker Corporation, a company that specializes in medical equipment.

10 *send us books* At the top of the list of books Richard thought he'd read at the hospital was *The Odyssey*.

11 *Richard has either* A concise evaluation of the factors related to the pathology of DPAM and PMCA, and the confusion around their biology and prognosis, can be found in Nakakura, "Pseudomyxoma Peritonei."

12 *By 7:20, his blood pressure* The timing of events in the ICU is confirmed by the hospital record and by subsequent interviews with nurses and resident interns on staff that evening.

## 2: compatriots

16 *Richard lived on Blue Mountain* Jozo Weider founded Blue Mountain in 1941, and the Weider family kept primary ownership until 2014, when they sold their shares to Intrawest. The 1970s were a period of

major expansion for the ski resort. Blue Mountain is now the third busiest ski resort in Canada.

19 *heart beating through my Wonderbra* Wonderbra was developed in Canada by the Canadian Lady Corset Company. Though the popular push-up style wouldn't be introduced in the United States until 1994, Canadian women have been donning its underwired perfection since 1961.

## 3: leaving

28 *"He's coding," Christie says* "Coding" is medical slang for the use of a crash cart or code cart during a cardiopulmonary arrest or other emergency requiring resuscitation and a coordinated all-hands-on-deck response on the part of medical personnel. *The Concise Dictionary of Modern Medicine* by J.C. Segen.

## 4: quilt

29 *walked the Bruce Trail* This trail, which follows the edge of the Niagara Escarpment, extends for over five hundred miles from Tobermory to Queenston, Ontario, including the areas around Blue Mountain, Georgian Bay, and Lake Ontario. See http://brucetrail.org/.

31 *graduated from high school* Ontario high school students choosing to enter college typically attended high school for five years. The final year, grade thirteen, represented a preparatory year before university. This practice was abolished by the province in 2003, to save money.

32 *a hundred thousand fans at Canada Jam* Canada Jam was an eighteen-hour concert held on August 26, 1978, in Mosport Park, east of Toronto. It was the biggest music event in the country's history at that time, attracting 110,000 visitors and featuring the Doobie Brothers, Kansas, the Commodores, and Triumph.

38 *a weekend retreat called Engaged Encounter* The archdiocese required anyone getting married in the Catholic Church to either take a program of instruction from a priest or attend a weekend retreat. We chose the latter, outside Toronto, on the grounds of the Sisters of the Good Shepherd.

## 5: cairn

48 *the five-day protocol of heated chemotherapy* For those wanting a greater understanding of HIPEC following cytoreductive surgery, a graphic video presentation by Dr. Temple at University of Calgary's Faculty of Medicine is available here: https://www.youtube.com/watch?v=U2FJpxIZ5yo#t=20.

The Journal of Clinical Oncology published a well-cited study of early medical research on the efficacy of HIPEC: Tristan D. Yan et al., "Systematic Review on the Efficacy of Cytoreductive Surgery Combined with Perioperative Intraperitoneal Chemotherapy for Peritoneal Carcinomatosis from Colorectal Carcinoma," Journal of Clinical Oncology 24, no. 24 (August 2006): 4011–19, doi: 10.1200/JCO.2006.07.1142.

The case for identifying the patients who might experience long-term benefits, and what the criteria for selection might be, is made in F. Mohamed et al., "A New Standard of Care for the Management of Peritoneal Surface Malignancy," Current Oncology 18, no. 2 (April 2011): 84–96, http://www.ncbi.nlm.nih.gov/pmc/articles/PMC3070715/.

A well-cited study of 2,298 patients treated with HIPEC is Chua et al., "Early- and Long-Term Outcome Data of Patients with Pseudomyxoma Peritonei."

More recent research can be found in A. C. Lord et al., "Recurrence and Outcome after Complete Tumour Removal and Hyperthermic Intraperitoneal Chemotherapy in 512 Patients with Pseudomyxoma Peritonei from Perforated Appendiceal Mucinous Tumours," European Journal of Surgical Oncology (September 2014): ii, doi: 10.1016/j.ejso.2014.08.476. The primary conclusion is that "approximately one in four patients develops recurrence after complete CRS and HIPEC for PMP of appendiceal origin. Selected patients can undergo salvage surgery with good outcomes."

A *New York Times* article on the impact of HIPEC on PMP and other cancers caused a debate within the PMP community, many of whom saw the piece as unnecessarily broad in treating all digestive cancers as one: Andrew Pollack, "Hot Chemotherapy Bath: Patients See Hope, Critics Hold Doubts," *New York Times*, August 11, 2011, http://www.nytimes.com/2011/08/12/business/heated-chemotherapy-bath-may-be-only-hope-for-some-cancer-patients.html?pagewanted=all&_r=0.

48 *PMP happens to one in a million* At the time of Richard's diagnosis, PMP was said to occur in one in a million people every year, though the numbers appear to be rising to two in a million a year. This may be due to greater knowledge and proper diagnosis of the rare cancer.

These figures can be confirmed in an early study: A. Mukherjee et al., "Pseudomyxoma Peritonei Usually Originates from the Appendix: A Review of the Evidence," *European Journal of Gynaelogical Oncology* 25, no. 4 (2004): 411–14, http://www.ncbi.nlm.nih.gov/pubmed/15285293. And in a more recent one: N. J. Carr, "Current Concepts in Pseudomyxoma Peritonei," *Annales de Pathologie* 34, no. 1 (February 2014): 9–13, doi: 10.1016/j.annpat.2014.01.011.

The statistic of one thousand cases diagnosed in the United States every year comes from PMP Pals, an advocacy organization.

56 *The dominant prognostic factor* PMP, as a rare and relatively unknown disease, has a variety of misconceptions attached to it. The pathology of PMP is one of the most troublesome aspects investigated by the medical community. Thus, misdiagnosis is one of the primary issues, with doctors failing to recognize the mucin as having originated from the appendix, erroneously attributing it to the ovaries in females, or calling it colon cancer, or providing no diagnosis. Likewise, many label PMP 'benign,' a terminology that does not communicate the seriousness of the cancer. PMP rarely spreads via the lymphatic system or the bloodstream.

One landmark research paper differentiated the pathology of PMP: B. M. Ronnett, et al., "Immunohistochemical Evidence Supporting the Appendiceal Origin of Pseudomyxoma Peritonei in Women," *International Journal of Gynecologic Pathology* 16, no. 1 (1997): 1–9, http://www.ncbi.nlm.nih.gov/pubmed/8986525. It stated a case for specifying the type of mucin-producing tumor, specifically identifying that low-grade disease has different mutations from those of high-grade disease. Did patients have a disseminated peritoneal adenomucinosis (DPAM, a low-grade mucinous adenocarcinoma) or a peritoneal mucinous carcinomatosis (PMCA, a high-grade mucinous adenocarcinoma), or some kind of cancer in between those varieties? The authors also clarified misconceptions related to PMP being attributed to ovarian cancer. They argued that only low-grade DPAM should be called PMP, whereas others used the term to describe the accumulation of mucin caused by either low- or high-grade disease.

Recent studies are adept in correlating the type of malignancy, surgical outcomes, and survival rates. See P. Dartigues et al., "Peritoneal Pseudomyxoma: An Overview Emphasizing Pathological Assessment and Therapeutic Strategies," *Annales de Pathologie* 34, no. 1 (February 2014): 14–25, doi: 10.1016/j.annpat.2014.01.012.

51 *an anoxic incident* Cerebral anoxia is a complete interruption of blood supply to the brain. Hypoxia is a partial interruption of blood flow to the brain. More information on hypoxic and anoxic brain injury can be found on the website of the Family Caregiver Alliance: https://www.caregiver.org/hypoxic-anoxic-brain-injury.

## 6: scout

56 *the Serious Moonlight tour* The set list from David Bowie's performance in Toronto on September 3, 1983, included "Modern Love" as an encore, as can be seen on Setlist.fm: http://www.setlist.fm/setlist/david-bowie/1983/cne-stadium-toronto-on-canada-4bd0ebfa.html.

62 *I climbed from Lake O'Hara* Lake O'Hara is located in Yoho National Park, near Lake Louise, Alberta, Canada. For more information visit Parks Canada: http://www.pc.gc.ca/eng/pn-np/bc/yoho/natcul/ohara/sentiers-trails.aspx.

## 7: serum

63 *to prevent blood clots from forming* Pulmonary embolism was a serious risk for Richard, who had undergone two surgeries and was immobile for a few days. More information on pulmonary embolism can be found on the website of Johns Hopkins Medicine: http://www.hopkinsmedicine.org/healthlibrary/conditions/respiratory_disorders/pulmonary_embolism_85,P01308/.

66 *a chemotherapy called 5FU, or fluorouracil* At the time of Richard's surgery, 5FU, or fluorouracil, was commonly combined with mitomycin C in intraoperative HIPEC, followed by five days of early postoperative intraperitoneal chemotherapy (EPIC) treatment for peritoneal carcinomatosis from appendiceal and other gastrointestinal malignancies. See Tristan D. Yan et al., "Perioperative Intraperitoneal Chemotherapy for Peritoneal

Surface Malignancy," *Journal of Translational Medicine* 4 (April 2006): 17, doi: 10.1186/1479-5876-4-17.

The University of Calgary published an eleven-year study of PMP patients, in which they argue that HIPEC combined with EPIC results in unnecessary complications: Y. J. McConnell et al., "HIPEC+EPIC versus HIPEC-Alone: Differences in Major Complications Following Cytoreduction Surgery for Peritoneal Malignancy," *Journal of Surgical Oncology* 107, no. 6 (May 2013): 591–6, doi: 10.1002/jso.23276.

68 *a letter to friends, written from the hospital* The letter was written on October 1, 2003.

70 *about ten thousand generations ago* This is an estimate I arrived at with the help of a Seattle Public Library researcher. Though our data selection was somewhat arbitrary, we used recent evidence of *Homo sapiens* appearing two hundred thousand years ago and assumed the average childbearing age to be twenty; this would add up to around ten thousand generations. (One of the reasons Seattle is an incredible place to live is that it provides research assistance as a free service to the public, through the library. Online help is available from librarians around the country twenty-four hours a day, seven days a week, 365 days a year. Librarians at the Seattle Public Library are usually available from 9:00 AM to 6:00 PM seven days a week.)

72 *twelve motor skills tests in five minutes* The hospital neurologist likely used a mini cognitive evaluation of ten verbal questions and twelve motor skills tests, the same brief tests commonly used to predict dementia in patients. According to one study: "While the benefits of the statistical probability–calculation approach are clear (maximizing detection while minimizing unnecessary investigation of healthy people), several drawbacks are also apparent. Many screening tests overemphasize memory dysfunction, the hallmark of Alzheimer's disease, to the neglect of other domains such as language, praxis or executive function" (Breda Cullen et al., "A Review of Screening Tests for Cognitive Impairment," *Journal of Neurology, Neurosurgery & Psychiatry* 78, no. 8 (August 2007): 790–99, doi: 10.1136/jnnp.2006.095414.)

## 8: undoing

79 *a terrific job working for the Whyte Museum* The Whyte Museum of the Canadian Rockies is an archive, art gallery, and educational facility oriented to mountain art and culture, especially that of the Canadian Rockies around Banff, Alberta.

85 *eligible for the subsidized food program* In the 1990s, nearly 50 percent of Memphis City schools had students on the free/reduced-price lunch program, and those numbers are about the same today. Poverty is so prevalent that the school district, under a federal program, now also serves breakfast and supper to children who would otherwise go hungry. (From the Kids Count Data Center, a project of the Annie E. Casey Foundation: http://datacenter.kidscount.org/data/Tables/2979-free-reduced-price-school-lunchprogram.)

## 9: shattered

92 *The first soldiers* On October 16, 2002, a year prior to the day of our return home, President Bush had initiated the call to war in Iraq.

97 *We need to get someone to clarify* Later, brain injury specialists would argue for a need to differentiate between traumatic brain injury (TBI) and anoxic insult, and a condition they would term hypoxic-ischemic injury (HII). The reason for the change in terminology was to suggest the severity of the injury and its most appropriate treatment. David B. Arciniegas, president of the International Brain Injury Association, argued for the diagnostic term HII in 2010. See Arciniegas, "Hypoxic-Ischemic Brain Injury," International Brain Injury Association, December 10, 2012, http://www.internationalbrain.org/articles/hypoxicischemic-brain-injury/.

100 *Mild to moderate brain injuries* Mild brain injury describes the kind of injury sustained, not the impact of that injury on the patient's life. A traumatic brain injury (TBI), is defined as an alteration in brain function caused by an external force while an acquired brain injury (ABI) is an injury to the brain caused by stroke, drowning, seizure disorders, electric shock, substance abuse, tumor, infectious disease, toxic exposure or oxygen deprivation (Hypoxia/anoxia). ). The annual incidence of TBI

is 1,700,000 while the annual incidence of ABI is 917,000, according to the Brain Injury Association of America. http://www.biausa.org.

TBI including all levels of severity, is a major cause of death and lifelong disability in the United States. Each year, an estimated 1.5 million Americans sustain a TBI, fifty thousand die from these injuries, and eighty to ninety thousand experience the onset of long-term disability. An estimated 5.3 million Americans live with a permanent TBI-related disability today. Information from the National Center for Injury Prevention and Control, Report to Congress on Mild Traumatic Brain Injury in the United States: Steps to Prevent a Serious Public Health Problem (Atlanta, GA: Centers for Disease Control and Prevention, 2003), http://www.cdc.gov/ncipc/pub-res/mtbi/mtbireport.pdf.

## 10: sobering

104 *We began therapy* The therapeutic work described in this chapter was done with a Gottman therapist. John Gottman is a University of Washington researcher renowned for his work on marital stability and divorce prediction. For more information visit the Gottman Institute, http://www.gottman.com/.

111 *Called a debulking* Debulking surgery is seen today as beneficial more for palliative care, but in 2000, very few doctors knew any other treatment for PMP. Debulking surgery is not performed with curative intent, while cytoreductive surgery is. See H. Andréasson et al., "Outcome Differences between Debulking Surgery and Cytoreductive Surgery in Patients with Pseudomyxoma Peritonei," *European Journal of Surgical Oncology* 38, no. 3 (October 2012): 962–8, doi: 10.1016/j.ejso.2012.07.009.

112 *The morbidity rate* The doctor who performed Richard's first surgery was likely referring to the rate of recurrence among those undergoing cytoreductive surgery and HIPEC. Tumor progression rates were high in 1994, as documented in Gough et al., "Pseudomyxoma Peritonei," *Annals of Surgery*.

Some doctors think the primary factor contributing to patients' recovery isn't HIPEC but instead the combination of good surgeons with well-chosen patients. An overview of the differences in opinion about how to treat PMP can be found in Charlotte Bath, "'Hot Chemotherapy'

Generates Heated Debate about Its Use with Cytoreductive Surgery to Manage Peritoneal Metastases," *ASCO Post* 2, no. 15 (October 2011), http://www.ascopost.com/issues/october-15-2011/hot-chemotherapy-generates-heated-debate-about-its-use-with-cytoreductive-surgery-to-manage-peritoneal-metastases.aspx.

Research on morbidity and mortality of HIPEC around the time of Richard's surgery was scarce. Among the doctors tracking patients between 1995 and 2003, one team placed morbidity at 34 percent, as reported in U. Schmidt et al., "Perioperative Morbidity and Quality of Life in Long-Term Survivors Following Cytoreductive Surgery and Hyperthermic Intraperitoneal Chemotherapy," *European Journal of Surgical Oncology* 31 (2005), doi: 10.1016/j.ejso.2004.09.011.

## PART TWO

### 11: servant

122 *group of Tibetan Buddhist monks* We would later learn of the controversy surrounding the Bowers Museum exhibit and the sand mandala constructed by the monks to celebrate its launch. See Daniel Yi, "Tibetan Exhibit Is More Political Artifice Than Art, Protesters Say," *Los Angeles Times*, February 22, 2004, http://articles.latimes.com/2004/feb/22/local/me-octibet22.

122 *grains of sand into a mandala* The monks built the mandala to honor victims of fire, and then later took the sand to the ocean to release their suffering.

122 *send the lama* Information on the lama can be found in documents about the monks' eighteen-month tour of the United States in 2003. Lharampa Geshe Ngawang Lungtok was the senior teacher at Garden Shartse monastery. See the websites of Tara House Meditation Center (http://www.tarahouse.org/monks.html#monks) and Gaden Shartse Lhopa Khangtsen (http://gadenlhopa.org/).

### 12: waiting

132 *I finally read the abstracts* Perry Shen et al., "Factors Predicting Survival after Intraperitoneal Hyperthermic Chemotherapy with

Mitomycin C after Cytoreductive Surgery for Patients with Peritoneal Carcinomatosis," *Archives of Surgery* 138, no. 1 (January 2003): 26–33, doi: 10.1001/archsurg.138.1.26; R. P. McQuellon et al., "Quality of Life after Intraperitoneal Hyperthermic Chemotherapy (IPHC) for Peritoneal Carcinomatosis," *European Journal of Surgical Oncology* 27, no. 1 (February 2001): 65–73, http://www.ncbi.nlm.nih.gov/pubmed/11237495.

132 *Chemotherapy with Mitomycin C* Mitomycin has been approved for use by the FDA since 1995; however, its use in HIPEC was often denied by insurance providers because the protocol was not approved. Although at the time of Richard's surgery, the evidence in favor of cytoreductive surgery and HIPEC as a "gold standard" of treatment was not established, several researchers would later state a compelling case to standardize its use. One, Laurie Todd, a PMP survivor herself, makes her argument in Chapter 18 of *The Sample Appeal: More Insurance Warrior Wisdom*, excerpted on the website of the Carcinoid Cancer Foundation, 2010: http://www.carcinoid.org/content/excerpt-18-experimental-seize-their-weapons.

In 2006, the perception of HIPEC was dramatically altered with the publication of a consensus statement by a group of seventy-five physicians: J. Esquivel et al., "Cytoreductive Surgery and Hyperthermic Intraperitoneal Chemotherapy in the Management of Peritoneal Surface Malignancies of Colonic Origin: A Consensus Statement," *Annals of Surgical Oncology* (2006), doi: 10.1245/s10434-006-9185-7.

135 *who specializes in Brain Gym* Brain Gym is a program of movements, exercises, and activities developed to assist children with learning challenges. See Josie M. Sifft and G. C. K. Khalsa, "Effect of Educational Kinesiology upon Simple Response Times and Choice Response Times," *Perceptual and Motor Skills* 73, no. 3 (1991): 1011–1015, doi: 10.2466/pms.1991.73.3.1011.

141 *According to a 2011 article* "The cost of the surgery and HIPEC, including hospitalization, ranges from $20,000 to more than $100,000, doctors said. While Medicare and insurers generally pay for the operation, the heated treatment may not be covered. But doctors added it may be if it is described merely as chemotherapy." From Pollack, "Hot Chemotherapy Bath," *New York Times*.

142 *Speech and Language Evaluation* Providence Speech and Hearing Center, Orange, California, report dated February 16, 2004.

## 13: virgin

153 *"I don't think so,"* Possibly Richard forgot his sexual history because he had difficulties with both long-term and short-term memory, a rarity. There's no medical information that we found to verify. We have our own experience. Yet sexual changes after traumatic brain injury are common. See Angelle M. Sander et al., *Sexual Functioning and Satisfaction after Traumatic Brain Injury: An Educational Manual* (Houston, TX: Baylor College of Medicine, 2011), http://www.tbicommunity.org/resources/publications/sexual_functioning_after_tbi.pdf.

## 14: mysterium

156 *First up: the entire soliloquy* *The Oxford Shakespeare: Hamlet*, ed. G.R. Hibbard (Oxford: Oxford University Press, 1987), Act II, Scene 2.

157 *out pops the announcer* The *Adventures of Superman* monologue was from the George Reeves–era television series, in black-and-white and color, which originally aired from 1952–58 and was syndicated during Richard's childhood.

164 *to get in to see Dr. L* Dr. David M. Lechuga, director, Neurobehavioral Clinical and Counseling Center, Lake Forest, California.

165 *three days of tests* An explanation of what's in a neuropsychological evaluation and why it's used for brain injury is available in Brenda Kosaka, "Neuropsychological Assessment in Mild Traumatic Brain Injury: A Clinical Overview," *British Columbia Medical Journal* 48, no. 9 (November 2006): 447–52, http://www.bcmj.org/article/neuropsychological-assessment-mild-traumatic-brain-injury-clinical-overview.

## 15: watershed

174 *To help you create compensatory strategies* Brain injury survivors use a range of compensatory strategies to cope with daily life, from memory logs, weekly planners, and task lists to recording devices, mo-

bile phones, and computer devices. Richard first used Post-it notes and a printed weekly planner. He progressed to a PalmPilot and then, later, when they were introduced, to an iPhone. Survivors must learn to manage fatigue, monitor their attention and concentration, process information, track their executive functioning, and work on their social skills.

177 *A railroad worker* An article by Malcolm Macmillan informed my understanding of aspects of Gage's story: Macmillan, "Phineas Gage: Unravelling the Myth," *Psychologist* 21, no. 9 (September 2008): 828–31, http://thepsychologist.bps.org.uk/volume-21/edition-9/phineas-gage-unravelling-myth.

180 *Memory is reconstitutive* Priscilla Long, "Remembering Abraham Lincoln," *American Scholar*, May 16, 2012, http://theamericanscholar.org/remembering-abraham-lincoln/.

## 16: pathless

189 *Pauline Boss* Boss's work helped me understand ambiguous loss, both the range and scope of the grief in such a circumstance. We were in what Boss calls Type Two, the kind characterized by physical presence and psychological absence, which can occur with addictions, dementia, depression. Type One is characterized by psychological presence and physical absence, which can be brought about by war, genocide, natural disasters, even adoption. See Boss, *Ambiguous Loss: Learning to Live with Unresolved Grief* (Cambridge: Harvard University Press, 2000). See also http://www.ambiguousloss.com.

Only recently has there been more significant study on relationships after brain injury. Ambiguous loss is a primary area of inquiry. See Emilie Godwin, Brittney Chappell, and Jeffrey Kreutzer, "Relationships after TBI: A Grounded Research Study," *Brain Injury* 28, no. 4 (April 2014): 398–413, doi: 10.3109/02699052.2014.880514.

193 *Nicholl Fellowship competition* In 2003, I placed in the quarterfinals of the Nicholl Fellowship, which, at that time, according to director Greg Beal, represented the top 5 percent of entries. This competition is overseen by the Academy Awards® and sponsored by Don and Gee Nicholl.

196 *Mr. Nace works with his sons and his wife* The Paulson & Nace firm practices in four states. More information about them can be found on their website, http://paulsonandnace.com.

201 *bed-and-breakfast where Allen Ginsberg slept* Ginsberg is said to have rested at Hotel Bohème, in the North Beach neighborhood of San Francisco.

## 17: pleasure

210 *We seek the legendary Brocéliande* In Arthurian legend, the Brocéliande is the forest where the Lady of the Lake supposedly kept Merlin. It's fictional, but is also said to be located southwest of Rennes, in the Paimpont forest, which still receives visitors to a tree where people hang requests and blessings addressed to Merlin. The forest was thirty minutes from our temporary home in Josselin.

## 18: friend

225 *be creative about ways in which you can access information* In Richard's rehabilitation, we focused primarily on working memory, short-term memory, and the executive and attention control required for its proper functioning. Attention is not only the ability to focus but also the ability to ignore sensory stimulation that prevents concentration. A poor working memory also prevents the acquisition of new information that would develop executive skills to enhance judgment. More recent research on these factors can be found in Keisuke Fukuda and Edward K. Vogel "Human Variation in Overriding Attentional Capture," *Journal of Neuroscience* 29, no. 27 (July 2009): 8726–33, doi: 10.1523/JNEUROSCI.2145-09.2009.

Richard used a variety of assistive technologies over the course of his rehabilitation from brain injury, including a PalmPilot, timers, iPhones, GPS devices, voice recordings, and written forms to guide his retrieval of patient information. The National Resource Center for Traumatic Brain Injury has more information at http://www.tbinrc.com/cognitive-rehabilitation-and-assistive-technology-resources.

229 *the Sufis in the Canadian Rockies* The Sufi Movement of Canada is not affiliated with any religion but is instead devoted to the ideals of love, harmony, and beauty as expressed by the philosopher Hazrat Inayat Khan. In the late twentieth century, they held retreats at Lake O'Hara, a UNESCO World Heritage wilderness site, high in the Canadian Rockies.

232 *brain scientists like Michael Gazzaniga* Dr. Gazzaniga is a leading researcher in cognitive neuroscience; his notion of a "fictional self" has influenced my understanding of how we construct our narratives. He says that memory is self-serving and unreliable; while the right brain "regurgitates" a remembered experience, the interpreter, located in the left brain, "remembers the gist of the story line and fills in the details by using logic, not real memories." See Gazzaniga, *The Ethical Brain: The Science of Our Moral Dilemmas* (New York: HarperCollins, 2006) and *The Mind's Past* (Berkeley and Los Angeles: University of California Press, 2000). An overview of Gazzaniga's work is available in Cathy Gere, "Hemispheric Disturbances: On Michael Gazzaniga," *The Nation*, December 5, 2011, http://www.thenation.com/article/164646/hemispheric-disturbances-michael-gazzaniga.

## 19: heat

242 *marital strategist John Gottman's parlance* Renowned for his work on marital stability and divorce prediction, John Gottman has conducted breakthrough research with thousands of couples over the past forty years. Gottman is the founder of the Love Lab at University of Washington and, with Dr. Julie Gottman, the Gottman Institute. For more information visit http://www.gottman.com/.

242 *sex columnist Dan Savage* Savage writes the internationally syndicated relationship and sex advice column *Savage Love*. He is the author of several books and, with his husband, Terry Miller, the founder of the It Gets Better project.

243 *Babeland* Claire Cavanah and Rachel Venning opened the first Babeland store in 1993 in response to the lack of women-friendly sex shops in Seattle. Babeland has a vital sexual education program and community.

## 20: lover

261 *We read* Sex at Dawn This book is about the evolution of monogamy in humans. Christopher Ryan and Cacilda Jethá, *Sex at Dawn: How We Mate, Why We Stray, and What It Means for Modern Relationships* (New York: HarperCollins, 2010).

262 *Married people, regardless of gender* Infidelity statistics come from Helen E. Fisher, "Serial monogamy and clandestine adultery: evolution and consequences of the dual human reproductive strategy," *Applied Evolutionary Psychology*, ed: S. Craig Roberts (Oxford: Oxford University Press, 2012), 94.

262 *Still, open marriages* Open marriage statistics are from Stephanie Pappas, "5 Myths about Polyamory Debunked," *Live Science*, February 14, 2014, http://www.livescience.com/27128-polyamory-myths-debunked.html.

271 *Dan Savage uses the term monogamish* This concept is covered well in Mark Oppenheimer, "Married, with Infidelities," *New York Times*, June 30, 2011, http://www.nytimes.com/2011/07/03/magazine/infidelity-will-keep-us-together.html?pagewanted=all.

278 *the cultural filter of an ironic view* Both David Foster Wallace, in his essay "E Unibus Pluram: Television and U.S. Fiction," and Adam Kelly, in his essay "David Foster Wallace and the New Sincerity in American Fiction," offer serious questions about the role of sincerity and authenticity in an increasingly self-conscious culture. Wallace, "E Unibus Pluram," *Review of Contemporary Fiction* 13, no. 2 (Summer 1993): 151–94; Kelly, "David Foster Wallace and the New Sincerity in American Fiction," *Consider David Foster Wallace: Critical Essays*, ed. David Hering (Los Angeles and Austin: Sideshow Media Group Press, 2010): 131–46.

## 21: wondering

282 *Still, I've read "The Median* Stephen Jay Gould, "The Median Isn't the Message," *Discover* 6 (June 1985): 40–42, http://www.cancerguide.org/median_not_msg.html.

283 *Richard's tests give us* All of this data is from a report generated by the University of Washington Medical Center's Brain Injury Rehabilitation Program.

283 *an interview with each of us by Dr. P* Dr. Mary Pepping, director of the University of Washington Medical Center's Neuropsychology Testing Service and outpatient Neuro-Rehabilitation Program until 2013.

297 *the brain-injured enter a liminal state* Liminality is a fascinating way to view the brain-injured and their caregivers. For more, see Suzanne Gibbons, Alyson Ross, and Margaret Bevans, "Liminality as a Conceptual Frame for Understanding the Family Caregiving Rite of Passage: An Integrative Review," *Research in Nursing and Health* 37, no. 5 (October 2014): 423–36, doi: 10.1002/nur.21622.

297 *neither "me" nor "not me."* But what theorists think identity is—all of the subjective processes by which they talk about the self, including the tendency to be biologically dominant in strategies—informs the therapy for patients with TBI. See David Segal, "Exploring the Importance of Identity Following Acquired Brain Injury: A Review of the Literature," *International Journal of Child, Youth & Family Studies* 1, no. 3/4 (2010): 293–314, http://journals.uvic.ca/index.php/ijcyfs/article/view/2093/738.

297 *We learn from our research* *The Medical Malpractice Myth* by Tom Baker (Chicago: University of Chicago Press, 2007), like the brilliant documentary *Hot Coffee* (dir. Susan Saladoff, 2011), provides a stunning dismantling of the rationale for tort reform. Baker, director of the Insurance Law Center, shows that the real cause of the rise in malpractice is "too much malpractice, not too much litigation." Though I didn't come to this book until after we won our case, I had to research malpractice mostly as a way to deal with the shame of fighting the medical system. I didn't understand that corporate health care wants patients to remain guilty and fearful. Corporate health care profits from a culture of hero-worship of doctors and unquestioning compliance among the families of patients. Even if their doctor or hospital made a mistake.

Recent reporting on tort reform includes Michael Hiltzik, "New Study Shows That the Savings from 'Tort Reform' Are Mythical," *Los Angeles Times*, September 20, 2014, http://www.latimes.com/business/hiltzik/la-fi-mh-another-study-shows-why-tort-reform-20140919-column.html.

304 *No one knows the cancer's cause.* There is initial research about the potential link between appendix cancer and geographic proximity to nuclear waste in the United States. Cancer forums identifying PMP patients in several investigations include an unusual cluster among people who have lived in North St. Louis County. The CDC is investigating this grouping. More information about this group can be found at Coldwater Creek Facts: http://www.coldwatercreekfacts.com/.

We would not know about this connection until ten years after Richard's diagnosis: Richard's father worked for the Canadian navy, in its nuclear engineering division, from the time that Richard was born until his parents' divorce when he was three years old.

310 *the world's largest act of faith* The Kumbh Mela is a massive Hindu pilgrimage that can attract one hundred million people. It is held every third year in one of four places: Haridwar, Allahabad, Nashik, and Ujjain, along the Ganges in India.

## Further Study

PMP Research Foundation, with links to research they've funded for a decade:

http://www.pmpcure.org/

Pseudomyxoma Survivor, a UK-based charity:

http://www.pseudomyxomasurvivor.org/

PMP Awareness Organization:

http://www.pmpawareness.org/

PMP Appendix Cancer Support Group, a Facebook group for caregivers and survivors. Membership is by invitation:

https://www.facebook.com/groups/PMPAppendixCancerSupportGroup/

Centers for Disease Control and Prevention, information on traumatic brain injury:

http://www.cdc.gov/traumaticbraininjury/

Brain Trauma Foundation:

https://www.braintrauma.org/

Brain Injury Association of America:

http://www.biausa.org/

Brain Injury Association of Canada:

http://biac-aclc.ca/